DiversITALY

Elementary Italian

with Inclusive Language & Gender Equality

Volume **1**

Francesca Calamita | Chiara De Santi

Kendall Hunt

publishing company

Cover image © Shutterstock.com

Kendall Hunt
p u b l i s h i n g   c o m p a n y

www.kendallhunt.com
Send all inquiries to:
4050 Westmark Drive
Dubuque, IA 52004-1840

Printed in the United States of America

INDICE

I CONTENUTI DEL TESTO

Chapters and themes	By the end of this chapter, students will be able...	Grammar Structures

Capitolo 1
 	
Iniziamo
	▪ to read in Italian with a correct pronunciation
	▪ to greet people when they meet and when they leave
	▪ to thank people
	▪ to ask how people are doing and respond to the question
		1.0 Iniziamo
		1.1 The Italian alphabet
		1.2 Sounds and pronunciation
		    1.2.1 How to pronounce C and G
		    1.2.2 The double consonants
		1.3 Greetings
		    1.3.1 Informal vs. formal
		    1.3.2 Greetings at the arrival
		    1.3.3 Greetings at the departure
		1.4 Thanking people
		1.5 Meeting people

Capitolo 2
 	
Il mondo dell'istruzione e del lavoro
	▪ to use verb **essere** [*to be*] in the present tense to ask who someone is
	▪ to use verb **essere** [*to be*] in the present tense to express nationalities
	▪ to ask for names and respond to the question
	▪ to ask for origin (country, town, etc.) and respond to the question
	▪ to meet people and have an introductory conversation
	▪ to understand the universe of nouns and their gender (m. or f.) and number (s. or pl.), and to use them with indefinite (*a/an* in English) and definite articles (*the* in English)
		2.0 Iniziamo
		2.1 Personal subject pronouns
		2.2 Verb *essere* [*to be*]
		2.3 Adjectives of nationality
		2.4 What's your name? Where are you from?
		    2.4.1 What's your name? My name is…
		    2.4.2 Where are you from? I am from…
		    2.4.3 Nice to meet you!
		2.5 Nouns in the singular
		2.6 Nouns in the plural
		2.7 Indefinite articles
		2.8 Definite articles

Capitolo 3
 	
Le famiglie italiane e le loro diversità
	▪ to count from zero to 100
	▪ to ask for phone numbers
	▪ to know money and specifically Euros
	▪ to use **c'è** [*there is*] and **ci sono** [*there are*] to express existence of someone or something in a certain space
	▪ to use adjectives, including colors, to describe people and things
	▪ to use verb **avere** [*to have*] in the present tense to express possession and relationship
	▪ to use the idiomatic expressions of verb **avere** [*to have*] in the present tense, including age
	▪ to use possessive adjectives and pronouns
	▪ to express the time via days of the week, months, and seasons
		3.0 Iniziamo
		3.1 Numbers from 0 to 100
		3.2 C'è [*there is*] and *ci sono* [*there are*]
		3.3 Adjectives
		    3.3.1 Groups of people
		    3.3.2 Physical and psychological traits
		    3.3.3 Colors
		    3.3.4 Eyes and hair
		3.4 Verb *avere* [*to have*]
		    3.4.1 The uses of avere
		    3.4.2 The idiomatic expressions with avere
		3.5 Possessive adjectives
		3.6 Possessive adjectives with some family members in the singular
		3.7 Days of the week, months, and seasons
		    3.7.1 Days of the week
		    3.7.2 Months
		    3.7.3 Seasons

Chapters and themes	By the end of this chapter, students will be able...	Grammar Structures

Capitolo 4
 	
La cucina italiana
	▪ to use verbs in **-are** in the present tense
	▪ to use irregular verbs in **-are** such as **andare** [*to go*], **dare** [*to give*], **fare** [*to do/to make*], and **stare** [*to stay/to remain*]
	▪ to use interrogatives when asking questions
	▪ to use **questo/a** [*this/this one*] and **quello/a** [*that/that one*] to indicate the proximity or not of someone or something
	▪ to use simple prepositions and their most used expressions to express of going or being in a place and the means of transportation one uses to go from a place to another
	▪ to ask and respond about time and when something happens (from when to when)
		4.0 Iniziamo
		4.1 Verbs in -*are* in the present tense
		   4.1.1 Regular verbs in -are
		   4.1.2 Other verbs in -are
		4.2 Irregular verbs in -*are*: *andare*, *dare*, *fare*, and *stare*
		4.3 Interrogatives
		4.4 Demonstrative pronouns and adjectives
		   4.4.1 Questo/a *as this/this one*
		   4.4.2 Quello/a *as that/that one*
		4.5 Simple prepositions
		4.6 What time is it?

Capitolo 5
 	
Viaggio nelle arti italiane
	▪ to use verbs in **-ere** in the present tense
	▪ to use verbs **sapere** and **conoscere** to say when we know (or we don't know) something or someone
	▪ to use verb **piacere** [*to like*]
	▪ to use verbs in **-ire** in the present tense
	▪ to use articulate prepositions and their most used expressions
	▪ to use verbs **andare** [*to go*] vs. **venire** [*to come*]
	▪ to use the partitive to express a part of something
	▪ to count from 100 onward
	▪ to use ordinal numbers
	▪ to express dates
		5.0 Iniziamo
		5.1 Verbs in -*ere* in the present tense
		   5.1.1 Regular verbs in -ere
		   5.1.2 Irregular verbs in -ere
		5.2 Verbs *sapere* and *conoscere*
		5.3 Verb *piacere*
		5.4. Verbs in -*ire* in the present tense
		5.5 Articulated prepositions
		5.6 Verbs *andare* vs. *venire*
		5.7 Partitive (some of)
		5.8 Numbers from 100 onwards, ordinal numbers, and dates
		   5.8.1 Ordinal numbers
		   5.8.2 Dates

Capitolo 6
 	
Ciak si gira: l'Italia e il cinema
	▪ to use modal verbs **dovere** [*must, to have to, to need to*], **potere** [*can, may, to be able to*], and **volere** [*want*] to express respectively **necessity** and **obligation, possibility** and **ability**, and **wish** and **determination**
	▪ to form and to use adverbs to specify how often, when, where, how, and how much one does something
	▪ to use the variable forms of **molto/a/i/e** [*much, many, a lot of, lots of*], **tanto/a/i/e** [*a lot of, many*], **troppo/a/i/e** [*too much, too many*], and **poco/a/pochi/poche** [*little, few, not many*]
	▪ to form and to use the past tense **passato prossimo** to express events happened in the past
	▪ to use **passato prossimo** of verbs such as **piacere, dovere, potere,** and **volere**
		6.0 Iniziamo
		6.1 Modal verbs *dovere* [*must, to have to, to need to*], *potere* [*can, may, to be able to*], and *volere* [*want*] in the present tense
		   6.1.1 Dovere
		   6.1.2 Potere
		   6.1.3 Volere
		6.2 Adverbs and *molto, tanto, troppo,* and *poco*
		   6.2.1 Adverbs in -mente *and others used frequently*
		   6.2.2 Molto, tanto, troppo, and poco
		6.3 Past participles of *essere* and *avere*, and regular and irregular verbs in -*are*, -*ere*, and -*ire*
		   6.3.1 Regular past participles
		   6.3.2 Irregular past participles
		6.4 Construction of past tense *passato prossimo*
		   6.4.1 The passato prossimo *of essere and* avere
		   6.4.2 The passato prossimo *with* avere
		   6.4.3 The passato prossimo *with* essere
		6.5 Other uses of *passato prossimo*
		   6.5.1 The passato prossimo *with* piacere
		   6.5.2 The passato prossimo *with* dovere, potere, *and* volere

Appendice: more on...	Culture	Gender Equality, Diversity, and Inclusion
■ Andare, dare, fare e stare ■ Gli interrogativi: quale/i ■ Gli interrogativi: quanto/a/i/e ■ Le preposizioni ■ Che ora è? Che ore sono?	**Note culturali** ■ L'esterofilia italiana ■ I piatti italiani (esempi di anti-pasti, primi, secondi, contorni e dolci) ■ Le discipline universitarie ■ La giornata con le 24 ore **La pagina culturale** ■ Mangiare all'italiana ■ L'Italia e le sue cucine regionali	**Le parole contano** ■ Chef vs Cuoca ■ Gender Studies in Italy ■ Terminology concerning abilities and disabilities
■ Verbi regolari in **-are**, **-ere** e **-ire** ■ Piacere ■ Le preposizioni articolate ■ I numeri ordinali	**Note culturali** ■ Gli alcolici in Italia ■ Le operazioni matematiche e le frazioni ■ Il mercato italiano **La pagina culturale** ■ L'arte in Italia	**Le parole contano** ■ Breaking the glass ceiling ■ Mi piace la lingua italiana inclusiva!
■ Il condizionale per esprimere *I would like* ■ I verbi in **-re** al presente e al passato prossimo	**Note culturali** ■ Il movimento #Metoo **La pagina culturale** ■ Il cinema italiano	**Le parole contano** ■ Asterisk and schwa in complex sentences

PREFAZIONE

WHY A BOOK LIKE THIS?

What does it mean to learn a new language? What kind of opportunities can a new language open up to you? A new language and its culture can open a world of possibilities! Communicating with people from other parts of the world, learning new vocabulary and its cultural features every day, becoming part of a new country you are fascinated by; these are a few of the many opportunities that might come to mind. However, *le parole contano* [*words matter*], and the way we use them shapes the way we think about others. As Italian writer Michela Murgia states, "il linguaggio è un'infrastruttura culturale che produce rapporti di potere [*language is an infrastructure that produces power relationships*]" (Michela Murgia, *Stai Zitta*, Einaudi, Torino 2020, p. 31), therefore words have power, and it is up to us to use them in an empowering way. Words can help to create a more inclusive and diverse world with less social injustice, to contribute to achieving gender equality, and to give visibility to those who have remained in the shadows for too long. As educators, we believe that it is part of our job to help our students to think critically about the world, and a language class—far from being reduced only to technical skills—offers a valuable opportunity to do it.

Many textbooks written and adopted to teach and learn Italian give more visibility to male protagonists of history, literature, cinema, and the arts, than to their female counterparts, favoring examples from the middle and upper classes, traditional families, and stereotypical gender roles. Despite still being kept hidden by the canonical curriculum, women and minorities have made history, contributed to literature, art, cinema, and much more. Therefore, the time has come to rethink the canon and the teaching of the Italian language, including more diverse perspectives which in turn might be more representative of the current world.

Italy has changed profoundly over the last 30 years, and with this textbook we would like to talk about Italy as it is today, by acknowledging its social challenges, its cultural achievements, and its continuing evolution. We are in need of a refreshed education that might help to dismantle socio-cultural patriarchal traditions through the language. *DiversITALY* teaches students conventional Italian grammar, yet it makes them aware of the evolving scenario and debate concerning inclusive language. With this textbook students will learn how to use Italian in a more inclusive way, including all professions declined in the feminine forms, the use of asterisks, slashes and schwa, as well as other forms of experimentation, as we believe that "considerare i femminili uno stravolgimento dell'italiano è [...] dovut alla paura del cambiamento" [*to consider feminines an upheaval of the Italian language is ... due to the fear of change*] (Vera Gheno, *Femminili singolari*, effequ, Firenze 2019, p. 78).

The authors of *DiversITALY* believe that learning a new language can have a predominant role in shaping globally-oriented generations who desire to improve the current social scenario and pursue gender equality, inclusion, and diversity at all levels; therefore, Departments of Italian Studies worldwide have an important role to play not only to recover from the decreased enrollment which has affected many institutions, but also to re-emerge from the current global health crisis as an essential humanities subject that can shape a better world. In other words, Italian language classes can give educators the opportunity to use words to explore present-day issues with their students in a frequently international and diverse setting, thus helping them to become global and active citizens of this evolving world. As a consequence, educators in this area have the opportunity to affirm their role as cross-cultural mediators and innovators, connecting people around the world and creating spaces where diversity, equity, inclusion, social justice, and gender equality are the norm rather than the exception. As Joan Clifford and Deborah S. Reisinger suggest: "As educators [...] it is our responsibility to maintain an atmosphere that does not discriminate, stereotype, tokenize, privilege, or somehow treat students unfairly" (*Community-Based Language Learning: A Framework for Educators*, Georgetown University Press, Washington D.C. 2019, p.114).

In this spirit, we are delighted to share with you *DiversITALY!*

Francesca Calamita and Chiara De Santi

THE STRUCTURE OF VOLUME 1

The first volume of *DiversITALY* is divided into six chapters; the first is an shorter introductory chapter where the alphabet and pronunciation are introduced. Each chapter concerns a different theme: from Italian families to Italian cuisine, from the Italian visual arts to Italian cinema, to list a few examples from volume 1. Each chapter starts with a dialogue, while the grammar structures are explained in detail through a variety of examples, and at times inductively. Often, more in-depth information on some grammar structures is given in the **Appendice** [*Appendix*] at the end of each chapter.

The chapters also include exercises that can be completed in class, and reviewed in pairs or groups. In the textbook, the exercises are organized into four different types:

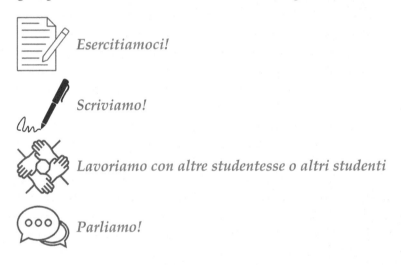

Esercitiamoci!

Scriviamo!

Lavoriamo con altre studentesse o altri studenti

Parliamo!

With **Esercitiamoci!** [*Let's practice!*] students practice the grammar structures through exercises that can be completed on an individual basis or in pairs/groups, to foster comprehension skills. With **Scriviamo!** [*Let's write!*] students improve their writing skills, while with **Parliamo!** [*Let's talk!*] students focus on strengthening their listening and comprehension skills through dialogues. The authors of *DiversITALY* believe in a communicative approach through which students are pushed to use the grammar structures learned in the textbook to communicate with other students. This is why there are many **Parliamo!** exercises in each section.

The exercises that are labeled as **Lavoriamo con altre studentesse o altri studenti!** [*Let's work with other female or male students!*] are designed for peer-review work to check over the exercises included in the **Esercitiamoci!** and **Scriviamo!** sections.

The first edition of the textbook also includes **il libro degli esercizi** [*workbook*] that is run through an online platform, and it is divided into six chapters following the structure of the textbook. Each chapter of the workbook includes ten auto-graded exercises so that the students can practice the grammar structures covered in the textbook.

Le note culturali [*Cultural Notes*] through the chapters and **Le pagine culturali** [*Cultural Pages*] at the end of each chapter play a leading role in this textbook, and are designed to teach students about Italian culture and society in the 21st century. Specifically, after each section of **La pagina**

culturale, there are exercises devoted to Italian culture. **Esercitiamoci con la cultura** [*Let's practice through culture*] is a way for students to explore some aspects of Italian culture. Each chapter also has a number of boxes titled **Le parole contano** [*Words Matter*], where we focus on issues of gender equality, diversity, and inclusion through language. Students learn how language changes and how its changes contribute to creating greater visibility for women, minorities and all those who have been hidden for too long. Topics range from grammar and visibility, such as the use of slashes, asterisks and schwa, to debates over words to promote gender equality, body positivity, and women's empowerment. Each chapter also includes a **Glossario** [*Glossary*] at the end.

We have adopted American spelling, yet you might find British words and expressions from New Zealand and Australia, which also represent the global backgrounds of the authors.

ACKNOWLEDGEMENTS

The authors of DiversITALY believe in cooperation and collaboration among colleagues to offer students of Italian language and culture the most updated learning experience. We are immensely grateful to the contributors who helped us in a variety of ways, while we all attempted to cope with the COVID-19 pandemic and its challenges. The contributors played a key role in providing exercises for the workbook, reading chapters, and giving precious suggestions to the authors. Of course, the authors are solely responsible for the final version of the textbook, yet we would not be able to offer this innovative textbook without the many suggestions we received. We extend a heartfelt thank you to **Enrico Cecconi** (University of Bath), **Laurie Detenbeck** (State University of New York at Fredonia), **Ida Ferrari** (University of Virginia in Siena), **Margherita Galofaro** (Farmingdale State College, SUNY), **Hiromi Kaneda** (University of Virginia), **Stella Mattioli** (University of Virginia), **Emanuele Occhipinti** (Drew University), **Vincenzo Selleri** (Farmingdale State College, SUNY), and **Michela Valmori** (University of Bologna). Other contributors from around the globe will join us for the second volume.

Francesca Calamita thanks all her empowering women around the world, without whom she could not have reached the same level of awareness on gender issues in Italian language, culture and beyond, in particular, her academic mothers Claudia Bernardi, Adalgisa Giorgio, Sally Hill, and Bernadette Luciano. She also thanks her mother, Mara Lanzi, as well as her best friends Claudia Casali, Mabel Richart-Marset, and Roberta Trapè for their endless support. Chiara De Santi deeply thanks her mother Alessandra Calamassi for having been a role model and for having taught her the core values of diversity, equity, inclusion, and social justice, and her husband Alex Caviedes and their daughters Julia and Sofia for the continuous love and support during the writing process, and for the respect they showed while *mamma* was locked in her study typing on her laptop. As authors, we especially thank Alex for having gone through the chapters, offering a last, attentive glance at the English language before submitting the work to the publisher. We also thank Sheri Hosek and Sue Saad from Kendall Hunt Publishing Company for their help and support during the whole process.

INIZIAMO

1

CAPITOLO

By the end of this introductory chapter, you will be able to sound words in Italian correctly, to read with correct pronunciation (although, you will still not have a full understanding of the content), to greet people, and understand formal versus informal situations. In terms of cultural elements, you will learn about the Italian regions, the Italian language, and the dialects, as well as the Italian gestures.

INIZIAMO

Read the dialogue below with another student, alternating roles:

Fen:	Buongiorno!
Alessandro:	Salve! Come stai?
Fen:	Sto molto bene, grazie, e tu?
Alessandro:	Sto così così.
Fen:	Ciao!
Alessandro:	Ciao! A presto!

Work with another student to understand the content of this short dialogue. Do you know what the words mean? If not, what do you think they might mean?

1.1 L'ALFABETO ITALIANO

The Italian alphabet consists of 21 letters. Some of them are pronounced differently in comparison with the English alphabet. A very important difference concerns the letter **H**: when it is at the beginning of a word, it is **not** pronounced in Italian! For instance, you read the word *hotel* like it was *otel*.

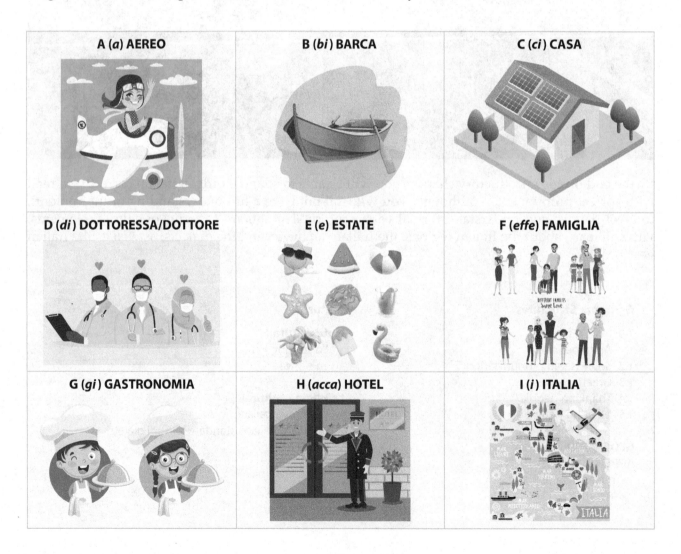

A (*a*) AEREO	B (*bi*) BARCA	C (*ci*) CASA
D (*di*) DOTTORESSA/DOTTORE	E (*e*) ESTATE	F (*effe*) FAMIGLIA
G (*gi*) GASTRONOMIA	H (*acca*) HOTEL	I (*i*) ITALIA

J K W X Y are part of the alphabet because they are found in foreign words commonly used by Italians, such as:

*The kiwi is a unique bird and the national icon of New Zealand. It symbolises the uniqueness of New Zealand's wildlife and it is considered a *taonga* (treasure) to Maori. Kiwi is the nickname for a New Zealander.

NOTA CULTURALE

Lo spelling in italiano. While spelling is often taught in school in Anglophone countries, in Italy spelling instruction is not considered part of the curriculum. However, when Italians need to spell out a word, in most cases they use Italian cities:

A come **Ancona**	M come **Milano**
B come **Bologna**	N come **Napoli**
C come **Como**	O come **Otranto**
D come **Domodossola**	P come **Palermo**
E come **Empoli**	S come **Savona**
F come **Firenze**	T come **Torino**
G come **Genova**	U come **Udine**
H come **hotel** *	V come **Venezia**
I come **Imola**	Z come **Zurigo** *
L come **Livorno**	

* Exceptions

To know how a word is spelled, one can ask: **Come si dice?** [*How do we say it?*]

To know how a word is written, one can ask: **Come si scrive?** [*How do we write it?*]

Locate all these cities above! Go online and locate them on a map of Italy. Have fun!

1.2 SUONI E PRONUNCIA

When students from different countries begin studying English, they often encounter challenges when dealing with pronunciation. Although very often one hears that Italian is pronounced as it is written, Italian has some rules that must be followed.

Below, you will find the basic rules of pronunciation in Italian. Vowels **E** and **O** can be pronounced **open** [*aperte*] or **closed** [*chiuse*], and this helps distinguish words with different meanings but written in the same way, such as **venti** [*twenty*], pronounced with a closed **E**, and **venti** [*winds*], pronounced with an open **E**.

1.2.1 COME PRONUNCIARE "C" E "G"

CA—CO—CU
[pronounced in English like K]

C has a hard sound when followed by the vowels **A**, **O**, and **U** (like in English *cat*).

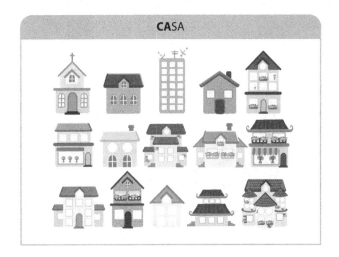

CASA

ECOLOGIA

CULTURA

CHE—CHI
[pronounced in English like K]

C followed by **HE** and **HI** also has a hard sound (like in English *Kentucky* and *kitchen*).

ORCHESTRA

CHIANTI

CHIANTI

NOTE that with foreign words, in most cases these combinations follow the rule of the language the word comes from (for instance, *cheeseburger* is pronounced like in English; *mise*, which means *outfit*, is pronounced like in French).

> SCA—SCHE—SCHI—SCO—SCU
> [pronounced in English like SK]

Also **SCA**, **SCHE**, **SCHI**, **SCO**, **SCU** have hard sounds.

SCACCHI

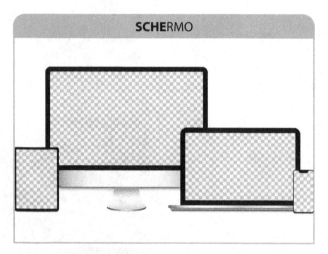

SCHERMO

DISCHI

SCOPPIO

SCUOLA

> QUA—QUE—QUI—QUO
> CQUA—CQUE—CQUI—CQUO
> [QU is pronounced in English like QU]

QU is pronounced like **CU** and like the English **QU** [*quartz*]: **QU**ADERNO, **QU**ESTO/A, A**QUI**-LONE, and **QUO**TA.

CQU is pronounced like **CU**: A**CQUA**—A**CQUE**RELLO—A**CQUI**STO—A**CQUO**LINA.

In Italian, the three nephews of Donald Duck, Huey, Dewey, and Louie, are called **Qui**, **Quo**, and **Qua**:

> CIA—CE—CI—CIO—CIU
> [pronounced in English like CH]

C has a soft sound when followed by the vowels **E** and **I** (like in English *chat* and *chitchat*).

CIABATTA

CENA

CITTÀ

CIOCCOLATO

CAC**CIU**CCO

SCIA—SCE—SCI—SCIO—SCIU
[pronounced in English like SH]

When **SC** is followed by the vowels **IA, E, I, IO,** and **IU,** the sound is soft. This combination of consonants and vowels is pronounced like the English sound *sh: sherif, she, shah, shopper, shoe.* There are certain exceptions, such as **sciare** [*to ski*], which is pronounced [shi-are] and not like [sha-re], and **sciatore/sciatrice** [*skier*], which are pronounced [shi-atore/shi-atrice]. **SCIE** in words are pronounced like **SCE:** among the most common words are **scienza** [*science*], **scienziata/o** [*scientist*], and **scientifico/a** [*scientific*].

<u>**NOTE**</u> that **SCE** (and **SCIE**) is pronounced like *sherif,* **SCI** is pronounced like *she,* **SCIA** is pronounced like *shampoo,* **SCIO** is pronounced like *shopper,* and **SCIU** is pronounced like *shoe.*

SCIAMANA/**SCIA**MANO

SCENEGGIATORE/**SCE**NEGGIATRICE

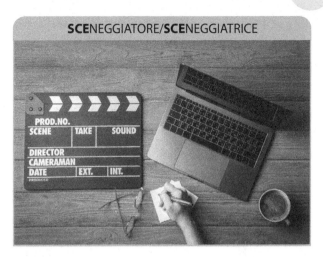

SCI

SCIOPERO

SCIU**SCIÀ**

The letter G follows the same rule of letter C.

> GA—GO—GU
> [pronounced in English like G]

G has a hard sound when followed by the vowels **A**, **O**, and **U** (like in English *gap*, *good*, *goat*, and *gulf*).

GATTO/**GA**TTA

GOL

DE**GU**STAZIONE

> GHE—GHI
> [pronounced in English like G]

When **G** is followed by **HE** and **HI**, the sound of the letters combined is hard (like in English *get* and *guitar*).

SPA**GHE**TTI

GHIACCIOLO

SGA—SGHE—SGHI—SGO—SGU
[pronounced in English like SG]

GIA—GE—GI—GIO—GIU
[pronounced in English like J]

Do not forget that **SGA**, **SGHE**, **SGHI**, **SGO**, and **SGU** also have hard sounds.

SGABELLO—**SGHE**MBO—**SGHI**GNAZZO— **SGO**NFIARE—**SGU**ARDO

G has a soft sound when followed by the vowels **E** and **I** (like in English *jazz* and *jeans*). There are certain exceptions, such as **magia** [*magic*], which is pronounced like [maj-ia] and not like [maj-a].

GIALLO/A

GELATERIA

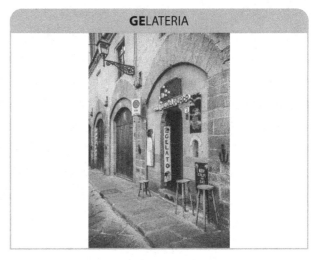

GITA

GIOCARE

GIUSTIZIA

GIU vs. GUI
[GIU is pronounced in English like J; GUI is pronounced in English like G]

GN and GL
[GN is pronounced in English like GN; GL is pronounced in English like Y]

Pay attention to the difference between **GIU** and **GUI**: **GIU**SEPPINA / **GIU**SEPPE (*Josephine/ Joseph*) and **GIU**STIZIA [*justice*] versus PIN-**GUI**NO [*penguin*] and LIN**GUI**NE.

GN—cognac, lasagna, gnocchi, cognome, giugno

GL—gli, aglio, scoglio, figlia / figlio, voglio, luglio

NOTA CULTURALE

Lo schwa. In linguistics, specifically in the field phonology and phonetics, the **schwa** is "(1) an unstressed mid-central vowel (such as the usual sound of the first and last vowels of the English word *America*); (2) the symbol ə used for the schwa sound and less widely for a similarly articulated stressed vowel (as in *cut*)" (Source: https://www.merriam-webster.com/dictionary/schwa). In the next chapters, we will learn more about the use of the schwa in Italian in connection with gender equality, inclusion and diversity. This sound is present in the Neapolitan dialect—for example, the word *mammeta* [*mammətə*] (tua madre) has two of them—as well as in the Piedmontese dialect.

 Esercitiamoci!

Listen to the following words and learn how to pronounce them. Continue to practice until you master the sounds.

CA — CHE — CHI — CO — CU
SCA — SCHE — SCHI — SCO — SCU

casa, cosa, maschera, scuola, chela, sconsolato/a, cascata, curiosare, scudo, che, colore, chiesa, calamita, maccheroni, schiuma, malachite, chi, coraggio, cuore, scansare, chiodo, scarpa, compagnia, caschetto, cultura, scheletro, scopa, custode

CIA—CE—CI—CIO—CIU

ceci, ciao, ciuffo, caciotta, mancia, cibo, cinepresa, ciambella, cioccolato, cipresso, ciondolo, ciurma, ciuccio, ciabatta, celeste, ciottolo, circo

SCIA—SCE—SCI—SCIO—SCIU

scetticismo, scenata, scivolo, sciame, pastasciutta, sciovinismo, sciupare, sciocchezza, asceta, scimmia, sciarpa, sciopero, scialle, cascina

GA—GHE—GHI—GO—GU
SGA—SGHE—SGHI—SGO—SGU

ghirlanda, ragazza, sgomento, sgherro, mago/a, mango, guardare, sgattaiolare, sghignazzo, sgommata, guizzo, ghiottoneria, sgarro, gola, sghiribizzo, sgualcito, gocciola, garage, guanciale, sgargiante, guscio, sgusciare, sguardo, ghepardo, sgorbio, ghianda

GIA—GE—GI—GIO—GIU

ginnastica, germe, mangiare, giullare, gente, ginepro, giardino, giocattolo, giornale, genitori, giudizio, giada, giovane, viaggio, ginestra, gemma, giallo/a, giusto/a, giaguaro, giaggiolo, magia

Lavoriamo con altre studentesse o altri studenti

With another student or in groups, look for words with the above sounds. Choose one word from each group among the ones listed above and look for its meaning in a dictionary, writing the definition next to the word:

	CHOSEN WORD	MEANING
CA—CHE—CHI—CO—CU		
SCA—SCHE—SCHI—SCO—SCU		
CIA—CE—CI—CIO—CIU		
SCIA—SCE—SCI—SCIO—SCIU		
GA—GHE—GHI—GO—GU		
SGA—SGHE—SGHI—SGO—SGU		
GIA—GE—GI—GIO—GIU		

 Lavoriamo con altre studentesse o altri studenti

A. Help B to complete his/her/their grid by dictating the words on your grid. Remember to spell each letter the second time you dictate the word.

AEREO	BARCA		DOTTORESSA		LINGUA
		ZONA BLU			
ITALIA		MARE	XILOFONO	OPERAIO	

B. Help A to complete his/her/their grid by dictating the words on your grid. Remember to spell each letter the second time you dictate the word.

		UNIVERSITÀ		VIAGGIO	
GASTRONOMIA	PASSAPORTO		REGIONE	QUARANTENA	FAMIGLIA
	IMPRENDITRICE				NONNA

1.2.2 LE CONSONANTI DOPPIE

In Italian, some words have similar spellings, but different meanings. When there are double consonants in one word, the pronunciation tends to be more accentuated. See some examples below:

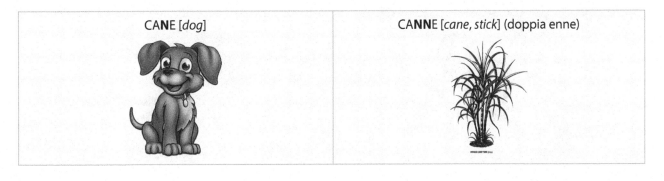

CANE [*dog*]   CANNE [*cane, stick*] (doppia enne)

CAPELLO [*hair*]

CAPPELLO [*hat*] (doppia pi)

CASA [*house, home*]

CASSA [*case, cashier*] (doppia esse)

COPIA [*copy*]

COPPIA [*pair, couple*] (doppia pi)

DITA [*fingers*]

DITTA [*firm*] (doppia ti)

NOTE [*notes*]

NOTTE [*night*] (doppia ti)

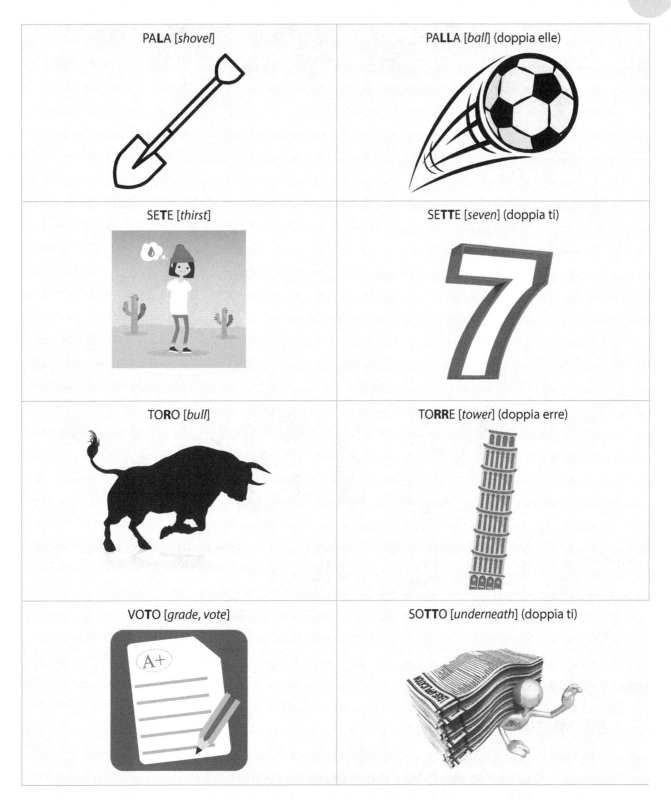

PALA [*shovel*]

PALLA [*ball*] (doppia elle)

SETE [*thirst*]

SETTE [*seven*] (doppia ti)

TORO [*bull*]

TORRE [*tower*] (doppia erre)

VOTO [*grade, vote*]

SOTTO [*underneath*] (doppia ti)

Make sure to practice the pronunciation of the double consonants.

Lavoriamo con altre studentesse o altri studenti

Find more double consonants in Italian (tip: **Google** "double consonants in Italian" in the **Images**). Write the word with one consonant on the left and the word with double consonants on the right:

UNA CONSONANTE	DOPPIA CONSONANTE

Share your findings with the class and practice your words as well as the words found by the other students. Do not forget to take notes.

1.3 I SALUTI

When interacting with someone in English, **formality** versus **informality** is made easier by the subject pronoun **you**. One uses it not only with a friend, a partner, a sibling, a relative, a parent, or another student, to name a few examples, but also with a professor, a doctor, the president of the university or of a nation. Like in many other languages, in Italian there are more distinctions and nuances in how and when one should be informal or formal. There are nuances that are also dictated by grammar structures. One should be aware that languages always evolve, and what is perceived as odd today might not be perceived as odd tomorrow. For example, think about **good** versus **well** in English: grammatically, it is correct to say *I am well*, however nowadays one often hears *I am good* rather than *I am well*.

1.3.1 INFORMALE E FORMALE

In Italian, there are two registers: formal and informal. One can be **INFORMAL** with family members, friends, classmates, someone who is much younger than us (a child), and peers of the same age (usually up to 25/30 years old). One should always be **FORMAL** with people who are older than the speaker, with peers of the same age (usually when one is older than 25/30 years old), people who one does not know well, professors, staff members, doctors, nurses, law enforcement, retailers, cleaners, taxi drivers, and so on. When one is not sure what register to use, one can be **SEMI-FORMAL** (see below what to use when).

Italians tended to be rather formal with greetings, however things are changing. Nowadays, one can witness more informality among younger generations, which was unimaginable only a few decades ago. In Italy, one might often hear *Buongiorno* [*good morning*] or *Buonasera* [*good evening*] followed by titles (Buongiorno, dottoressa/dottore; Buongiorno, professoressa/professore;

Buongiorno, signora/signore; Buonasera, avvocato/a; Buonasera, ingegnere/a; Buonasera, architetto/a). By saying **Buona giornata** or **Buona serata**, you are wishing someone a good day and a good evening.

1.3.2 I SALUTI ALL'ARRIVO

When you meet someone or a group of people, you greet the person or the group. In English, one often hears **How are you?** (or alike) as a way of saying **Hi/Hello**; In Italian, this expression does not mean *hi/hello*. In Italian, when one asks someone *How are you?* [**Come stai?/Come sta?/Come state?**], it means that one really wants to know how the person is doing. Because of this cultural difference, it is suggested that you always reply to this question, saying how you are actually doing. Furthermore, if you respond to an Italian that you are not doing so well, expect to have a long conversation!

When one meets someone (or a group of people), one uses the greetings below, utilising them differently based on the situations, namely if one is in a formal, informal, or semi-formal situation.

INFORMAL	FORMAL	SEMI-FORMAL
Buongiorno, Buon giorno	Buongiorno, Buon giorno	Buongiorno, Buon giorno
Ciao	Buon pomeriggio	Salve
	Buonasera, Buona sera	

Esercitiamoci!

Fill in the blanks with the greetings, paying attention to the context to evaluate what kind of situation it is, namely if it is formal, informal, or semi-formal:

Two friends meet: what would one say?

_____, Chiara!

_____, Francesca!

You meet your professor: what would you say?

_____, Professoressa!

_____, Liam!

At 9 am, you meet your 70-year-old neighbour: what would you say?

_____, signor Attilio!

_____, Abdul!

 Lavoriamo con altre studentesse o altri studenti

Check the sentences above with another student to make sure that they are correct. Do not forget that it is common to make mistakes: it is part of the learning process!

 Parliamo!

Time to speak! Greet as many students as possible in your class.

1.3.3 I SALUTI ALLA PARTENZA

Now that you have learned how to greet someone, you also need to learn to tell the person or the group of people goodbye. **What to use when** also depends on the level of formality and informality of the situation. Look at the chart below:

INFORMAL	FORMAL	SEMI-FORMAL
Ciao	Arriveder**La** (*one person*)	Arrivederci
Ci vediamo, Ci vediamo presto	Arriveder**ci** (*two or more people*)	A presto
A domani	A domani	A domani
Buona giornata	Buona giornata	Buona giornata
Buona serata	Buona serata	Buona serata
Buonanotte, Buona notte	Buonanotte, Buona notte	Buonanotte, Buona notte

See the dialogues below:

— Ciao Angelo, a domani!
— A domani, Pietro! Buon viaggio [*Have a safe trip*!]!

— Buonanotte, Luigi! Sogni d'oro [*Sweet dreams*]!
— Buonanotte, mamma!

Scriviamo!

Fill in the speech bubbles with the saluti you have just learned:

Esercitiamoci!

Fill the blanks with the greetings. Pay attention to the context to evaluate what kind of situation is:

After class: what would you say?

_____, Professoressa/Professore!

_____, Igiaba!

After the gym with your friend: what would you say?

_____, Steven!

_____, Melissa!

After an evening out: what would you say?

_____, Xin!

_____, Bojing and Ai!

Lavoriamo con altre studentesse o altri studenti

Check over the exercises above with another student or group of students to make sure that they are correct. Do not forget that it is common to make mistakes: it is part of the learning process!

 Parliamo!

Time to speak! Say **goodbye** to as many students as possible in your class.

1.4 I RINGRAZIAMENTI

It is now time to learn how to thank people and how to respond to **thank you**. Once again, the level of formality and informality might impact what you would say.

Thank you!

INFORMAL	FORMAL	SEMI-FORMAL
Grazie	Grazie	Grazie
Grazie mille	Grazie mille	Grazie mille
Ti ringrazio/**Vi** ringrazio	**La** ringrazio/**Vi** ringrazio	

You are welcome!

INFORMAL	FORMAL	SEMI-FORMAL
Prego	Prego	Prego
Di niente	Di niente	Di niente
Non c'è di che	Non c'è di che	Non c'è di che
Ci mancherebbe/Ci mancherebbe altro	Ci mancherebbe/Ci mancherebbe altro	Ci mancherebbe/Ci mancherebbe altro
Figura**ti**	**Si** figuri	

Esercitiamoci!

Fill in the blanks with the greetings. Pay attention to the context to evaluate what kind of situation it is:

When you borrow a book from a classmate: what would you say?

_____, Maddalena!

_____, Giorgio!

When your professor gives you back your exam: what would you say?

_____, Professore!

_____, Trinity!

Attenzione!

Always **PAY ATTENTION TO PUNCTUATION:** when they are used, there is always a reason. Punctuation includes period [*punto*], comma [*virgola*], colon [*due punti*], semicolon [*punto e virgola*], exclamation point/mark [*punto esclamativo*], and question point/mark [*punto interrogativo*].

 Lavoriamo con altre studentesse o altri studenti

Check over the exercise above with another student or group of students to make sure it is correct. Do not forget that it is common to make mistakes: it is part of the learning process!

 Parliamo!

Time to speak! Thank as many students as possible in your class and respond to thanks and continue to practice.

1.5 GLI INCONTRI

Now that you know how to greet people, how to say goodbye, and how to thank them. It is now time to ask them how they are doing.

When you **meet a friend**, you want to ask *how your friend is doing* [*Come stai?*], right?

Read the dialogue below:

— Ciao, Giulia!

— Ciao, Qing!

— Come stai?

— Bene, grazie, e tu?

— Anch'io bene, grazie!

— Ciao!

— Ciao!

When you **meet your professor**, you may want to ask *how your professor is doing* [*Come sta?*], and your professor wants to know *how all the students are doing* [*Come state?*].

Read the dialogue below:

— Buongiorno, ragazze e ragazzi!

— Buongiorno, Professoressa!

— Come state?

— Bene, grazie, e Lei come sta?

— Molto bene, grazie!

How are you doing? How are they doing?

One cultural aspect that you need to know is about the level of pain or happiness: in Italian, there is not a **pain scale level** such as in Australia, Canada, New Zealand, the UK, and the United States, as pictured below:

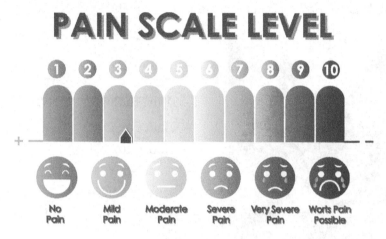

If you go to a doctor in Italy, the doctor might not ask you how much pain you are feeling from 1 to 10. Vice-versa, Italians who go to a doctor in the above-mentioned countries might not be able to give the doctor an exact diagnosis of their level of pain simply because they have not learned how to assess their level of pain from 1 to 10. It is a cultural nuance.

IO STO...	I AM..
Bene	Well
Molto bene	Very well
Benissimo	Very, very well
Non c'è male	It is not bad
Non male	Not so bad
Non troppo male	Not too bad
Così così	So so
Male	Bad
Molto male	Very bad
Malissimo	Very, very bad

 Scriviamo!

Create a dialogue based on a meeting with someone, a friend, or a professor. Please, use the greetings that we have learned in this chapter and the expressions of feeling.

 Lavoriamo con altre studentesse o altri studenti

Check the dialogue above with another student or group of students to make sure that it is correct. Do not forget that it is common to make mistakes: it is part of the learning process!

 Parliamo!

Time to speak! Using the above dialogue, speak with as many students as possible, and continue to practice.

LA PAGINA CULTURALE

Very often, when one thinks about language learning, grammar structures are the first things to come to mind. However, a language is not only grammar and words, but also it is culture and social elements. Above all, words matter and they shape the way we think about the world. Since a language is spoken by people, a language represents them, what they do, how they think, and how they see the world. Knowing a language means gaining a passport to know other people and their cultures, to open us up to diversity, to be more inclusive, and to foster equality and respect for all, while also understanding stereotypes as a limited way to represent the world we live in. The cultural messages that words bring with them have the power to shape your choices, widen your horizons, and in turn contribute to creating a more inclusive and diverse world with less social injustice.

Nigerian writer **Chimamanda Ngozi Adichie**, author of *Purple Hibiscus* (2003), *Half of a Yellow Sun* (2006), and *Americanah* (2013), delivered a wonderful TEDGlobal Talk in 2009: ***The Danger of a Single Story***. Watch the video online (https://www.ted.com/talks/chimamanda_ngozi_adichie_the_danger_of_a_single_story?language=en) and discuss it in class. This talk will help you understand the importance of cultures, intercultural communication, and sociolinguistics, which are the basis of studying a new language and interacting with people who are different from us.

As you learn how to read, listen, speak, and write in Italian, you will also discover Italy with the goal of taking a virtual trip to this fascinating country in the shape of a boot. You will deconstruct stereotypes, understanding them as a limited version of the story of humanity, and renegotiate meanings even in your own language. Knowing others is one of the best ways to know ourselves a little bit better as individuals and as a group of people and global citizens of the world.

In particular, in this first founding chapter, you will discover about the Italian regions and their names, the Italian language and its dialects, and the Italian gestures. Certainly, they are not exhaustive and you are encouraged to look for more information. Be curious and be open to the unknown! The world is at your fingertips!

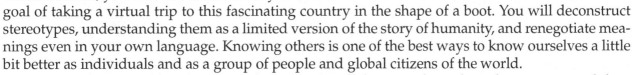

LE REGIONI ITALIANE

Look at the map above and respond to the following questions:

Quante [*How many*] regioni ci sono [*there are*] in Italia? _____

Quali [*What*] sono i nomi delle regioni? Scrivi [*Write*] i nomi delle regioni in italiano da Sud a Nord:

LA LINGUA ITALIANA STANDARD E I SUOI DIALETTI

The Italian standard language and the Italian dialects derive from Latin with influences from ancient Greek and other languages, such as Spanish and French. The Italian dialects are true languages that are very different from one another. Many Italian dialects/languages get their nouns from the regions, the city or town, or the Italian area where they are spoken.

Roma ⇒ il dialetto romano or romanesco
Firenze ⇒ il dialetto fiorentino
la Sicilia ⇒ il dialetto siciliano

Often, there are middle grounds. For instance, in the Tuscia area, in the Northern part of the Lazio region, there is a mixed dialect with influences from Rome, Southern Tuscany, and Umbria.

Choose five regions from the ones listed in the previous part and write their dialects next to them:

LA REGIONE	IL DIALETTO

I GESTI ITALIANI

Italians are well known for using gestures and we often say that they speak with their hands: **con le mani**. However, gestures are very informal. Here are some famous Italian gestures:

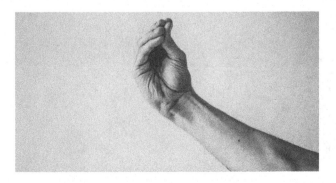

(**ma che dici?**—when you do not agree)

(**quando una cosa è perfetta**—the best of the best)

(**scusi/scusa**—to call for attention)

(**buonissimo/a**—to refer to food)

Now it is your turn: **Cosa significano questi gesti?** [*What do these gestures mean?*]. Let's practice them:

Look for more images of gestures on **Google** and for videos on **YouTube**. What gestures did you find? Share your findings with the class.

ESERCITIAMOCI CON LA CULTURA

A. What is culture and why is it important for the identity of a country and its people? Write all Italian words, expressions, and concepts you know that you can associate with Italian culture.

B. Lingua e dialetti. Look up the difference between a *lingua* and a *dialetto* on the net. Then find out what languages are spoken in Italy, how many *regioni* there are, and the names of some dialects that are spoken in those regions. Report what you find out to the class.

Exercises Credits

[1] Activity primarily contributed by Emanuele Occhipinti. Copyright © Kendall Hunt Publishing Company.

GLOSSARIO

Nomi [*Nouns*]

cultura [*culture*]

dialetto/i [*dialect/dialects*]

gesto/i [*gesture/gestures*]

inglese [*English*]

Italia [*Italy*]

italiana/o [*Italian*]

lingua/e [*language/languages*]

regione/i [*region/regions*]

Saluti [*Greetings*]

a domani [*till tomorrow*]

a presto [*till soon*]

arrivederci [*see you all—formal*]

arrivederLa [*see you—formal*]

buona giornata [*have a good day*]

buonanotte, buona notte [*good night*]

buonasera, buona sera [*good evening*]

buona serata [*have a good evening*]

buongiorno, buon giorno [*good morning*]

buon pomeriggio [*good afternoon*]

ciao [*hi, bye—informal*]

ci vediamo [*see you—informal*]

salve [*hello—semi-formal*]

Ringraziamenti [*Thanks*]

ci mancherebbe [*don't mention it*]

ci mancherebbe altro [*don't mention it*]

di niente [*you are welcome*]

figurati [*you are welcome—informal*]

grazie [*thank you*]

grazie mille [*thanks a million*]

La ringrazio [*thank you—formal*]

non c'è di che [*don't mention it*]

prego [*you are welcome*]

si figuri [*you are welcome—formal*]

ti ringrazio [*thank you—informal*]

vi ringrazio [*thank you all*]

Come stai/sta/state? [*How are you?*]

Come stai? [*How are you? —informal*]

Come sta? [*How are you? —formal*]

Come state? [*How are you all?*]

Sto... [*I am...*]

bene [*well*]

benissimo [*very well*]

così così [*so so*]

male [*bad*]

malissimo [*very, very bad*]

molto male [*very bad*]

non c'è male [*it's not too bad*]

non male [*not so bad*]

non troppo male [*not too bad*]

APPENDICE

IN-CLASS USEFUL WORDS

In a classroom, there are words that can be useful to learn in order to ask questions and respond to them:

PER L'INSEGNANTE/FOR THE EDUCATOR	
ITALIANO	**INGLESE**
Aprite il libro	Open the book
Aprite il libro a pagina...	Open the book at page...
Chiudete il libro	Close the book
Lavorate a coppie	Work in pairs
Lavorate in gruppi	Work in groups
Lavorate in gruppi di 2-3 studenti/studentesse	Work in groups of 2-3 students
Scrivete	Write
Leggete	Read
Ascoltate	Listen
Parlate	Speak/Talk
Compiti	Homework

PER LA CLASSE /FOR THE CLASS	
ITALIANO	**INGLESE**
Come si scrive PENNA?	How is PENNA [*pen*] written/spelled?
PENNA si scrive PI-E-ENNE-ENNE-A	PENNA is written/spelled as...
Come si pronuncia PENNA?	How is PENNA pronounced?
Non ho capito	I didn't understand
Può ripetere, per favore?	Could you repeat, please?
Ho capito	I understood
Posso uscire?	May I leave the class?

ACCENTS

In Italian, when the accents are present, they always fall on the last vowel of a word, and they are always graphic signs, which means that you have to include them. There are two types of accents, *acuto* (to the right) and *grave* (to the left): their direction is especially important when one types.

Look at the differences:

È (accento grave)	the pronunciation of the E is wide open
É (accento acuto)	the pronunciation of the E is closed
è vs. é—**è** [*is*] and **perché** [*why, because*]	

In most cases, the vowels A, I, O, and U have accents that are *grave*: città [*city*], colibrì [*hummingbird*], oblò [*porthole*], giù [*down*].

STRESS

In Italian, the stress can fall on different syllables (always vowels) within a word. However, if the (graphic) accent falls on the last syllable, these words are called *tronche*. If the stress falls on the second to last syllable, these words are called *piane* (most words in Italian are *piane*). If the stress falls on the third to last syllable, they are called *sdrucciole*. If the stress falls on the fourth from last syllable, they are called *bisdrucciole*.

The words that are *bisdrucciole* are mostly conjugated verbs. See the examples below:

Parole tronche (last syllable): **u-ni-ver-si-tà**
Parole piane (second to last): **e-du-ca-zio-ne**
Parole sdrucciole (third to last): **ba-si-li-co**
Parole bisdrucciole (fourth from last): **fab-bri-ca-no**

As a final note, when one asks questions in Italian, the stress is placed at the end of the question, right before the question marks.

IL MONDO DELL'ISTRUZIONE E DEL LAVORO

2

CAPITOLO

By the end of this chapter, you will be able to use the verb **essere** [*to be*] to express who you are, your nationality, and where you come from; to say your name and ask for the names of others; and to use **indefinite and definite articles** with **nouns**, both in the **singular** and **plural** forms. In terms of cultural elements, you will learn about the Italian education system and the world of work.

INIZIAMO

Read the dialogue below with another student, alternating roles:

Karim:	Ciao! Come ti chiami?
Marcella:	Mi chiamo Marcella, e tu come ti chiami?
Karim:	Io sono Karim. Piacere!
Marcella:	Piacere mio!
Karim:	Di dove sei?
Marcella:	Sono di Olbia, e tu di dove sei?
Karim:	Io sono di Marrakech. Sono marocchino.
Marcella:	Io sono italiana. Cosa fai?
Karim:	Sono un dottore. E tu cosa fai?
Marcella:	Sono una dentista. Come stai?
Karim:	Sto bene, grazie. E tu come stai?
Marcella:	Anch'io sto bene, grazie.
Karim:	A presto!
Marcella:	Ciao!

Work with another student to understand the content of this short dialogue. What do the words mean?

2.1 I PRONOMI PERSONALI SOGGETTO

In English, subject pronouns (**I, you, she/he/it, we, you all, they**) are mandatory in a sentence. However, in Italian, one can understand from the conjugated verb who is performing the action. Therefore, subject pronouns are not used in all sentences. They are used only to emphasize who exactly is doing the action or to highlight an opposition, such as "**Io** sono una dentista, **tu** sei un dottore [*I am a dentist, you are a doctor*]."

ENGLISH	ITALIAN
I	IO
YOU (one person)	TU
SHE/IT	LEI
HE/IT	LUI
WE	NOI
YOU ALL (two or more people)	VOI
THEY	LORO

What do you notice in the table? What are the differences between English and Italian? Why is it important to distinguish between **you** and **you all** to understand the subject pronouns in Italian? Prepare notes and have a class discussion.

Lavoriamo con altre studentesse o altri studenti

Look at the picture below with other classmates:

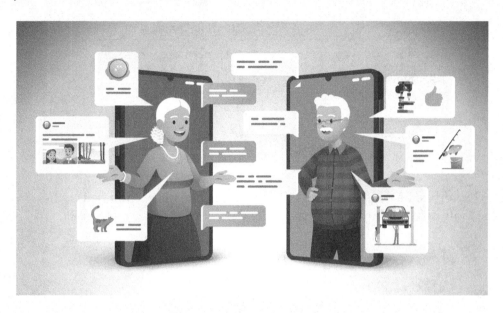

What subject pronouns do they use to communicate? Prepare notes and have a class discussion.

 ## LE PAROLE CONTANO

Choosing pronouns between two options, such as **lei/lui** [*she/he*], is limiting. This is particularly true for queer people who do not define themselves within the binary system. English is more flexible than Italian and other Romance languages. Indeed, the plural pronoun **they** is used in English to avoid the imposition of choosing only gender binary options. Furthermore, the recently coined **ze** has become popular in the Anglophone world. Yet, there is still much debate and cultural resistance. In this textbook, you will learn about alternative options to the standard grammar rules to make the Italian language more inclusive. You will discover that a language is in constant evolution and that words matter. Words can make women and minorities more visible, validate some behaviours, or stigmatize others. Learning a language is a powerful instrument to make the world more inclusive and sensitive to gender equality; make sure to read through all the boxes titled **LE PAROLE CONTANO** [*words matter*] since you will get many tips to use Italian in an inclusive and empowering way.

2.2 IL VERBO ESSERE

The verb **essere** [*to be*] is an **auxiliary verb** and is fundamental for communication in both English and Italian. As an experiment, try not to use the verb **to be** for a few hours: are you able to express yourself well, or does it limit your speaking?

Below, you will find the conjugations of this auxiliary verb. In both languages, this verb is **irregular**, which means that **it does not follow the regular pattern**.

TO BE	ESSERE
I AM	IO SONO
YOU ARE	TU SEI (informal)
YOU ARE	LEI È (formal)
HE/SHE/IT IS	LUI/LEI È
WE ARE	NOI SIAMO
YOU ALL ARE	VOI SIETE
THEY ARE	LORO SONO

To make the verb **to be** negative (**to not be**) in Italian, one places **non** before the conjugated verb. Complete the table below following the example.

NON ESSERE	
IO **NON** SONO	NOI
TU	VOI
LUI/LEI	LORO

As learned in the previous chapter (see its Appendix), accents are important in Italian. Look at the specific example with the verb essere:

Attenzione

E with or without accent has two different meanings:

È → IS (HE/SHE/IT IS)

E → AND

 Lavoriamo con altre studentesse o altri studenti

Answer the following questions with another classmate:

1. Do you know what **TO** (as part of the verb **to be**) indicates in English grammatically?
2. What does **CONJUGATING A VERB** mean?
3. **To be or not to be**: can you describe the **NEGATION RULE** in English and in Italian?
4. Think about the verb **TO BE** in English: how and when do you use it?

Like in English, in Italian one uses the verb **essere** to say the names, such as **I am Carine; I am Mark**. In the space below, write in Italian who you are:

_____

WHO IS WHO? or INDOVINA CHI		
To ask someone who he/she is (informally), in Italian one says:	**Chi sei?**	**Who are you?**—one person, informal
To ask someone who she/he is (formally), in Italian one says:	**Chi è (Lei)?**	**Who are you?**—one person, formal
To ask who someone is (she), in Italian one says:	**Chi è (lei)?**	**Who is she?**
To ask who someone is (he), in Italian one says:	**Chi è (lui)?**	**Who is he?**
To ask a group of people who they are, in Italian one says:	**Chi siete (voi)?**	**Who are you all?**—two or more people, formal and informal
To ask who multiple people are (they), in Italian one says:	**Chi sono (loro)?**	**Who are they?**

Why are the subject pronouns in parenthesis? What is the difference between **Chi è (Lei)?** and **Chi è (lei)?**

Scriviamo!

What do you ask when you want to know who someone is or who a group of people are?

You meet a professor and you want to know from her/him who the professor is:

_____

You meet a group of professors and you want to know from them who they are:

_____

You meet a new student and you want to know from him/her who the new student is:

_____

You want to know from a friend who is a professor: how do you ask this?

Option 1:_____

Option 2: _____

Why are there two options in the example above?

 Lavoriamo con altre studentesse o altri studenti

With another student, check over the answers to the previous exercise to make sure that they are correct. Then, share your thoughts about options 1 and 2 with the class.

Parliamo!

Ask your closest classmates who they are and say who you are, as in the example below:

— Ciao! Chi sei?

— Sono Sara. E tu chi sei?

— Sono Marco. Ciao!

— Ciao!

2.3 LE NAZIONALITÀ

In Italian, to express nationality, one uses the verb **essere.** Conventionally, nationality is formalized by a passport, however often people—particularly those who moved from one country to another and those whose parents were born in another place from where they live—also belong emotionally to other nations. Moreover, for example someone can be a first-generation Italian, American, or Australian; someone else might possess two nationalities; others might have multiple origins because of their ancestors or parents. Deciding who we are and where we come from is often a complex process.

How many times does one hear expressions such as *I am Italian and American, I am Canadian and Indian, I am French and Mexican*? With large-scale **emigrations from** different countries, **immigrations into** countries, or **migrations within** countries, the sense of belonging to one place or another is defined not only by a legal status (as formalized by a passport), but also by our feelings and identity. Since it is important to be able to express our identities and say who we are, you will learn how to define yourself in Italian along nationality lines. See the examples below:

> **Io sono/Tu sei/Lei è italiana**
> **Io sono/Tu sei/Lui è italiano**

What is the difference between **italiana** and **italiano**? What do you think the two endings might implicate?

Altri esempi:

Io sono albanese	Io sono australiano/a	Io sono cinese
Io sono americano/a	Io sono austriaca/o	Io sono eritreo/a
Io sono argentina/o	Io sono canadese	Io sono francese

Io sono indiana/o	Io sono neozelandese	Io sono salvadoregno/a
Io sono inglese	Io sono pachistano/a	Io sono spagnola/o
Io sono marocchino/a	Io sono portoghese	Io sono tedesco/a
Io sono messicana/o	Io sono portoricana/o	Io sono venezuelana/o

What do you notice from the sentences above? Why are there often two options? Respond to this question and then share your thoughts with the class.

The nationalities mentioned above are described based on countries; however, one can also express belonging to a continent or to a specific region:

Io sono africana/o	Io sono asiatica/o	Io sono europea/o
Io sono arabo/a	Io sono nordamericano/a	Io sono sudamericano/a

The various nationalities mentioned above are in the singular form, while those in the plural form are below:

Noi siamo/Voi siete/Loro sono italian<u>e</u>
Noi siamo/Voi siete/Loro sono italian<u>i</u>

What is the difference between **italian<u>e</u>** and **italian<u>i</u>**? What do you think the two endings might implicate?

Altri esempi:

Noi siamo albanesi	Noi siamo austriache/ austriaci	Noi siamo eritrei/e
Noi siamo americani/e		Noi siamo francesi
Noi siamo argentine/i	Noi siamo canadesi	Noi siamo indiane/i
Noi siamo australiani/e	Noi siamo cinesi	Noi siamo inglesi

Noi siamo marocchini/e   Noi siamo portoghesi   Noi siamo tedeschi/tedesche
Noi siamo messicane/i   Noi siamo portoricane/i   Noi siamo venezuelane/i
Noi siamo neozelandesi   Noi siamo salvadoregni/e
Noi siamo pachistani/e   Noi siamo spagnole/i

What do you notice from the sentences above? Take notes and then share your thoughts with the class.

 Lavoriamo con altre studentesse o altri studenti

Look at the sentences below and decide if the adjectives are in the masculine (m.) or feminine (f.) form, and in the singular (s.) or plural (pl.) form:

Io sono Italiana	f.	m.	s.	pl.
Io sono italiano	f.	m.	s.	pl.
Noi siamo italiane	f.	m.	s.	pl.
Noi siamo italiani	f.	m.	s.	pl.

Check over your answer with another student.

 Lavoriamo con altre studentesse o altri studenti

Look for more nationalities with another student.

Nationalities in Italian   **Their translation into English**

_____   _____

_____   _____

_____   _____

_____   _____

_____   _____

_____   _____

Share your findings with the class.

Write in Italian who you are based on your nationality (or nationalities) following the example: *Io sono italiana*; or *Io sono italiano*.

_____

Parliamo!

Ask some of your classmates about their nationalities. See some examples below:

- Sei italiana/o?

To answer the above question, respond:

- Sì, sono italiana/o.

OR

- No, non sono italiana/o. Sono americana/o.

LE PAROLE CONTANO

Using the slash (/) is a way to write in a more inclusive way. The ending in **a/o** or **o/a** addresses both feminine and masculine forms. You will learn more about this topic in the next chapters, however in this textbook the authors alternate **a/o** and **o/a** without always giving precedence to the conventional masculine form.

2.4 COME TI CHIAMI? DI DOVE SEI?

In this part of the chapter, you will learn how to ask for names and origin(s) when you are introduced to people who you do not know.

2.4.1 COME TI CHIAMI? MI CHIAMO…

To ask for names, one uses the expression **Come ti chiami?** [*What's your name*]. To this latter expression, one replies with **Mi chiamo…** [*My name is…*]. If you would like to reply with the verb **essere**, you could also say **Il mio nome è**… [*My name is…*] or **Sono**… [*I am…*].

To ask someone or a group of people about the first names:

ENGLISH	ITALIAN
What's your name?	**Come ti chiami?**—one person, informal
What's your name?	**Come si chiama (Lei)?**—one person, formal
What's her name?	**Come si chiama (lei)?**
What's his name?	**Come si chiama (lui)?**
What are your names?	**Come vi chiamate (voi)?**—two or more people, formal and informal
What are their names?	**Come si chiamano (loro)?**

How to respond to the questions above:

COME TI CHIAMI? MI CHIAMO…	
Come ti chiami?	**Mi chiamo…**
Come si chiama (Lei)?	**Mi chiamo…**
Come si chiama (lei)?	**Si chiama…**
Come si chiama (lui)?	**Si chiama…**
Come vi chiamate (voi)?	**Ci chiamiamo…**
Come si chiamano (loro)?	**Si chiamano…**

What do you notice from the two tables above? What are the differences between informal and formal registers? Share your thoughts with the class.

Read the two dialogues below:

— Ciao, mi chiamo Mira. Tu come ti chiami?
— Io mi chiamo Mario!
— Piacere!
— Piacere mio!

— Salve, come si chiama?
— Mi chiamo Hassan. Lei come si chiama?
— Mi chiamo Carolina!
— Piacere!
— Piacere!

What do you notice from the two dialogues above? What do you think **Piacere** means? Take notes and then share your findings with the class.

2.4.2 DI DOVE SEI? SONO DI...

To ask someone informally where that person is from, one uses the expression **Di dove sei?** [*Where are you from?*]. As mentioned earlier, when talking about nationalities, the answer is open to various options. Indeed, it is about identity and a sense of belonging to a certain place. To the question above, you can respond with (1) the town where you were born, (2) the town where you live now if it identifies your origin, (3) the town or city where you studied, (4) the town, the county/province, state/region that identifies you the best, (5) the country (or countries) you have your passport from, or (6) the continent you come from.

To ask someone or a group of people about their origins:

ENGLISH	ITALIAN
Where are you from?	**Di dove sei?**—one person, informal
Where are you from?	**Di dov'è (Lei)?**—one person, formal
Where is she from?	**Di dov'è (lei)?**
Where is he from?	**Di dov'è (lui)?**
Where are we from?	**Di dove siamo (noi)?**
Where are you all from?	**Di dove siete (voi)?**—two or more people, formal and informal
Where are they from?	**Di dove sono (loro)?**

How to respond to the questions above:

DI DOVE SEI? SONO DI...	
Di dove sei?	**Io sono di...**
Di dov'è (Lei)?	**Io sono di...**
Di dov'è (lei)?	**Lei è di...**
Di dov'è (lui)?	**Lui è di...**
Di dove siamo (noi)?	**Noi siamo di...**
Di dove siete (voi)?	**Noi siamo di...**
Di dove sono (loro)?	**Loro sono di...**

What do you notice from the two tables above? What are the differences between informal and formal registers? Share your thoughts with the class and then read the two dialogues below:

1. — Ciao, sono Mira. E tu come ti chiami?
   — Io sono Mario! Di dove sei, Mira?
   — Sono di Tirana, la capitale dell'Albania. E tu di dove sei, Mario?
   — Sono di Bari.

2. — Salve, come si chiama?
   — Sono Hassan. Lei come si chiama?
   — Io sono Carolina! Di dov'è, Hassan?
   — Sono di Dubai, una città negli Emirati Arabi. E Lei di dov'è, Carolina?
   — Sono di Tropea, in Calabria.

What do you notice about formal and informal tone from the two dialogues above? Take notes and then share them with the class.

Scriviamo!

Write below in Italian who you are and where you come from, reflecting on your family origins and background.

_____

_____

Check over your sentence(s) with another classmate and tell a classmate (in English) more about your family's origins and background.

Parliamo!

Ask some of your classmates about their origins (*Di dove sei? Sono di...*) and their nationalities (*Sei italiana/o? Sì, sono italiana/o; No, non sono italiana/o, sono neozelandese*); also, respond to their questions. Take notes on your interviews and then share your findings with the class (example: *Antonio è di Melbourne. Lui è australiano*).

2.4.3 PIACERE!

When one meets someone for the first time, in English one would conventionally say **Nice to meet you**. In Italian, one says **Piacere,** and the two shake hands.

NOTA CULTURALE

Incontri all'italiana. In formal situations, Italians shake hands. If they know each other well and have not seen each other for a long time, when they meet, they exchange two kisses on their cheeks. Italians usually do not hug as a form of greeting.

INFORMAL	FORMAL
Piacere!	Piacere!
Piacere di conoscer**ti**	Piacere di conoscer**La**

When you are in a **formal** situation, you can say **Piacere** or **Piacere di conoscerla** to the person in front of you. However, if you write formally, you would need to write: **Piacere di conoscerLa**. The capitalized **L** is a way to be formal in writing; as today the capitalized **L** is used less and it might disappear in the upcoming years.

Piacere mio means *It is my pleasure!* and it is usually used when replying to someone who already said **Piacere**. See below the dialogue from earlier in this chapter (2.4.1):

— Ciao, mi chiamo Mira. Tu come ti chiami?
— Io mi chiamo Mario!
— **Piacere!**
— **Piacere mio!**

Che piacere! means *What a pleasure!* It is used in the same way as it is used in English. For example: **Che piacere vederti, Giulia!** [*What a pleasure to see you, Giulia!*].

Esercitiamoci!

Complete the dialogue below:

— Ciao, mi chiamo Samantha Cristoforetti. Sono italiana. Sono un'astronauta. E tu?

_____

— _____.

— Piacere di conoscerti!

— Piacere di conoscerla!

Why does Samantha say **Piacere di conoscerti** while the interlocutor responds **Piacere di conoscerla**? What is the difference between the two? Take notes and then share them with the class.

Scriviamo!

1. Create a dialogue with the context provided here: You meet a new classmate. After having greeted the new classmate, ask for their name, introduce yourself by also saying your nationality and where you come from, then ask how the classmate is doing, say how you are doing, and say goodbye.

2. Create a dialogue with the context provided here: You meet a new professor. After having greeted the professor, ask for their name, introduce yourself by also saying your nationality and where you come from, then ask how the professor is doing, say how you are doing, and say goodbye.

 Lavoriamo con altre studentesse o altri studenti

Check over the two dialogues above with another student to make sure that they are correct. Do not forget that making mistakes is part of the learning process. **This is a fearless classroom!**

 Parliamo!

Talk to your closest classmates:

1. Greet them (see 1.3.2).
2. Ask for their names and introduce yourself, saying your first name and your nationality or nationalities (see 2.3 and 2.4).
3. Ask where they come from (see 2.4.2).
4. Do not forget to say **Piacere**, possibly shaking hands (see 2.4.3).
5. Ask how they are doing and say how you are doing (see 1.5); do not forget to thank them (see 1.4 and 1.5).
6. Say goodbye (see 1.3.3).

2.5 I NOMI AL SINGOLARE

By definition, English, like Danish and Swedish, is a natural gender language: for example, nouns referring to objects or things do not have a grammatical gender; however, specific pronouns in accordance with gender exist. Furthermore, some words and expressions are highly gendered and reveal the biological sex of a person: think about the words **chairman** or **policeman** that have been used for a long time and, sometimes, are still in use. Thanks to feminist linguists, queer activists, and campaigns over the past few decades, the vocabulary has become more inclusive to also adopt terms such as **chairwoman** or **chairperson** and **policewoman** or **police officer**. Moreover, words to describe professions with the embedded words **man** or **woman** have been recently replaced by **person**, thus addressing everyone, such as, **chairperson**; sometimes, the reference to gender has been dropped entirely, as in the case of **chair** as the **chair** of a Department in an American university. However, there is still much cultural resistance, and one might hear a variety of options and expressions such as **mankind** rather than **humankind**.

In Italian, like in other Romance languages, every noun has a grammatical gender; not only people, pets, and animals, but also objects. More neutral expressions **without gender-related specifications** exist, and you will learn about them throughout the textbook. As in English, words can indicate a singular number (just one), and these are **singular nouns**, or plurality (two or more), and these are **plural nouns**. In most cases, through the endings (and the context) one is able to identify the grammatical gender of a noun—if **feminine (f.)** or **masculine (m.)**—and its number, namely if it is **singular (s.)** or **plural (pl.)**.

In Italian, most nouns end with vowels:

1. In most cases, if a noun ends in **-O**, it is **masculine**; if it ends in **-A**, it is **feminine**.

2. In Italian, most **first names** also follow this rule: if a first name ends in -O, it most likely belongs to a man (*Stefano*); if it ends in -A, it most likely belongs to a woman (*Camilla*). Furthermore, with many immigrants from different countries having moved to Italy, one can also encounter foreign names that follow the rule of their native language, and one might not know from the ending their grammatical gender.

3. In Italian, there also are many nouns that end in **-E and they can be either feminine or masculine**. Through practice and by looking at a dictionary one can learn about their grammatical gender. However, there are some basic rules:

   a. If a noun ends in **-IONE**, such as *regione* and *televisione*, very likely it is a **feminine** noun.

   b. If a noun that ends in **-E has a graphic accent**, such as *caffè* or *tè*, the noun is very likely **masculine**.

   c. If a noun ends in **-TORE**, such as *viaggiatore* and *attore*, the noun is very likely **masculine**. If a noun ends in **-TRICE**, such as *viaggiatrice* and *attrice*, the noun is very likely **feminine**.

4. In Italian there are also **shorter versions of longer nouns**, like in English when one utilises *photo* for *photograph* or *bike* for *bicycle*. Look at the five words below and write next to them what gender you think they are, based on their endings:

CINEMATOGRAFO _____   MOTOCICLETTA _____

FOTOGRAFIA _____   AUTOMOBILE _____

BICICLETTA _____

When one shortens these words, their gender remains the same. Based on this rule, write down the grammatical gender of the five words below and check your answers with another student:

CINEMA _____   MOTO _____

FOTO _____   AUTO _____

BICI _____

There are also words that, once shortened, have the same ending, such as *aereo* (m.) from *aeroplano* (m.).

As in the cases above, in Italian there are **exceptions**: we highly recommend checking them in the **Appendix** at the end of this chapter.

See below a recap of the basic rule of the grammatical gender:

> **-O—masculine (m.s.)**
>
> **-A—feminine (f.s.)**
>
> **-E—feminine (f.s.) or masculine (m.s.)**

-O	amico
	cugino
	zio
	libro
	tavolo
-A	amica
	cugina
	studentessa
	zia
	penna
	sedia
-E	ape (f.)
	chiave (f.)
	regione (f.)
	televisione (f.)
	studente (m.)
	cane (m.)
	tè (m.)
	caffè (m.)

Nouns are very important in Italian since their grammatical gender (feminine or masculine) and their number (singular or plural) determine articles (definite and indefinite), adjectives, and at times also the conjugation of verbs, as you will learn throughout the study of the language.

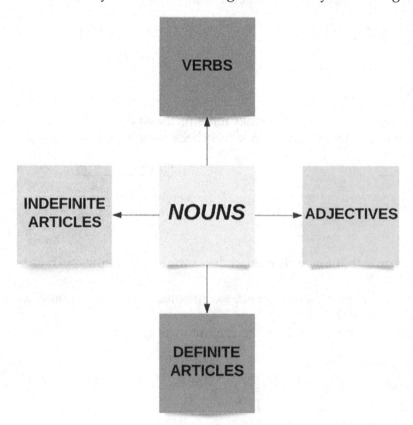

Esercitiamoci!

Look at the words below and write if they are **feminine (f.)** or **masculine (m.)**. To complete the exercise, do not forget to check the exceptions in the Appendix:

zaino _____	tesi _____	safari _____	mano _____
computer _____	Marco _____	mano _____	dito _____
lezione _____	ipotesi _____	crisi _____	stagione _____
classe _____	paese _____	cinema _____	sport _____
programma _____	regione _____	foto _____	film _____
sistema _____	provincia _____	bici _____	autobus _____
Sara _____	panorama _____	Nicola _____	tavolo _____
errore _____	virtù _____	auto _____	sedia _____
sbaglio _____	tabù _____	moto _____	scrivania _____
tema _____	Andrea _____	macchina _____	
problema _____	brindisi _____	radio _____	

Lavoriamo con altre studentesse o altri studenti

Check over your answers above with the class.

Attenzione

Certain words in English and in Italian look very similar in how they are spelled; however, they have different meanings: these words are called **false friends**. Do not be tricked by them!

- **argument** [*discussione*] vs. **argomento** [*topic*]
- **education** [*istruzione*] vs. **educazione** [*good manner, being polite*]
- **factory** [*fabbrica*] vs. **fattoria** [*farm*]
- **library** [*biblioteca*] vs. **libreria** [*bookshelf* and *bookstore/bookshop*]
- **magazine** [*giornale*] vs. **magazzino** [*warehouse*]
- **parent** [*genitore**] vs. **parente** [*family member*]
- **stamp** [*francobollo*] vs. **stampa** [*the press*]

* Note that **genitore** is masculine singular and **genitori** is masculine plural; the feminine singular is **genitrice** and the feminine plural is **genitrici**.

2.6 I NOMI AL PLURALE

Before looking at the rule for the pluralization of singular nouns in Italian, think about how you pluralize nouns in English: in most cases, you add an *s* at the end of a word; however, there also are special plural nouns (the exceptions) such as *women*, *men*, or *mice*. In Italian, there are different endings for nouns based on their grammatical gender, as the endings of the singular words are changed into plural endings, as indicated below:

-O (m.s.) → -I (m.pl.)

-A (f.s.) → -E (f.pl.)

-E (m.s. or f.s.) → -I (m.pl. or f.pl.)

-O → -I	amico → **amici** cugino → **cugini** zio → **zii** libro → **libri** tavolo → **tavoli**
-A → -E	amica → **amiche** (to keep the hard sound of the C) cugina → **cugine** studentessa → **studentesse** zia → **zie** penna → **penne** sedia → **sedie**
-E → -I	ape (f.) → **api** chiave (f.) → **chiavi** regione (f.) → **regioni** televisione (f.) → **televisioni** studente (m.) → **studenti** cane (m.) → **cani** tè (m.) → **tè*** caffè (m.) → **caffè***

* Tè and **caffè** are an exception since they do not change in the plural because of the graphic accent at their ends.

Beyond the two mentioned above, there are more **exceptions** when pluralizing nouns: check these in the Appendix at the end of this chapter.

LE PAROLE CONTANO

Persona (f.s.) [*person*] is often used as a gender-neutral term. Indeed, if you say **persona**, the biological sex of the person is not revealed, like in this example: **C'è una persona in giardino** [*There is someone in the garden*]. While the grammatical gender of **persona** is feminine, by using this term there are no references to biological sex as would be the case with **donna** [*woman*] or **uomo** [*man*]. In the plural, **persone** can also be used to describe a group of people without revealing further details about them, like in this example: **Ci sono molte persone in piazza** [*There are many people in the square*].

Another gender-neutral term that is used is **gente** (f.s.) [*people*], which means people as a group. While the grammatical gender of **gente** is feminine, this term, like **persona**, does not include references to biological sex. Look at the example: **C'è molta gente in giardino** [*There are many people in the garden*].

Esercitiamoci!

Beside the following words, write their plural and indicate if they are **f.pl.** or **m.pl.**, circling one of the two. Do not forget to look in the Appendix for the exceptions:

tabù _____ f.pl./m.pl.

caffè _____ f.pl./m.pl.

tesi _____ f.pl./m.pl.

città _____ f.pl./m.pl.

ipotesi _____ f.pl./m.pl.

hotel _____ f.pl./m.pl.

hamburger _____ f.pl./m.pl.

brindisi _____ f.pl./m.pl.

bar _____ f.pl./m.pl.

gioventù _____ f.pl./m.pl.

safari _____ f.pl./m.pl.

università _____ f.pl./m.pl.

tè _____ f.pl./m.pl.

crisi _____ f.pl./m.pl.

problemi _____ f.pl./m.pl.

cinema _____ f.pl./m.pl.

Lavoriamo con altre studentesse o altri studenti

Check over the exercises above with another student.

2.7 GLI ARTICOLI INDETERMINATIVI

Indefinite articles (in English **a/an**) refer to an unspecified person, place, idea, or thing. **Gli articoli indeterminativi** [*indefinite articles*] change in accordance with the gender of the noun they refer to, and they can be used only with singular nouns.

A/AN	
MASCHILE SINGOLARE	
UN	UN libro UN amico
UNO	UNO studente UNO gnomo UNO zio
FEMMINILE SINGOLARE	
UNA	UNA penna UNA studentessa
UN'	UN'amica UN'ape

What do you notice in the table above? When are **un, uno, una, un'** used in Italian? Take notes and share them with the class. Check the rules below and compare them with your guess:

LE REGOLE	
MASCHILE SINGOLARE	
UN	is used before nouns that are masculine singular beginning with vowels (a, e, i, o, u) or consonants.
UNO	is used before nouns that: 1. are masculine singular beginning with **S**+**consonant** (**st**adio, **st**udente, **sp**azio) 2. are masculine singular beginning with **Z** (**z**aino, **z**io, **z**oo). 3. are masculine singular beginning with two consonants such as **gn**, **pn**, **ps**, and **sc** (**gn**omo, **pn**eumatico, **ps**icologo, **sc**iatore).
FEMMINILE SINGOLARE	
UNA	is used before nouns that are feminine singular beginning with consonants.
UN'	is used before nouns that are feminine singular beginning with vowels (a, e, i, o, u).

Esercitiamoci!

First, fill in the blanks with the correct indefinite article:

_____ studentessa   _____ vacanza

_____ coppia   _____ psicologo

_____ amico   _____ direttrice

_____ radio   _____ programma televisivo

_____ cinema   _____ studente

_____ foto   _____ vespa

_____ tesi   _____ bici

_____ operaio   _____ zia

_____ arancia   _____ amica

Then, help identify items that one can buy in a grocery store, creating a **lista della spesa** [*shopping list*]. Look at the pictures and then write the noun of the item with the correct indefinite article.

Finally, make your own **lista della spesa**: what do you need? Write down five items not listed above together with their indefinite articles.

1. _____

2. _____

3. _____

4. _____

5. _____

 Lavoriamo con altre studentesse o altri studenti

Check over the exercises above with another student.

Esercitiamoci di più!

When you travel around the world, there are essential items that you need to fly internationally. First, look at the picture and add the correct indefinite articles.

_____ passaporto

_____ visto

_____ valigia

_____ adattatore

_____ biglietto aereo

Then, write down what you would bring with you beyond the items listed above (do not forget to include the indefinite articles):

1. _____

2. _____

3. _____

4. _____

5. _____

Check over the exercises above with another student.

Fai buon viaggio intorno al mondo!

2.8 GLI ARTICOLI DETERMINATIVI

Definite articles (in English **the**) refer to a specified person, place, idea, or thing. **Gli articoli determinativi** [*definite articles*] change in accordance with the gender and number of the noun(s) they refer to. They can be used with singular and plural nouns.

THE	
MASCHILE SINGOLARE	
IL	IL libro IL primo ministro
LO	LO studente LO gnomo LO zio
L'	L'amico L'argomento

MASCHILE PLURALE	
I	I libri I primi ministri
GLI	GLI studenti GLI gnomi GLI zii GLI amici GLI argomenti
FEMMINILE SINGOLARE	
LA	LA studentessa LA prima ministra
L'	L'amica L'ape
FEMMINILE PLURALE	
LE	LE studentesse LE prime ministre LE amiche LE api

What do you notice in the chart above? When are **il, lo, l', la, i, gli, le** used in Italian? Take notes and share them with the class. Now check the rules below and compare them with your guesses:

LE REGOLE	
MASCHILE SINGOLARE	
IL	is used before nouns that are masculine singular beginning with consonants.
LO	is used before nouns that: 1. are masculine singular beginning with **S**+**consonant** (**st**adio, **st**udente, **sp**azio) 2. are masculine singular beginning with **Z** (**z**aino, **z**io, **z**oo). 3. are masculine singular beginning with two consonants such as **gn, pn, ps**, and **sc** (**gn**omo, **pn**eumatico, **ps**icologo, **sc**iatore).
L'	is used before nouns that are masculine singular beginning with vowels (a, e, i, o, u).
MASCHILE PLURALE	
I	is used before nouns that are masculine plural beginning with consonants.
GLI	is used before nouns that: 1. are masculine plural beginning with vowels (a, e, i, o, u). 2. are masculine plural beginning with **S**+**consonant** (**st**adi, **st**udenti, **sp**azi) 3. are masculine plural beginning with **Z** (**z**aini, **z**ii, **z**oo). 4. are masculine plural beginning with two consonants such as **gn, pn, ps**, and **sc** (**gn**omi, **pn**eumatici, **ps**icologi, **sc**iatori).
FEMMINILE SINGOLARE	
LA	is used before nouns that are feminine singular beginning with consonants.
L'	is used before nouns that are feminine singular beginning with vowels (a, e, i, o, u).
FEMMINILE PLURALE	
LE	is used before nouns that are feminine plural beginning with consonants or vowels (a, e, i, o, u). LE does not elide in front of nouns.

Contrary to English, in Italian, countries are preceded by definite articles following the standard rules: **l'Italia, la Nuova Zelanda, il Portogallo, lo Sri Lanka, i Paesi Bassi**, or **gli Stati Uniti**. When a country is a smaller island, such as **Cuba, Porto Rico**, or **Capo Verde**, or a microstate such as **Andorra** or **San Marino**, they do <u>not</u> require a preceding article. However, if the country consists of a group of islands, definite articles are required like in the case of **le Maldive**. Continents are also preceded by definite articles: **l'Europa, l'Africa**, or **l'Australia**.

While cities do <u>not</u> require articles, Italian regions require them: **la Toscana, il Lazio, l'Umbria, la Sicilia**, or **la Sardegna.** Minor islands such as **Lampedusa, Capri**, or **Long Island** do <u>not</u> require articles. It is best to double check with your professor or with a dictionary if you are unsure about the use of articles with certain geographical terms.

I lavori (m.pl.)

LE professioni (f.pl)

LE PAROLE CONTANO

Many nouns of professions ending in **-e** can be often used for both masculine and feminine forms, such as **il presidente** (m.s.) and **la presidente** (f.s.), **il cantante** (m.s.) and **la cantante** (f.s.); however, not all of them. Think about **professore** (m.s.) and **professoressa** (f.s.), **dottore** (m.s.) and **dottoressa*** (f.s.), **infermiere** (m.s.) and **infermiera** (f.s.). When professions and roles exercised by women are coined with the ending in **-essa**, such as **studentessa** or **poetessa**, and are widely used in Italian, we suggest to continue using them; however, some words ending in **-essa** had negative connotations in the past and were used to diminish women's accomplishments, such as **presidentessa**: in this particular case, it is suggested to use **la presidente**.

Laura Boldrini, in passato è stata *[she was]* la presidente della Camera

***Medico** has been used for a long time for both female and male doctors; an alternative to this practice is to use **dottoressa** (f.s.) and **dottore** (m.s.). If one decides to use **medico**, it is suggested to use **medico** (m.s.) and **medici** (m.pl.), and **medica** (f.s.) and **mediche** (f.pl.): in this case, one is applying the same logic and grammar rule used for **operaio/a** and **avvocata/o.**

Esercitiamoci con le professioni!

First, fill in the blanks with the correct **definite article** in the **singular**:

_____ attore; _____ attrice

_____ scrittrice; _____ scrittore

_____ pittore; _____ pittrice

_____ o _____ barista (f. & m.)

_____ o _____ collega (f. & m.)

_____ o _____ regista (f. & m.)

_____ o _____ macchinista (f. & m.)

_____ poliziotto; _____ poliziotta

Although they are not professions:

_____ viaggiatrice; _____ viaggiatore

_____ o _____ turista (f. & m.)

Where would you like to travel soon? Write in Italian three countries that you would like to visit, and do not forget to add the definite article as in the example: **l'Italia**.

1. _____

2. _____

3. _____

Fill the blanks with the correct **definite article** in the **singular and plural**:

_____ operaia	_____ operaie
_____ operaio	_____ operai
_____ dottore	_____ dottori
_____ dottoressa	_____ dottoresse
_____ giudice (f.s.)	_____ giudici (f.pl.)
_____ giudice (m.s.)	_____ giudici (m.pl.)
_____ contadino	_____ contadini
_____ contadina	_____ contadine
_____ agricoltrice	_____ agricoltrici
_____ agricoltore	_____ agricoltori

_____ avvocata	_____ avvocate
_____ avvocato	_____ avvocati
_____ meccanico	_____ meccanici
_____ meccanica	_____ meccaniche

 ## LE PAROLE CONTANO

When referring to a female mechanic, you can simply say **meccanica**; for a group of female mechanics, you can say **meccaniche**. This way, one is applying the same logic and grammar rule used for **contadino/a** and **avvocata/o**.

_____ ingegnere   _____ ingegneri

_____ ingegnera   _____ ingegnere

_____ pilota (f.s.)   _____ pilote (f.pl.)

_____ pilota (m.s.)   _____ piloti (m.pl.)

 ## LE PAROLE CONTANO

With the increasing numbers of women in aviation, it has become necessary to address them with a feminine noun to describe their profession, such as **la comandante** (f.s.) and **le comandanti** (f.pl.), which were originally used only in the masculine forms, such as **il comandante** (m.s.) and **i comandanti** (m.pl.). The same applies to **l'assistente di volo** [*flight attendant*], a profession currently also widely performed by men: one can say **l'assistente**

di volo (m.s. & f.s.) and **gli assistenti di volo** (m.pl) and **le assistenti di volo** (f.pl). The English expressions **air hostess** and **air steward/ stewardess** are also gradually being phased out in favour of the neutral **flight attendant**.

Amelia Earhart, la prima pilota a tentare di fare il giro del mondo

In un aereo Alitalia

_____ operatore ecologico

_____ operatori ecologici

_____ operatrice ecologica

_____ operatrici ecologiche

_____ architetta   _____ architette

_____ architetto   _____ architetti

LE PAROLE CONTANO

As in the example of **medico** [*medical doctor*], **architetto** [*architect*] has often been used to also refer to a woman in the profession; currently one can use **architetta** (f.s.) and **architette** (f.pl.), applying the same logic and rules learned so far. An association of Italian female architects called **Rebel Architette** is advocating to use the two words in the feminine forms in all official documents. Google their name if you want to know more about them; since spring 2021 they have been able to use the first official **timbro** [*seal*] and have been recognized as **architetta/e**.

Lavoriamo con altre studentesse o altri studenti

Check over the exercise above with another student.

Scriviamo!

Write down five professions in the singular using a definite article.

1. _____

2. _____

3. _____

4. _____

5. _____

Now it is your turn! In the space below, write who you are or you would like to be using an indefinite article and a profession of your choice. Example: **Io sono un pompiere** [*firefighter*] or **Io vorrei essere** [*I would like to be*] **una regista**.

_____

There is another way to say what you do (or would like to do) for a living as in this example: **Io faccio il pompiere** [*firefighter*] or **Io vorrei fare la regista**. In the space below, write what you do or you would like to do for a living using the formulation with **fare** instead of **essere**.

_____

Lavoriamo con altre studentesse o altri studenti

Check over the exercise above with another student.

Parliamo!

Ask your classmates who they are or who they would like to be in terms of professions. You can ask questions such as:

Esempio #1:

— Chi sei?

— Sono un parrucchiere/una parrucchiera [*hairdresser*].

Esempio #2:

— Cosa vorresti essere? [*What would you like to be?*]

— Vorrei essere un'insegnante/un insegnante [*teacher*].

Esempio #3:

— Cosa fai o cosa vorresti fare? [*What do you do or would you like to do?*]

— Faccio/Vorrei fare l'avvocata/l'avvocato.

LE PAROLE CONTANO

As you might have gauged by now, for a long time, some nouns referring to professions were used only in the masculine forms, even if a woman performed that particular job. This was particularly the case with prestigious professions such as **ministro**, **medico**, and **ingegnere**. You might hear people still using the masculine nouns to refer to a woman who is a minister, a doctor, or an engineer and in other positions of power. However, to pursue gender equality, it is recommended that you use the feminine form, such as **la ministra**, **la medica**, **l'ingegnera**, **l'architetta**, etc.

Jacinda Arden, la prima ministra neozelandese

LA PAGINA CULTURALE

IL MONDO DELL'ISTRUZIONE

The education system in Italy goes from **il nido** [*nursery*] to **l'università** [*university*]. Schools and universities are mostly funded by the state, therefore they are public. There also are private schools and universities, however they are few in number. As Italy has gone through several reforms of the school system, school is now compulsory up to the first two years of high school; however, in the past, it was mandatory only up to middle school.

- The **nido** (up to 3 years old) is not compulsory.

■ Da 3 a 6 anni (tre anni di frequenza) [*from 3 to 6 years old: three years of attendance*]: **scuola dell'infanzia** [*kindergarten*]. It is not compulsory.

■ Da 6 a 11 anni (cinque anni di frequenza) [*from 6 to 11 years old: five years of attendance*]: **scuola elementare** or **scuola primaria** (prima, seconda, terza, quarta e quinta elementare). **Le insegnanti e gli insegnanti** [*teachers*] are called and addressed as **maestra** and **maestro**. It is compulsory.

■ Da 11 a 14 anni (tre anni di frequenza) [*from 11 to 14 years old: three years of attendance*]: **scuola media inferiore** or **scuola secondaria di primo grado** (prima, seconda e terza media). **Gli insegnanti e le insegnanti** are called and addressed as **professore** and **professoressa**. It is compulsory.

- Da 15 a 19 anni (cinque anni di frequenza) [*from 15 to 19 years old: five years of attendance*]: **scuola media superiore** or **scuola secondaria di secondo grado**. This cycle of studies has three options: **licei, istituti tecnici**, and i**stituti professionali** (prima, seconda, terza, quarta e quinta liceo/istituto tecnico/istituto professionale). Educators are called and addressed as **professoressa** and **professore**. The first two years are compulsory.

At the end of the five years of **la scuola media superiore** (the first two years of which are compulsory for all), there is an exam, which is the same for every Italian taking it in the same kind of high school.

In Italy there is not just one type of high school, but several different, highly specialized ones. The others include:

- **Liceo scientifico** with an emphasis on sciences, but also offering history, philosophy, mathematics, languages, and Latin courses. It is a preparatory high school toward university.
- **Liceo classico** with an emphasis on classics (Latin and Greek), but also offering sciences, history, philosophy, mathematics, and languages courses. It is a preparatory high school toward university.
- **Liceo linguistico** with an emphasis on languages. It is a preparatory high school toward university.
- **Liceo tecnologico** with an emphasis on technology. It is a preparatory high school toward university.
- **Istituto commerciale** with an emphasis on business.
- **Istituto professionale** with an emphasis on preparing students for trade professions such as electricians and plumbers.

After high school, one can continue with the university path.

During the last twenty years, the university system went through changes; nowadays, university is mostly divided into two parts:

- **Primo ciclo (laurea triennale)**: tre anni (equal to a BA)
- **Secondo ciclo (laurea magistrale)**: due anni (equal to an MA)

Several professional paths follow the 3+2-year structure, such as law school and engineering, while medical school is six years. In college, there are no General Education or Core Curriculum courses as they are covered in high school. In Italy, both high school and university are highly specialized and already focus on the chosen curriculum; this means that a doctor, a lawyer, an architect, or an engineer starts with their curriculum immediately after high school.

After the **laurea magistrale**, a student might continue toward a PhD in an Italian university (usually a three-year program). While only after a PhD can one be addressed as **Dottoressa** or **Dottore di Ricerca**—which corresponds to the title **Dr.** in the Anglophone countries—, already after the **laurea triennale** one holds the title of **Dottore** or **Dottoressa.**

Attending a public university in Italy is not free: although it is not as expensive as it is in anglophone countries, particularly in the United States, students pay tuition and fees based on their incomes or their parent(s) incomes, as in other European countries.

IL MONDO DEL LAVORO

In Italy, **il mondo del lavoro** [*the world of work*] is different from anglophone countries. For a long time, Italians sought to get a job for life, the so-called **posto fisso** or **a tempo indeterminato**. With **il**

posto fisso, it was very difficult to fire someone, and therefore with it came economic security. Most Italians worked only one job and did not change jobs as frequently as seen today in anglophone countries. With **il posto fisso**, which includes a working week (usually, Monday through Friday) of 40 hours, Italians had benefits, such as sick leave, maternity leave, paid vacation, and holidays off. With the Economic Boom (1958–1963), Italians in large numbers started to enjoy time off during weekends and summer vacation (in the past, in August many businesses shut down entirely, and many Italians enjoyed several weeks of vacation by the sea). Yet, owners of small businesses rarely had all these privileges, for example sick and maternity leaves or long vacations.

Nowadays, the circumstances have changed; it is more difficult to get **un posto a tempo indeterminato** (a contract for life up to retirement). Many jobs are **a tempo determinato** (for a few months or years), and the contracts are not as stable nor with all benefits as in the past; following a global trend, workers are often asked to be more flexible and treated more disposably. While for a long time one could get a job with a specialized high school diploma, currently it is not easy to find a good job even with a university degree, similar to many other places in the world.

Small businesses have started to disappear; while they have been the engine of the Italian economy for a long time, many **microimprese** [*small businesses*] cannot compete with big corporations. In an attempt to look for job security, many Italians currently prefer to be employed by a company or a firm rather than being self-employed, since they receive benefits such as sick and maternity leaves or paid vacations that they would not have as owners of small businesses.

In Italy, Labor Day is celebrated on May 1st.

ESERCITIAMOCI CON LA CULTURA

L'intervista. Read the interview below, look for the words that you do not know, and then answer the questions in Italian.

Il mondo della scuola e del lavoro

Chiara:	Salve, mi chiamo Chiara. Lei come si chiama?
Barbara:	Io sono Barbara. Lui è Mario, mio [*my*] marito.
Chiara:	Di dove siete?
Barbara e Mario:	Siamo di San Gimignano, una piccola città in Toscana tra [*between*] Siena e Firenze.

Chiara:	Come state?
Barbara e Mario:	Stiamo bene, grazie, e Lei?
Chiara:	Anch'io sto bene, grazie. Chi sono loro?
Barbara:	Loro sono i nostri [*our*] figli: si chiamano Giorgia e Giacomo.
Chiara:	Ciao, Giorgia! Ciao, Giacomo! Quanti anni avete [*how old are you*]?
Giorgia:	Io ho [*I am*] 20 anni.
Giacomo:	Io ho 12 anni.
Chiara:	Che classe fai [*In what grade are you*], Giacomo?
Giacomo:	Io sono in prima [*first year*] media [*middle school*].
Chiara:	Giorgia, tu vai [*go*] all'università? Che liceo hai fatto [*did you attend*] prima?
Giorgia:	Ho fatto il liceo delle scienze umane [*human sciences*]. Dopo l'esame di maturità [*after the final exam*], ho iniziato [*I have started*] l'università.
Chiara:	Cosa studi [*do you study*]?
Giorgia:	Adesso [*now*] studio storia, ma poi per la laurea triennale voglio [*I want*] studiare antropologia.
Chiara:	Barbara, che lavoro fa [*what do you do for a living*]?
Barbara:	Ho [*I have*] un negozio [*store*] a San Gimignano con Mario: il negozio si chiama *I Vecchi Sapori Toscani*. Mario e io vendiamo [*sell*] prodotti gastronomici. Abbiamo [*we have*] una commessa [*salesperson*].

Chiara:	Cosa vendete [*do you sell*]?
Barbara:	Pasta, vino, olio d'oliva, salse, salumi, formaggi e dolci tipici.
Chiara:	Vendete soprattutto [*mostly*] ai turisti?
Barbara:	Vendiamo molto [*a lot*] non solo [*not only*] ai turisti, ma anche [*but also*] ai locali.
Chiara:	Ci sono [*are there*] molti [*many*] turisti a San Gimignano?
Barbara:	Sì, ci sono molti turisti a San Gimignano, specialmente d'estate.
Chiara:	Che studi ha fatto [*what did you study*], Barbara?

Barbara:	Il liceo, e poi all'università ho studiato [*I studied*] scienze politiche.
Chiara:	Grazie mille a tutti e due per l'intervista!
Barbara e Mario:	Grazie a Lei e a presto!

Rispondi alle seguenti domande:

1. Come si chiamano i membri della famiglia? _____

_____

2. Dove vivono? _____

3. Dov'è la città dove vivono? _____

4. Quanti anni ha Giorgia? _____

5. Quanti anni ha Giacomo? _____

6. Che classe fa Giacomo? _____

7. Che liceo ha fatto Giorgia? _____

8. Cosa studia Giorgia all'università? _____

9. Cosa fanno Barbara e Mario? _____

10. Come si chiama il negozio? _____

11. Cosa vendono Barbara e Mario? _____

_____

12. A chi vendono Barbara e Mario? _____

13. Ci sono molti turisti a San Gimignano? _____

14. Quando ci sono i turisti a San Gimignano? _____

15. Cosa ha studiato Barbara? _____

16. L'intervista è formale o informale? _____

GLOSSARIO

auto/automobile [*automobile, car*]

bici/bicicletta [*bike/bicycle*]

che piacere! [*what a pleasure!*]

cinema/cinematografo [*cinema*]

è [*she/he is*]

e [*and*]

foto/fotografia [*photo/photograph*]

lista della spesa [*shopping list*]

moto/motocicletta [*motorcycle*]

passaporto [*passport*]

piacere [*nice to meet you*]

piacere di conoscerLa [*nice meeting you—formal*]

piacere di conoscerti [*nice meeting you—informal*]

piacere mio [*it is my pleasure*]

scuola [*school*]

studentessa/studente [*student*]

turista [*tourist*]

università [*university*]

viaggiatrice/viaggiatore [*traveller*]

Domande [*Questions*]

Chi sei? [*Who are you?*]

Come ti chiami? [*What's your name?*]

Cosa fai? [*What do you do?*]

Cosa vorresti essere? [*What would you like to be?*]

Cosa vorresti fare? [*What would you like to do?*]

Di dove sei? [*Where are you from?*]

Nazionalità [*Nationality/Nationalities*]

africana/o [*African*]

albanese [*Albanian*]

americana/o [*American*]

araba/o [*Arab*]

argentina/o [*Argentinian*]

australiana/o [*Australian*]

austriaca/o [*Austrian*]

canadese [*Canadian*]

cinese [*Chinese*]

eritrea/o [*Eritrean*]

europea/o [*European*]

francese [*French*]

greca/o [*Greek*]

indiana/o [*Indian*]

inglese [*English*]

irlandese [*Irish*]

italiana/o [*Italian*]

marocchina/o [*Moroccan*]

messicana/o [*Mexican*]

neozelandese [*New Zealander*]

pachistana/o [*Pakistani*]

portoghese [*Portuguese*]

portoricana/o [*Puerto Rican*]

salvadoregna/o [*Salvadorian*]

spagnola/o [*Spanish*]

sudamericana/o [*South American*]

tedesca/o [*German*]

venezuelana/o [*Venezuelan*]

Il mondo del lavoro [*the world of work*]

agricoltrice/agricoltore/ [*farmer*]

architetta/o [*architect*]

assistente di volo [*flight attendant*]

assistente sociale [*social worker*]

attrice/attore [*actor/actress*]

avvocata/o [*attorney*]

barista [*bartender*]

cantante [*singer*]

collega [*colleague*]

comandante [*captain*]

contadina/o [*farmer*]

dottoressa/dottore [*doctor*]

giudice [*judge*]

infermiera/e [*nurse*]

ingegnera/e [*engineer*]

insegnante [*teacher*]

macchinista [*driver*]

maestra/o [*teacher*]

meccanica/o [*mechanic*]

medica/o [*medical doctor*]

operaia/o [*worker*)]

operatrice ecologica/operatore ecologico [*waste collector*]

parrucchiera/e [*hairdresser*]

pilota [*pilot*]

pittrice/pittore [*painter*]

poetessa/poeta [*poet*]

poliziotta/o [*police officer*]

presidente [*president*]

professoressa/professore [*professor*]

regista [*film director*]

scrittrice/scrittore [*writer*]

APPENDICE

NOMI AL SINGOLARE: ECCEZIONI

1. In Italian, there are exceptions: there are first names that end in **-a** and belong to men, such as **Andrea** (in Italy, this first name used to be for men and not for women; its Italian feminine version was **Andreina**; however, recently, Andrea as a woman's name has become common) and **Nicola** (the feminine version of Nicola is **Nicoletta**). Certain feminine names, such as **Consuelo**, which is a woman's first name ending in **-o**, are also widely used. When a first name ends in **-i**, such as **Luigi** or **Giovanni**, or in **-e**, such as **Giuseppe** or **Emanuele**, it usually belongs to men.

2. Other **exceptions** that are usually **masculine** can be found below:

   a. Nouns ending in a consonant, such as **hotel, bar**, or **hamburger**, are of foreign origin and, in most cases, they are masculine.

   b. If a noun has only one syllable such as **re** (but also **tè** that has a graphic accent and it also is monosyllabic), it is very likely masculine.

   c. If a noun derives from the Greek language, it might end in **-a** and be masculine, such as **tema, problema**, or **programma**: please note that these words do not end simply in **-a**, but in **-ma**. Still, not many words ending in **-ma** are masculine: most of them are feminine, such as **mamma** or **palma** [*palm*].

   d. Other masculine words ending in **-a** are words such as **poeta** (its original feminine version is **poetessa**, however **la poeta** has started to be commonly used too).

   e. **Papà** [*dad*] in some Italian regions and **Papa** [*Pope*] are masculine: pay attention to the graphic accent (adding or not adding it changes the meaning of the word). **Babbo** [*dad*] in some other Italian regions is masculine.

   f. if a noun ends in **-i** such as **brindisi, taxi**, or **safari,** it might be a masculine word. See below for words ending in **-i** that are feminine.

3. See below for **exceptions** of words that are usually **feminine**:

   a. If a noun that ends in **-a** or **-u** has a graphic accent, such as **università, città, gioventù**, or **tabù**, it is very likely a feminine noun.

   b. There are words ending in **-o** that are feminine, such as **mano** or **radio**.

   c. As mentioned previously, there are also words ending in **-i** in the singular that are derived from Greek and are usually feminine, such as **tesi, crisi**, or **ipotesi**.

I PLURALI: ECCEZIONI

In the first chapter, you studied the sounds and learned that certain combinations have a hard sound (such as CA, CO, CU, SCA, SCO, SCU, CHE, CHI, SCHE, SCHI, GA, GO, GU, SGA, SGO, SGU, SGHE, SGHI) while others have a soft sound (CIA, CE, CI, CIO, CIU, SCIA, SCE, SCI, SCIO, SCIU, GIA, GE, GI, GIO, GIU). Because of these phonetic rules, there are cases when one must add an **H** when pluralizing a noun to keep its **hard sound**:

a. Masculine nouns ending in -CO pluralize in **-CHI** and -GO pluralize in **-GHI**: banco (m.s.) → **banchi** (m.pl.); disco (m.s.) → **dischi** (m.pl.); albergo (m.s.) → **alberghi** (m.pl.); mago (m.s.) → **maghi** (m.pl.). *Exceptions*: amico (m.s.) → **amici** (m.pl.); greco (m.s.) → **greci** (m.pl.); medico (m.s.) → **medici** (m.pl.); psicologo (m.s.) → **psicologi** (m.pl.); archeologo (m.s.) → **archeologi** (m.pl.).

b. Feminine nouns ending in -CA pluralize in **-CHE** and -GA pluralize in **-GHE**: amica (f.s.) → **amiche** (f.pl.); archeologa (f.s.) → **archeologhe** (f.pl.); psicologa (f.s.) → **psicologhe** (f.pl.).

Regarding the **soft sounds**:

a. Feminine nouns ending in -CIA pluralize in **-CIE** and -GIA pluralize in **-GIE** if -CIA and -GIA are preceded by a vowel or if the vowel **I** is stressed: magia (f.s.) → **magie** (f.pl.); farmacia (f.s.) → **farmacie** (f.pl.); acacia (f.s.) → **acacie** (f.pl.); camicia (f.s.) → **camicie** (f.pl.); ciliegia (f.s.) → **ciliegie** (f.pl.); valigia (f.s.) → **valigie** (f.pl.).

b. Feminine nouns ending in -CIA pluralize in **-CE** and in -GIA pluralize in **-GE** when **C** and **G** are preceded by consonants: ascia (f.s.) → **asce** (f.pl.); biscia (f.s.) → **bisce** (f.pl.); boccia (f.s.) → **bocce** (f.pl.); pioggia (f.s.) → **piogge** (f.pl.); spiaggia (f.s.) → **spiagge** (f.pl.).

c. Masculine nouns ending in -CIO pluralize in **-CI** and -GIO pluralize in **-GI**: cappuccio (m.s.) → **cappucci** (m.pl.); formaggio (m.s.) → **formaggi** (m.pl.).

Regarding the shorter versions of longer nouns:

a. The longer versions of the nouns follow the rule: **cinematografi** (m.pl.), **fotografie, motociclette, automobili,** and **biciclette** (all f.pl.).

b. The shorter versions do **not** change in the plural and keep the original gender: cinema (m.s.) → **cinema** (m.pl.); foto (f.s.) → **foto** (f.pl.); moto (f.s.) → **moto** (f.pl.); auto (f.s.) → **auto** (f.pl.); bici (f.s.) → **bici** (f.pl.). One knows if a word is plural or singular from the context and other parts of the sentence.

Below, find the nouns that **do <u>not</u> change in the plural**:

a. a noun (f. or m.) with a graphic accent (**città, università, tè, caffè, papà, virtù, gioventù, tabù**);

b. a noun ending with a consonant (**hotel, hamburger, sport, autobus**);

c. a noun with only one syllable (**re, sci**);

d. a noun ending with -i (m. or f.) (**sintesi, tesi, brindisi, safari, tesi, crisi, ipotesi, taxi**);

e. **radio** (f.s.) does not change in the plural: **radio** (f.pl.).

The exceptions confirming the rule:

Nouns ending in -a that are masculine are pluralized as if they were nouns ending in -o: problema (m.s.) → **problemi** (m.pl.); tema (m.s.) → **temi** (m.pl.); poeta (m.s.) → **poeti** (m.pl.); programma (m.s.) → **programmi** (m.pl.); Papa (m.s.) → **Papi** (m.pl.). Note that if **poeta** is used in its feminine form, the feminine plural is **poete**.

Other exceptions:

a. The plural of **mano** (f.s.) is **mani** (f.pl.).

b. The plural of **dito** (m.s.) is **dita** (f.pl.). **Diti** (m.pl.) refers to the *toes* and not to the fingers of a hand.

c. The plural of **uomo** (m.s.) is **uomini** (m.pl.).

d. The plural of **uovo** (m.s.) is **uova** (f.pl.).

e. The plural of **miglio** (m.s.) is **miglia** (f.pl.).

f. The plural of **paio** (m.s.) is **paia** (f.pl.).

SOURCES FOR EDUCATORS

If you would like to learn more about gender equality and Italian grammar, you should look at the works by Alma Sabatini, in particular *Il sessismo nella lingua italiana* (1987), and, more recently, the works by Cecilia Robustelli. You can download a free pdf guide from the net: *Donne, Grammatica e Media. Suggerimenti per l'uso dell'italiano* (2014) edited by Robustelli and in collaboration with G.I.U.L.I.A (Giornaliste Unite, Libere, Autonome) journalists: in the appendix, you will find a long list of professions in both feminine and masculine forms, which are helpful for addressing issues of grammar and gender equality in the classroom.

https://www.lettere.uniroma1.it/sites/default/files/1134/donne_grammatica_media.pdf

Furthermore, make sure to look at Annalisa Somma and Gabriele Maestri (edited by), *Il sessismo nella lingua italiana. Trent'anni dopo Alma Sabatini* (2020), *Femminili singolari* (2019) by Vera Gheno and *Gender, Discourse and Ideology in Italian* (2018) by Federica Formato.

If you would like to learn more about gender equality and second language acquisition, see also: Francesca Calamita, "Post-pandemic Messages of Gender Equality, Inclusion and Diversity in Italian Language Courses and Beyond: Yes, You Can (too)!", in *Beyond* (ISI-Florence and Umbra Institute-Perugia), n. 4, October 2021, pp. 8-20; and Francesca Calamita & Roberta Trapè, "Virtual Exchanges and Gender-inclusive Language: An Intercultural Citizenship Project to Foster Equality", in *Blended Learning and the Global South*, edited by Giovanna Carloni, Christopher Fotheringham, Anita Virga, and Brian Zuccalà (Edizioni Ca' Foscari, University of Venice: Venice, 2021), pp. 115-130.

LE FAMIGLIE ITALIANE E LE LORO DIVERSITÀ

CAPITOLO 3

By the end of this chapter, you will be able to count up to 100, to use **c'è** [*there is*] and **ci sono** [*there are*], to learn the adjectives and the verb **avere** [*to have*], including its most common idiomatic expressions, to use possessive adjectives, and to refer to expressions of time such as days of the week, months, and seasons. Do not forget that a language builds on previous knowledge, therefore refer back to the previous chapters when needed. In terms of cultural elements, you will learn about Italy and its diverse families.

INIZIAMO

Read the dialogue below with another student, alternating roles:

Ravina:	Ciao, Martin! Come stai?
Martin:	Ciao, Ravina! Sto bene, grazie, e tu?
Ravina:	Anch'io sto bene, grazie. Che piacere, Martin! Sono contenta di vederti [*to see you*]!
Martin:	Anch'io sono contento. Hai i capelli rossi adesso?
Ravina:	Sì, ho i capelli rossi. Avevo bisogno di cambiare [*I needed to change*].
Martin:	Sono belli! Ti stanno bene [*They fit you*].
Ravina:	Grazie! Che caldo [*So hot*]! Ho sete.
Martin:	Anch'io ho sete. C'è un bar. Andiamo [*let's go*]!
Ravina:	Sì, andiamo. Oggi devo studiare [*I have to study*] molto, ma una pausa per un espresso è perfetta! E poi quando ci sono gli amici, è sempre un piacere!
Martin:	Hai ragione!
Ravina:	Ho sempre ragione!
Martin:	Hai lo stesso numero di telefono?
Ravina:	Sì, e tu?
Martin:	Io ho un nuovo numero: 345 7341638.
Ravina:	Grazie!
Martin:	Prego!

Work with another student to understand the content of this short dialogue. Do you know what the words mean? Look up their meanings if you do not know them.

3.1 I NUMERI DA ZERO A 100

In this chapter, you will explore numbers up to 10, then up to 20, and finally up to 100. Below you will find the first group with numbers from 1 to 10 (**zero** in Italian is also spelt like in English):

UNO	DUE	TRE	QUATTRO	CINQUE
SEI	SETTE	OTTO	NOVE	DIECI

For the numbers from 11 to 20, think about English first: for instance, what does *seventeen* mean? Exactly: *seven+ten*! In Italian, one forms the numbers from 11 to 19 in the same way:

UNDICI	DODICI	TREDICI	QUATTORDICI	QUINDICI
SEDICI	DICIASSETTE	DICIOTTO	DICIANNOVE	VENTI

Check the Appendix for some tips on how to remember the numbers from 11 to 19 in Italian. Furthermore, the numbers from 21 to 29 are formed like in English. Complete the table below:

VENTUNO	VENTIDUE	VENTITRÉ		
		VENTOTTO		TRENTA

As you can see from the table above, **venti** drops its final vowel with **-uno** and **-otto**: this pattern repeats with all the numbers in the teens. The addition of three (**tre**) requires an accent, like in the example of **ventitré**.

Like in English, in Italian, the **tens** (twenty, thirty, forty, etc.) are reminiscent of the numbers from 1 to 10. Complete the table below:

TRENTA	QUARANTA		SESSANTA
			CENTO

The pronunciation of **sessanta** and **settanta** can be challenging, pay attention to it!

Now, write the numbers from 61 to 69 in the following table:

	SESSANTADUE			
				SETTANTA

The number **uno** changes in accordance with the noun it precedes. The forms of the indefinite article **uno/una/un'/un** and the number **uno** are the same:

un gatto [a/one male cat]	un amico [a/one male friend]	uno zio [a/one uncle]
una gatta [a/one female cat]	un'amica [a/one female friend]	una zia [a/one aunt]

In the same way, you must pluralize nouns and adjectives when you have two or more in number.

due gatti   cinque amici   otto zii

tre gatte   sette amiche   dieci zie

Virgole, punti e numeri. In Italy, one uses commas and periods/full stops with numbers, but with a reverse of the English practice. Instead of writing 1.50 as in English, in Italian one writes **1,50** (**uno virgola cinquanta**). For large numbers, one uses periods: instead of 1,000 as in English, in Italian one writes **1.000** (**mille**).

Scriviamo!

Write the Italian words for each number:

7 _____   71 _____

15 _____   77 _____

33 _____   82 _____

44 _____   93 _____

58 _____   95 _____

66 _____   87 _____

69 _____   45 _____

Lavoriamo con altre studentesse o altri studenti

Check over the numbers above with another student. Do not forget that it is part of the learning process to make mistakes. **This is a fearless classroom!**

NOTA CULTURALE

I numeri di telefono in italiano e la messaggistica. In Italian phone numbers there are no minuses or parentheses, as in **0039 010 9213118**: 0039 is the country code, 010 is the city code, and 9213118 is the local phone number. One reads it as: zero zero trentanove, zero dieci, novantadue tredici undici otto. This means putting together digits in pairs, but when there is a single unit remaining, you read it by itself (like the number 8 at the end of the example above). You might also hear **più trentanove**, as internationally 00 can be replaced by a + for all countries, such as +39 for Italy and +44 for the UK.

Many Italians exchange messages via Apps such as **WhatsApp**, **Telegram**, or **Viber**. Furthermore, many Italians use social media, such as Facebook, Instagram, Twitter, and TikTok, to name a few, to keep in touch with friends, family members, and acquaintances, as in many other parts of the globe. Traditional text messages (called **SMS: esse emme esse**) were used heavily in the past, but less frequently today.

Lavoriamo con altre studentesse o altri studenti

In pairs, take turns reading the following phone numbers aloud:

1. Il numero di telefono di Anna è 0039 081 935466
2. Il numero di telefono di Simon è 001 731 5647767
3. Il numero di telefono di Laila è 0033 25 276897
4. Il numero di telefono di Rebecca è 0064 30 3848476

5. Il numero di telefono di Arun è 0091 48 4567889
6. Il numero di telefono di Yoon-Hwa è 0082 67 304386
7. Il numero di telefono di Khalid è 00212 57 300498
8. Il numero di telefono di Rosibel è 00503 06 4533075

0039 is the country code for **Italy**	**0091** is the country code for **India**
001 is the country code for the **USA**	**0082** is the country code for **South Korea**
0033 is the country code for **France**	**00212** is the country code for **Morocco**
0064 is the country code for **New Zealand**	**00503** is the country code for **El Salvador**

 Parliamo!

First, ask your classmates for their phone numbers:

— **Qual è il tuo numero di telefono?**

— Il mio numero di telefono è...

Then, ask them if they know other country codes:

— Quali altri prefissi internazionali conosci [*you know*]?

— Nigeria: 00234.

La moneta. Being able to express numbers in Italian will help you out with transactions. In Italy, people paid with **lire** before the euro became the currency of the European Union starting on January 1, 2002. At that time, **le lire** (**lira** in the singular) became part of Italian economic history, and they were exchanged at a rate of **1.936,27 lire** for **un euro**:

Le monete [*coins*] are: **2 euro, 1 euro, 50 centesimi, 20 centesimi, 10 centesimi, 5 centesimi, 2 centesimi**, and **1 centesimo**.

Euros have several denominations. **Le banconote** [*bills*] are in denominations of **500 euro, 200 euro, 100 euro, 50 euro, 20 euro, 10 euro**, and **5 euro**.

In Italian, **euro** is not capitalized unless it begins a new sentence, and it does not change in the plural: **un euro, dieci euro**. Cents are **centesimi** and they pluralize: **un centesimo, dieci centesimi**.

3.2 C'È E CI SONO

In English, **c'è** can be translated as *there is* and **ci sono** as *there are*; how do you use *there is* and *there are* in English? Are they followed by singular nouns or plural nouns? Take notes and share them with the class.

In Italian, one uses **c'è** (always followed by a singular noun) and **ci sono** (always followed by plural nouns or by a list of things) to indicate existence and availability in a certain space, physical or figurative:

THERE IS	THERE ARE
C'È + SINGULAR NOUN	**CI SONO + PLURAL NOUNS OR A LIST OF THINGS (SINGULAR OR PLURAL)**

How could you translate *there is not* and *there are not* into Italian? Look at the examples below and then rewrite the sentences in the negative form:

C'È and CI SONO	NON C'È and NON CI SONO
C'è un libro sul [*on the*] tavolo	
C'è un'università a [*in*] Bologna	
Oggi c'è il sole	

C'È and CI SONO	NON C'È and NON CI SONO
C'è la professoressa in classe [*in the classroom*] 	
In classe ci sono le studentesse e gli studenti 	
Nel frigorifero ci sono il latte e le uova 	
Ci sono molte persone al [*at the*] bar 	

Modo di dire [*common saying*]: Quando il gatto non c'è, i topi ballano!

What do you think it might mean?

Esercitiamoci!

Fill in the blanks with **c'è** or **ci sono**:

	_____ un gatto sul tetto.
	_____ la famiglia di Kim.
	_____ Virio e Vanda al parco.
	Mohammed, sbrigati [*hurry up*]! _____ AnnaMaria al telefono!
	_____ gli ingredienti per fare [*to bake*] la torta al cioccolato?

Look at the picture and write what **c'è/non c'è** or **ci sono/non ci sono** in the classroom:

COSA C'È?

_____

_____

_____

_____

COSA NON C'È?

_____

_____

_____

_____

Lavoriamo con altre studentesse o altri studenti

Check over the exercises above with another student.

Scriviamo!

Form five complete sentences in Italian with **c'è** (or **non c'è**) and five with **ci sono** (or **non ci sono**) using the definite articles (**il, lo, l', la, l', i, gli, le**) or the indefinite articles (**un, uno, una, un'**):

C'È/NON C'È + SINGULAR NOUN

1. _____

2. _____

3. _____

4. _____

5. _____

CI SONO/NON CI SONO + PLURAL NOUNS OR A LIST OF THINGS (SINGULAR OR PLURAL)

1. _____

2. _____

3. _____

4. _____

5. _____

Lavoriamo con altre studentesse o altri studenti

Check over the ten sentences above with another student.

Parliamo!

Ask another student the questions below, alternating roles and using both **c'è** and **ci sono**.

1. Cosa c'è in un'aula? [*What is there in a classroom?*]
2. Cosa c'è in una casa? [*What is there in a house?*]
3. Cosa c'è in un supermercato? [*What is there in a supermarket?*]
4. Cosa c'è in un ristorante? [*What is there in a restaurant?*]
5. Cosa c'è in un aeroporto? [*What is there in an aeroport?*]

Before asking and answering questions, take notes.

3.3 GLI AGGETTIVI

Adjectives are used to qualify people, pets, or all kinds of things; in other words, to give more information about them and to describe them both physically and emotionally. For example, when one says that *Sarah is tall*, the adjective *tall* (**alta/o** in Italian) gives us more information about Sarah. In both English and in Italian, one uses the verb **essere** to express the quality of people, pets, and things. In Italian, adjectives agree in gender and number with the nouns they are referring to; furthermore, most adjectives are placed **after** the nouns they are qualifying or referring to.

In Italian, there are three categories of adjectives in the singular: the adjectives ending in **-O** (*alto, bravo*) are used with a masculine noun; adjectives ending in **-A** (*alta, brava*) are used with a feminine noun; and adjectives ending in **-E** (*grande, intelligente*) are used with a feminine noun or a masculine noun. When one needs to **pluralize** an adjective, one changes the ending: from **-O** to **-I** (*alti, bravi*), from **-A** to **-E** (*alte, brave*), and from **-E** to **-I** (*grandi, intelligenti*).

> **-O** → **-I** (m.pl.)
> **-A** → **-E** (f.pl.)
> **-E** → **-I** (f.pl. or m.pl.)

-O → -I	allegro → allegri biondo → biondi rosso → rossi simpatico → simpatici
-A → -E	allegra → allegre bionda → bionde rossa → rosse simpatica → simpatiche
-E → -I	forte → forti grande → grandi intelligente → intelligenti verde → verdi

What does the above rule remind you of? Check the previous chapters and take note of where you can find a similar rule in the textbook: pp. _____ .

Beyond the three main categories mentioned above, there also are some adjectives that end in **-ISTA** or **-ASTA** (*ottimista, pessimista, altruista, femminista, entusiasta*) and that can be used with masculine and feminine nouns:

— una donna ottim**ista**/pessim**ista**/altru**ista**/femmin**ista**/entusi**asta**
— un uomo ottim**ista**/pessim**ista**/altru**ista**/femmin**ista**/entusi**asta**

In the plural, however, **-ISTA** changes to **-ISTI** for **m.pl.** and to **-ISTE** for **f.pl.** (same with **-ASTA**):

— le donne ottim**iste**/pessim**iste**/altru**iste**/femmin**iste**/entusia**ste**
— gli uomini ottim**isti**/pessim**isti**/altru**isti**/femmin**isti**/entusia**sti**

As learned in Chapter 2, one can use **persona** rather than **uomo** or **donna** to describe someone without revealing further details about their biological sex: **una persona femminista**.

Do you remember the **nationalities** studied in Chapter 2? Nationalities are also adjectives, and they follow the rule described above. You can describe a person or a group of people based on her/his or their nationalities.

3.3.1 I GRUPPI DI PERSONE

When one describes or addresses a **group of people constituting only men**, one uses the **masculine plural** (*gli amici, gli studenti*). If the **group is constituting only women**, one uses the **feminine plural** (*le amiche, le studentesse*). According to the traditional grammar rule, when one describes or addresses a **group of people consisting of women and men**, one should use the **masculine plural** (*gli amici, gli studenti*).

Please note that if one describes or addresses groups of people with adjectives, the adjectives also follow the above rule: *gli amici simpatici, gli studenti simpatici, le amiche simpatiche, le studentesse simpatiche.*

LE PAROLE CONTANO

The grammar rule for pluralization is problematic; as stated above, according to the rule, when one refers to a mixed group of people one should use the masculine plural form, even if the group is composed of many women and only one man. The use of **maschile universale** [*universal masculine*] is currently under discussion by sociolinguistics working on gender and language as well as public opinion in an attempt to find a more inclusive solution. For example, if in the room there are twenty-five female students (**studentesse**) and two male students (**studenti**), in the past the only available option was to describe this group as *gli studenti*. Thanks to feminist collectives and scholars who have started to question this rule, today we can say **le studentesse e gli studenti** or **gli studenti e le studentesse**. Many people still use only the masculine plural form to describe or to address a mixed group, and some others will tell you that repeating the plural in the feminine and masculine form is redundant. However, if one wants to promote gender equality, using both (*gli studenti e le studentesse* or *le studentesse e gli studenti*) is a good way to pursue it. To give more visibility to women, who have stood in the shadows for too long in a variety of languages and cultures, including Italian, the formula *le studentesse e gli studenti* should be preferred. Furthermore, one should be aware that there are options also to include those people who do not identify themselves with the gender-binary option. In this case one might opt for using the **asterisco** [*asterix*] or the schwa /ə/. This is common practice in emails, for example with the formulas: **car* tutt*** or **carə tuttə** [*dear all*]; however, the asterisk does not have a pronunciation. The schwa is an unstressed mid-central vowel and is present not only in English, such as in the American English pronunciation of "American [Amerəcən]," but also in Neapolitan dialect. Transfeminist and queer collectives and scholars have also experimented with other solutions, such as the vowel "**u**". When addressing a group of people by email, you could start with:

Care tutte e cari tutti	**Cari/e tutti/e**	**Caru tuttu**
Cari tutti e care tutte	**Car* tutt***	**Care.i tutte.i**
Care/i tutte/i	**Carə tuttə**	**Car3 tutt3**

3.3.2 I TRATTI FISICI E CARATTERIALI

To describe a person, a group of people, or sometimes a pet, it is important to be able to master the adjectives. To describe the physical traits of a person, a pet, or a thing, one can use adjectives such as:

I TRATTI FISICI	
ALTA/O (for people and things)	BASSA/O (for people and things)
LUNGA/O (for things)	CORTA/O (for things)
GRANDE (for things and people)	PICCOLA/O (for things and people)
GIOVANE (for people and sometimes for things)	ANZIANA/O (for people)
NUOVA/O (for things and people)	VECCHIA/O (for things)
BUONA/O (for things and people)	CATTIVA/O (for things and people)
CALDA/O (for things)	FREDDA/O (for things and people)
LISCIA/O (for things)	RUVIDA/O (for things)
LISCIA/O (for hair)	RICCIA/O (for hair)
MORBIDA/O (for things)	DURA/O (for things and people)

Be careful when using adjectives describing physical and psychological traits of people to avoid offending others; this is important in Italian as well as any other language.

I TRATTI CARATTERIALI	
SIMPATICA/O	ANTIPATICA/O
ATTIVA/O	PIGRA/O
OTTIMISTA	PESSIMISTA
ALTRUISTA	EGOISTA
BUONA/O, BRAVA/O	CATTIVA/O
ALLEGRA/O	TRISTE
FELICE	INFELICE
CONTENTA/O	SCONTENTA/O
CALMA/O	ARRABBIATA/O
DIVERTENTE	NOIOSA/O
ESTROVERSA/O	INTROVERSA/O
GENTILE	SCORTESE
SENSIBILE	INSENSIBILE
ORDINATA/O	DISORDINATA/O

The examples above are not exhaustive of all the adjectives that can be used to describe a person both emotionally and/or physically; however, they are a good starting point. Other adjectives that can be added are **intelligente, interessante, cordiale, furba/o, generosa/o, impulsiva/o,** and **riflessiva/o.**

Simpatico/a e bravo/a in italiano e inglese. Simpatico (like **bravo**) is an adjective that has entered the Anglophone world and is used often in its masculine singular form; however, more frequently, English-speaking feminist collectives on social media use the form **simpatica** (and **brava**) when it refers to a woman. Merriam-Webster's dictionary offers two meanings: (1) agreeable, likable, and (2) like-minded, sympathetic (having shared qualities, interests, etc.). In Italian, the adjective **simpatica/o** is used in the first instance, and it characterizes someone who is friendly, pleasant to be with, easygoing, and possibly with a sense of humor. Merriam-Webster's dictionary further explains its origin: *"Simpatico,* which derives from the Greek noun *sympatheia,* meaning 'sympathy,' was borrowed into English from both Italian and Spanish. In those languages, the word has been chiefly used to describe people who are well-liked or easy to get along with; early uses of the word in English reflected this, as in Henry James's 1881 novel *The Portrait of a Lady,* in which a character says of another's dying cousin, 'Ah, he was so simpatico. I'm awfully sorry for you.' In recent years, however, the word's meaning has shifted. Now we see it used to describe the relationship between people who get along well or work well together."

(https://www.merriam-webster.com/dictionary/simpatico).

Someone might wonder why the word **simpatico** and **bravo** were borrowed by English (and French) from Italian only in their masculine forms; this is a good example of sexism in languages, which has many shapes, including very soft forms that seem invisible on a first reading for nonnative speakers.

Do not forget that words matter in any language. They evolve with the language and contribute to the socio-political discourse of the time.

LE PAROLE CONTANO

Italy was a country with limited immigration until a few decades ago. However, migrations (mostly from Southern to Northern Italy and from the countryside to the cities) have been part of Italian history for a long time. Therefore, most of the Italian population has grown up among native Italians, yet at the same time, Italians have been exposed to diversity in terms of regional dialects and habits. However, with immigrants from Africa, Eastern Europe, China, and Southern America, the Italian population has been diversified in all aspects over the past decades. The initial unease toward diversity has also influenced the language and the culture. As in English, derogatory terms and adjectives, which in turn have contributed to create stereotypes, have been used to describe people from other ethnicities, especially making references to the color of the skin or the shape of the eyes. Today, people exercise greater caution in defining people whose origins are from other countries. We recommend using the correct terminology to describe people's faith, orientations, and views:

- For religious views: **atea/o, buddista, cattolica/o, cristiana/o, ebrea/o, evangelica/o, induista, musulmana/o, protestante, testimone di Geova,** etc.

- For sexual orientation: **bisessuale, eterosessuale, gay** and **lesbica, omosessuale, transgender. Queer** is an umbrella term also used in Italian for sexual and gender minorities who are not heterosexual and cisgender.
- For political views (without being specific with different political affiliations since they change from one country to another): **centrista**, **conservatrice** and **conservatore**, **progressista**, **radicale**, etc.

In Italy, the adjective **liberale** is not used with the meaning of *liberal* (as opposed to *conservative*), but it is mostly used to define the political and economic doctrine of *liberalismo* and the thoughts at its base.

In Italy, people tend to talk about politics a lot: you might hear Italians talking about it in cafès, bars, streets, and grocery stores; indeed, Italians like debating different points of view.

Esercitiamoci: caccia agli aggettivi!

Look for more adjectives with another student:

_____   _____

_____   _____

_____   _____

_____   _____

_____   _____

Share your findings with the class and take notes of adjectives learned from your classmates.

Scriviamo!

1. **Describe yourself** both physically and emotionally. Write full sentences in Italian (do not forget that we use the verb **essere**) and use at least five different adjectives.
2. **Describe one of your friends** both physically and emotionally. Use at least five different adjectives other than the adjectives used in #1.
3. **Describe your university**. Use at least three different adjectives other than the adjectives used in #1 and #2.
4. **Describe one thing of your choice**. Use at least three different adjectives other than the adjectives used in #1, #2, and #3.

Lavoriamo con altre studentesse o altri studenti

Check over the exercises above with another student.

3.3.3 I COLORI

Like in English, in Italian **colors** are adjectives and they agree in gender and number with the nouns they refer to:

ARANCIONE	GIALLA/O	ROSSA/O
AZZURRA/O	GRIGIA/O	VERDE
BIANCA/O	MARRONE	
CELESTE	NERA/O	

However, there are colors that do not change in gender and number, meaning that they are invariable:

BLU   **NOCCIOLA**   **VIOLA**
FUCSIA   **ROSA**

Look at the descriptions below:

1. Il divano è verde.

2. La macchina è bianca.

3. Le penne sono rosse.

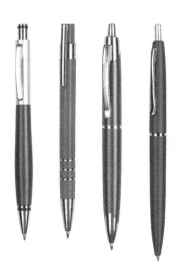

4. Le foglie sono marroni.

5. I fogli sono marroni.

NOTA CULTURALE

Le famiglie arcobaleno. When you hear or read the expression **le famiglie arcobaleno** [*rainbow families*], it refers to LGBTQ+ families. **La bandiera arcobaleno** symbolizes lesbian, gay, bisexual, transgender, and queer (LGBTQ) pride. The flag was invented in San Francisco; however, it is now used worldwide. The most common variant consists of six stripes: **rosso**, **arancione**, **giallo**, **verde**, **blu**, and **viola**. The stri-

ped-horizontal-flag with red at the top resembles the color transition of a natural rainbow. In Italian, the English expression **Gay Pride** is also used to indicate the annual event. One of the most important events is the Gay Pride in Rome usually held in June.

Esercitiamoci con i colori!

Look at the palette and write the colors beginning from the top left:

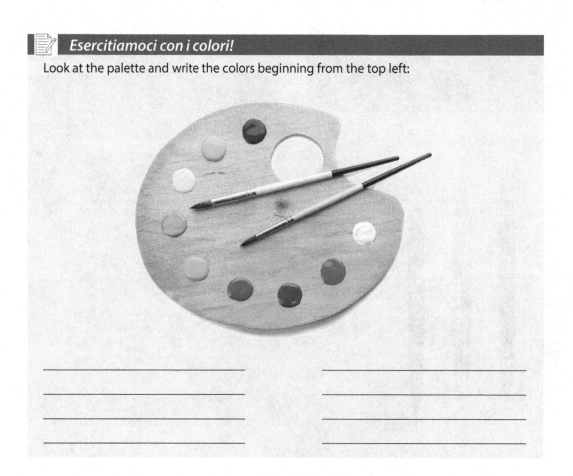

_____   _____

_____   _____

_____   _____

_____   _____

Scriviamo!

Write three sentences in Italian describing the color of one item and three sentences describing the color of multiple items. Use six different adjectives and pay attention to gender and number.

 Lavoriamo con altre studentesse o altri studenti

Check over the exercises above with another student.

 Parliamo!

With another student, describe the colors of ten items around you.

Example: (indicating a desk) – È marrone; (indicating pens) – Sono rosse.

3.3.4 GLI OCCHI E I CAPELLI

In Italian, the verb **avere** [*to have*] is used to describe a person's hair and eyes; for example: Io ho gli occhi verdi [*I have green eyes*]; Lei/Lui ha i capelli neri [*She/He has black hair*]. However, one can also use the verb **essere** to describe them with possessive adjectives: I miei occhi sono verdi [*My eyes are green*]; I suoi capelli sono neri [*Her/His hair are black*]. You can also say: **I capelli sono…**, **Gli occhi sono…** If you want to specify the person, you can say: **I capelli di Michela** [*Michela's hair*] **sono…**, **Gli occhi di Federico** [*Federico's eyes*] **sono…**

To describe **i capelli** [*hair*], one can use the following adjectives:

I CAPELLI (m.pl.)	
MARRONI	brown
CASTANI	light/chestnut brown
BIONDI	blond
NERI	black
BIANCHI	white
ROSSI	red
GRIGI	gray
VERDI	green
BLU	blu
VIOLA	violet

Certainly, **i capelli** can be described in other ways beyond color: such as **corti** [*short*], **lunghi** [*long*], **lisci** [*straight*], **ricci** [*curly*], **ondulati/mossi** [*wavy*], **afro** [*Afro*], **intrecciati** [*braided*].

To describe **gli occhi** [*eyes*], one can use the following adjectives:

GLI OCCHI (m.pl.)	
MARRONI	dark brown
NOCCIOLA	hazelnut
CELESTI/AZZURRI	light blue

GLI OCCHI (m.pl.)	
BLU	dark blue
VERDI	green
NERI	black
GRIGI	gray
ROSSI	red

If you want to generalize, without being specific about a particular nuance of hair and eyes, you can also say: **capelli chiari** [*fair hair*] or **capelli scuri** [*dark hair*]; **occhi chiari** [*fair eyes*] or **occhi scuri** [*dark eyes*].

If one wears **gli occhiali** [*glasses*] or **le lenti a contatto** [*contact lenses*] or simply **lenti** (f.pl.), one says **porto gli occhiali** [*I wear glasses*] or **porto le lenti a contatto.**

If one has tattoos, one says: **ho un tatuaggio; ho i tatuaggi.**

Scriviamo!

Com'è? Come sono? Now describe this group of students' physical traits.

Write five full sentences in Italian, one for each student. Use at least ten different adjectives, two per each student, and do not forget that we use the verb **essere**.

Lavoriamo con altre studentesse o altri studenti

Check over the exercise above with another student.

Parliamo!

With another student, describe the groups in the photos below:

1.

3.

2.

4.

Before starting to speak, take notes.

Body positivity e la terminologia della salute mentale. Body-shaming someone is an act of bullyism, and it consists of criticizing someone based on the shape, size, or appearance of their body. In the 2010s, to fight this social practice, the body positivity movement was launched around the world on social media, TV, and other forms of cultural expression. According to the movement, all human beings should have a positive body image, while at the same time they should question the socio-cultural impositions related to the

body. The movement also advocates for the acceptance of different sizes, genders, races, and appearance. When one learns a new language, one learns new words, and some of them, like adjectives to describe physical appearance, might help us reflect on what we could do to create a body-positive approach to talk about other people. Words such as **grassa/o** [*fat*] and **paffuta/o** [*chubby*] are not offensive *per se*, but they might become offensive in the western contemporary context where fatphobia dominates narratives. This also includes the Italian context. In Italy, famous brands such as Moschino and Gucci have started to support the cause, like other international companies. For example, Gucci created a new campaign for its lipstick with an "imperfect" smile, which reminds us that the so-called "Hollywood smile"

is an artificial product and everyone has different smiles. This change on the part of fashion brands is particularly valuable since the fashion industry has dominated narratives on ideal body shapes for a long time and is also responsible for the stigmatization of certain body types. However, pinkwashing—the promotion of women's and LGBTQ empowerment through the selling of products—is also on the rise.

Similarly, when describing someone emotionally one should pay attention to the misuse of adjectives to describe mental illness. Words such as **anoressica/o** [*anorexic*] or **bulimica/o** [*bulimic*] should not be used to describe someone according to their body size and false myths on eating disorders, but rather, one should remember that they are adjectives to be used only in a medical diagnosis.

3.4 IL VERBO AVERE

Like in English, in Italian, the verb **avere** [*to have*] is an auxiliary verb. Below, you can find the conjugations of the verbs *to have* and **avere** both in English and in Italian, which are considered **exceptions** (meaning that **they do not follow the regular conjugation patterns**) in both languages.

TO HAVE	AVERE
I HAVE	IO HO
YOU HAVE	TU (informal) HAI
YOU HAVE	LEI (formal) HA
HE/SHE/IT HAS	LUI/LEI HA
WE HAVE	NOI ABBIAMO
YOU ALL HAVE	VOI AVETE
THEY HAVE	LORO HANNO

For the verb **avere**, the negation **non** [*do not, does not*] is placed before the conjugated verb as one would do for **essere**. Complete the table below following the example.

NON AVERE	
IO **NON** HO	NOI
TU	VOI
LUI/LEI	LORO

In Italian, **avere** is used to express possession (*I have a car*) and relationship (*I have a friend*).

Scriviamo!

Answer the questions below with complete sentences in Italian like in the example below.

Example: Che cosa [*What*] hai nell'astuccio [*in the case*]? <u>Ho le penne, la gomma e tre matite.</u>

Che cosa hai nello zaino [*in the backpack*]?

_____

Che cosa hai sulla scrivania [*on the desk*]?

_____

Che cosa hai sul comodino [*on the night table*]?

_____

Che cosa hai nel frigorifero [*in the fridge*]?

_____

Lavoriamo con altre studentesse o altri studenti

Check over the exercise above with another student.

3.4.1 GLI USI DI AVERE

As stated above, in Italian, the verb **avere** is used to express **possession** (*ho una macchina*) and **relationship** (*ho un'amica/un amico*), as in English. Look at the examples below:

- Ho una macchina rossa.
- Abbiamo una casa bianca e verde.
- Avete uno zaino giallo.
- Hai molti amici e molte amiche.

- Claire ha due madri.
- Marco ha uno zio e tre cugini.
- Professoressa, Lei ha quattro colleghe e colleghi.

As you have already learned, one uses the verb **avere** to say what kind of **hair** and **eyes** one has; however, pay attention: in Italian **capelli**, **occhi**, and **baffi** [*mustache*] are masculine plural, therefore, as a consequence the adjectives must be masculine plural, while **barba** [*beard*] is feminine singular:

- Yinan ha i capelli lunghi, lisci e neri.
- Sahib ha gli occhi castani, i capelli corti, marroni e ricci, e i baffi marroni.
- Caterina ha i capelli biondi e gli occhi nocciola.
- Piero ha gli occhi verdi e i capelli scuri.
- Carmelo ha la barba bianca e i baffi grigi.

Check the Appendix for more adjectives to describe hair, eyes, and face.

 Scriviamo!

1. **Describe your hair and eyes.** Write two full sentences in Italian to describe your hair and eyes. Use the verb **avere** and the definite articles. Do not forget to make the agreements.

    Example: (1) Ho i capelli neri. (2) Ho gli occhi verdi.

    1. _____

    2. _____

2. **Describe the hair and eyes of one of your friends.** Write two full sentences in Italian.

    1. _____

    2. _____

Esercitiamoci!

Chi sono? [*Who are they?*] and **Come sono?** [*How are they?*]. Look at the pictures, read the short bio, and briefly describe them in the column on the right with the adjectives for physical traits, including **occhi** and **capelli**. Use verbs **essere** and **avere** accordingly.

Chi sono? Come sono?		
	Rosa Parks è un'attivista afroamericana di diritti civili e simbolo della lotta contro il razzismo. Per commemorarla [*to commemorate her*], nel 2015 in molte città italiane i mezzi pubblici avevano [*had*] uno slogan breve che diceva [*stating*] "60 Rosa Parks."	
	Federico Fellini è un regista italiano famoso nel mondo. *La dolce vita* è un suo capolavoro [*masterpiece*], come *8 ½* e *Amarcord*.	
	Frida Kahlo è una pittrice messicana nota al pubblico internazionale. A Roma c'erano [*there were*] in mostra i suoi dipinti dall'ottobre 2019 al marzo 2020.	

Chi sono? Come sono?		
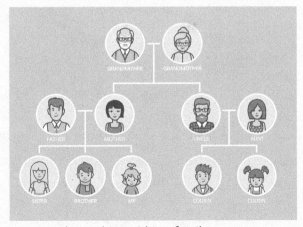	**Michelangelo** è un artista italiano del Rinascimento amato in ogni parte del mondo. Il suo *David* è a Firenze e milioni di persone lo ammirano [*admire it*] ogni anno.	
	Dacia Maraini è una scrittrice italiana famosa in tutto il mondo. *Donna in guerra* è un suo [*one of her*] capolavoro femminista; è un'autrice di letteratura, teatro e giornalismo.	
	Tiziano Ferro è un cantante italiano conosciuto nel mondo. Canta [*sings*] anche in spagnolo e in inglese. È un'icona gay della musica pop italiana.	

 Lavoriamo con altre studentesse o altri studenti

Check over the exercises above with another student.

 ## LE PAROLE CONTANO

Italy has been often perceived as a family-oriented country influenced by Catholic values. Socio-cultural circumstances have changed greatly from the past; in present-day time, there are many kinds of families, including those without children and child-free.

Below, you can find nouns to express relationships within a family:

- **bisnonna** [*great grandmother*]
- **nonna** [*grandmother*]

- **bisnonno** [*great grandfather*]
- **nonno** [*grandfather*]

- **madre** [*mother*]
- **mamma** [*mom*]
- **genitrice** [*parent*]
- **genitrice adottiva** [*adoptive parent*]
- **figlia** [*daughter*]
- **sorella** [*sister*]
- **nipote** [*granddaughter, niece*]
- **zia** [*aunt*]
- **cugina** [*female cousin*]
- **moglie** [*wife*]
- **compagna** [*female partner*]
- **cognata** [*sister-in-law*]
- **suocera** [*mother-in-law*]

- **padre** [*father*]
- **papà/babbo** [*dad*]
- **genitore** [*parent*]
- **genitore adottivo** [*adoptive parent*]
- **figlio** [*son*]
- **fratello** [*brother*]
- **nipote** [*grandson, nephew*]
- **zio** [*uncle*]
- **cugino** [*male cousin*]
- **marito** [*husband*]
- **compagno** [*male partner*]
- **cognato** [*brother-in-law*]
- **suocero** [*father-in-law*]

To say adopted children in Italian, one adds the adjective **adottiva/o** after the noun: **figlia adottiva** and **figlio adottivo**. Children in foster care are **figlia/o in affido** or **figlia/o in affidamento**. The person who takes care of them is **affidataria/o**. **Adottiva/o** and **in affido** are used to make a legal distinction, but in everyday situations one tends not to be specific.

The terms used in Italian for half-brother and step-brother [***fratellastro***], half-sister and step-sister [***sorellastra***], step-mother [***matrigna***] and step-father [***patrigno***], have a derogatory connotation and tend not to be used anymore. Instead of **sorellastra** and **fratellastro**, one can use respectively **sorella** and **fratello**.

To specify a second marriage or partnership of a parent, one can define the wife, husband, or partner of the parent as: **la seconda moglie** [*the second wife*], **il secondo marito** [*the second husband*], **la seconda compagna** [*the second female partner*], or **il secondo compagno** [*the second male partner*]. Although when one says **la moglie/il marito/la compagna/il compagno di mio padre/mia madre**, they already imply that the person is not the parent of whom is speaking. If one does not want to specify the number, one could say **il marito successivo** [*the next husband*], **la moglie successiva** [*the next wife*], **la compagna successiva** [*the next female partner*] or **il compagno successivo** [*the next male partner*]. It is common to hear the word **partner** in Italian: this imported word allows people to talk about their significant others without adding too many details in terms of gender. Usually, **la/il partner** is used for a stable relationship.

In Italian, *boyfriend* and *girlfriend* are respectively **ragazzo** and **ragazza**. The correspondent of the English term *fiancé* is **fidanzata/o;** however, it is considered old-fashioned and not used frequently in current conversations.

Esercitiamoci!

Fill in the blanks with the conjugated verb of **avere**. Pay attention to the subject pronouns.

1. Marcella, Cesare e io _____ un fratello; si chiama Domenico.

2. Io _____ tre gatti; si chiamano Rosmarino, Timo e Basilico.

3. Tu e Juan _____ uno zio e una zia a [*in*] New York; si chiamano John e Marcelle.

4. Lucilla _____ un amico di [*from*] Torino; si chiama Patrizio.

5. Tu _____ una sorella; si chiama Livia.

6. Gianni _____ due amiche di Firenze; si chiamano Yan e Qing.

7. Ilaria e Paolo _____ una cugina a Parigi; si chiama Florence.

8. Pamela _____ una nipote e un nipote a Los Angeles; si chiamano Jessie e Carlos.

Lavoriamo con altre studentesse o altri studenti

Check over the exercise above with another student.

Parliamo!

With another classmate, talk about your family and describe its members answering these questions:

1. Chi [*whom*] c'è nella tua [*in your*] famiglia?
2. Come sono fisicamente e di carattere? [*How are they in terms of physical appearance and personality?*]

Example: (1) Nella mia famiglia ci sono una madre, un padre e due figlie. (2) La madre ha i capelli biondi e corti, il padre ha i capelli castani e ricci, una figlia ha i capelli marroni e ondulati e una figlia ha i capelli biondi e lisci. (3) La madre ha gli occhi marroni, il padre ha gli occhi celesti, una figlia ha gli occhi marroni e una figlia ha gli occhi celesti. (4) La madre è piccola e simpatica, il padre è alto ed estroverso, una figlia è alta e allegra e la sorella è piccola e disordinata.

3.4.2 LE ESPRESSIONI IDIOMATICHE CON AVERE

The verb **avere** also helps to form idiomatic expressions; these expressions cannot be translated literally into another language. For instance, in Italian, one uses the verb **avere** (and not **essere** like in English) to express **l'età** [*the age*]:

- Elisabetta ha ventitré anni.
- Roger ha trentacinque anni.
- Karen ha sessantadue anni.
- Karim ha novanta anni.

To ask one's age, in Italian one says: **Quanti anni hai?** or **Quanti anni ha?** The first question is used in informal situations and the second one in formal settings. See the dialogues below:

Giulia: Quanti anni hai?

Carlos: **Ho diciannove anni**! E tu?

Giulia: Ho ventidue anni.

Juan: Quanti anni ha?

Simanti: **Ho ottantaquattro anni**. E Lei?

Juan: Ho ottantatré anni.

There are several other idiomatic expressions that are built with **avere**:

ENGLISH	ITALIAN
to be X years old	**AVERE X ANNI**

ENGLISH	ITALIAN
to be hungry	**AVERE FAME**

ENGLISH	ITALIAN
to be thirsty	**AVERE SETE**
to be sleepy	**AVERE SONNO**
to be scared/afraid (of)	**AVERE PAURA (DI)**
to be/feel hot	**AVERE CALDO**
to be/feel cold	**AVERE FREDDO**

ENGLISH	ITALIAN
to be wrong	**AVERE TORTO**
to be right	**AVERE RAGIONE**
to be in a hurry	**AVERE FRETTA**
to feel like doing or having something	**AVERE VOGLIA DI**
to need	**AVERE BISOGNO DI**

Esercitiamoci!

Fill in the blanks with **le espressioni idiomatiche con avere**.

1. Giovanni e Riccardo _____ di un gelato al cioccolato.

2. Oggi ci sono trentacinque gradi [*celsius*]! Tu _____.

3. Luda non dorme bene [*sleeps well*]. Lei _____.

4. Alessandro, AnnaMaria e io _____. Siamo in ritardo per la lezione di italiano.

5. Oggi nevica [*snows*]. Voi _____.

6. I genitori di Stella e Jessica _____: se non studiano [*if they do not study*], non passano [*pass*] l'esame.

7. Io _____ quarantaquattro anni.

8. Hiromi _____. Non mangia [*eats*] da ieri [*since yesterday*]!

Le unità di misura. In Italy, one uses **Celsius** (rather than Fahrenheit), **kilometers** (rather than miles), **meters** and **centimeters** (rather than feet and inches), **kilos** and **grams** (rather than pounds and ounces), and **liters** and **milliliters** (rather than gallons and liquid ounces). To cook, Italians do not use cups and spoons, but the units (kilos, grams, liters, and milliliters).

grado [*Celsius*]

chilometro [*kilometer*]

metro [*meter*]

centimetro [*centimeter*]

chilo/chilogrammo [*kilo*] and **grammo** [*gram*]

Comparison of Units of Weight

I Ounce   I Gram   I Lb.   I Kilo

litro [*liter*] and **millilitro** [*milliliter*]

Scriviamo!

Look at the picture and use idiomatic expressions to describe the feelings of the characters with full sentences in Italian.

1.

_____

2.

_____

3.

_____

4.

_____

5.

_____

 Scriviamo!

Write one full sentence in Italian for each idiomatic expression (twelve sentences in total).

 Lavoriamo con altre studentesse o altri studenti

Check over the exercises above with another student.

 Parliamo!

Ask as many classmates as you can about their ages.

 Parliamo!

Now talk to your closest classmate. Ask and answer these questions:

1. Quanti anni hai?
2. Hai fame?
3. Hai sete?
4. Hai sonno?
5. Di cosa hai paura?
6. Hai caldo?

7. Hai freddo?
8. Hai spesso [*often*] ragione?
9. Hai spesso torto?
10. Hai spesso fretta?
11. Di cosa hai voglia?
12. Di cosa hai bisogno?

Ask two more questions among the ones listed above using a formal register:

1. _____

2. _____

3.5 GLI AGGETTIVI E I PRONOMI POSSESSIVI

Gli aggettivi possessivi [*possessive adjectives*] specify possession, ownership, and relationship: *this is my book*; *this is my best friend*. Like all adjectives in Italian, possessive adjectives must agree in gender and number with the thing possessed (not with the possessor) or with the person, people, or pets we are in a relationship with. In most cases, possessive adjectives precede the nouns they modify. Complete the table below, paying attention to gender and number:

	Maschile singolare	Femminile Singolare	Maschile plurale	Femminile plurale
my	il mio	la mia	i miei	le mie
your	il tuo		i tuoi	
his/her/its		la sua		le sue
our	il nostro			le nostre
your		la vostra	i vostri	
their	il loro	la loro		le loro

The adjective **loro** [*their*] never changes; however, the articles preceding it agree in gender and number with the thing that is owned or the person, people, or pets one is in a relationship with.

In the table below, insert the correct possessive adjective **my** in Italian in the column on the left, paying attention to the gender and number of the items listed in the right column:

	libri
	amiche
	penna
	amico

Look at the examples below with **my**:

1. Il mio <u>attore</u> preferito è Toni Servillo.

2. La mia <u>attrice</u> preferita è Virna Lisi.

3. I miei <u>registi</u> preferiti sono Gianfranco Rosi e Federico Fellini.

4. Le mie <u>registe</u> preferite sono Alina Marazzi e Alice Rohrwacher.

In the table below, insert the possessive adjective **our** in Italian in the column on the left, paying attention to the gender and number of the items listed in the right column:

	scuola
	vicini
	matite
	cane

Look at the examples below with **our**:

1. **La nostra** <u>amica</u> si chiama Michela.
2. **Il nostro** <u>amico</u> si chiama Giorgio.
3. **Le nostre** <u>amiche</u> si chiamano Claudia e Tomoko.
4. **I nostri** <u>amici</u> si chiamano Luigi e Marco.

Possession and relationship can also be built with the simple preposition **di** [*of*], which in English can be also translated with the Anglo-Saxon genitive, such as in the sentence *Amanda's pen* [**La penna di Amanda**]. Look at the examples below and translate them into English:

1. Questa è la penna **di** Sabrina.

_____

2. La mamma **di** Sam si chiama Rosaria.

_____

Esercitiamoci!

Fill in the blanks with possessive adjectives in the **singular** form:

1. Il mio/La mia

   a. _____ astuccio

   b. _____ matita

   c. _____ penna

2. Il tuo/La tua

   a. _____ amica

   b. _____ amico

   c. _____ gatta

3. Il suo/La sua

   a. _____ opera

   b. _____ libro

   c. _____ film

4. Il nostro/La nostra

   a. _____ pranzo

   b. _____ cena

   c. _____ colazione

5. Il vostro/La vostra

   a. _____ maestro preferito

   b. _____ materia preferita

   c. _____ regista preferita

6. Il loro/La loro

   a. _____ casa

   b. _____ appartamento

   c. _____ villa

Now fill in the blanks with possessive adjectives in the **plural** form:

1. I miei/Le mie

   a. _____ quaderni

   b. _____ caramelle

   c. _____ pennarelli

2. I tuoi/Le tue

   a. _____ zie

   b. _____ zii

   c. _____ cani

3. I suoi/Le sue

   a. _____ bici

   b. _____ cugini

   c. _____ case

4. I nostri/Le nostre

   a. _____ foto

   b. _____ fiori

   c. _____ piante

5. I vostri/Le vostre

   a. _____ materie preferite

   b. _____ cibi preferiti

   c. _____ amiche

6. I loro/Le loro

   a. _____ amici

   b. _____ vacanze

   c. _____ pizzerie preferite

Esercitiamoci di più!

Fill in the blanks with possessive adjectives in the singular or in the plural form:

1. Martina, dove sono _____ occhiali?

2. Ecco Silvana: questi sono _____ cani.

3. Le studentesse e gli studenti hanno una professoressa italiana: _____ docente si chiama Alessia Palazzoli.

4. La mia famiglia e io andiamo [go] sempre in Italia inestate: queste sono _____ vacanze preferite!

5. Carolina e Matt, quali sono _____ film preferiti?

6. Ciao! Sono Claudia. _____ libro preferito è *Il maestro e Margherita* di Mikhail Bulgakov.

7. Mi chiamo Tobia e _____ pasta preferita sono i bucatini all'amatriciana.

Scriviamo!

Form six complete sentences in Italian using possessive adjectives in the **singular** and six complete sentences in Italian using possessive adjectives in the **plural**.

 Lavoriamo con altre studentesse o altri studenti

Check over the exercises above with another student.

Parliamo!

Ask another student the questions below, alternating roles. Take note of the answers of your classmate and share them with the class.

1. Chi è la tua migliore amica o il tuo migliore amico? Come si chiama o come si chiamano se più di una o uno [*if more than one*]?
2. Chi sono i tuoi professori e le tue professoresse questo semestre?
3. Qual è il tuo corso preferito questo semestre?
4. Qual è il tuo corso preferito in generale?
5. Qual è il tuo piatto preferito?
6. Qual è il tuo ristorante preferito o la tua pizzeria preferita?
7. Qual è il tuo film preferito? Se più di uno, quali sono i tuoi film preferiti?
8. Quali sono le tue attrici preferite e i tuoi attori preferiti?
9. Qual è il tuo regista preferito o la tua regista preferita?
10. Per una vacanza, qual è la tua destinazione preferita?
11. Qual è il tuo libro preferito?
12. Qual è la tua cantante preferita o il tuo cantante preferito? Qual è il tuo gruppo musicale preferito?

Ask your classmate three more questions of your choice. Write them below before starting:

1. _____

2. _____

3. _____

Finally, ask two more questions among the ones listed above using a formal register:

1. _____

2. _____

3.6 GLI AGGETTIVI POSSESSIVI CON ALCUNI MEMBRI DELLA FAMIGLIA AL SINGOLARE

Possessive adjectives follow a particular rule with some family members (mostly relatives via blood) in the singular, such as mother and father, brother and sister.

LE PAROLE CONTANO

The idea of family varies broadly, and families can be very different from each other. The grammar rule about possessive adjectives introduced in this chapter pertains only to some family members, mostly members labeled as such by blood relationship and/or the traditional context. Grammatically, this rule cannot be applied to partners, boyfriends and girlfriends, fiancés, stepmothers and stepfathers, stepbrothers and stepsisters, and half-brothers and half-sisters as well as pets. For this reason, the authors of the textbook have decided to write in the subtitle of the chapter *gli aggettivi possessivi con alcuni membri della famiglia*, in contrast with the traditional grammar

rule, which would say *gli aggettivi possessivi con i membri della famiglia* as a statement to our commitment to teach Italian in an inclusive way, which also reflects the idea of family in the 21st century. You will also note *some family members* vs. *family members* as a reminder that this rule only applies to certain family members indeed! L'aggettivo *alcuni* [some] fa la differenza!

When some family members are in the singular (without other qualifications), such as **madre**, **padre**, **nonna**, **nonno**, **figlio**, **figlia**, **zio**, **zia**, **cugino**, **cugina**, **nipote**, **suocera**, **suocero**, **cognato**, and **cognata**, do **not** include the definite articles **il** and **la** with possessive adjectives (**mia**, **tuo**, **sua**, **vostro**, and so on), except for **loro**. With **loro**, always include the articles even when describing the above family members in the singular. Look at the examples below:

1. **Mia madre** si chiama Jill e **mio padre** si chiama Daniele.
2. **Tuo fratello** è creativo e **tua sorella** è intelligente.
3. **Mia figlia** è molto brava a scuola.
4. **Sua cugina** si chiama Dacia e **suo cugino** si chiama Dario.
5. **Mio nonno** si chiama Pietro e **mia nonna** si chiama Rosa.
6. **Mio zio** è simpatico e **vostra zia** è divertente.
7. **Il loro nipote** è un infermiere, mentre **la loro nipote** è una dottoressa.
8. **La loro madre** è un'architetta e **il loro padre** sta a casa con il loro figlio e le loro figlie.

Attenzione

With the words **mamma**, **babbo**, **papà**, one must include the definite articles: **la mia mamma**, **il mio babbo**, **il mio papà**. Do not forget that **babbo** and **papà** mean *dad* and they are used regionally. While **papà** is widely used in most Italian regions, **babbo** is mostly used in **Toscana**, **Romagna**, **Umbria**, Northern **Lazio**, **Marche**, and **Sardegna**.

The concept expressed by the whole family does not fit in this rule, and for this reason it remains as **la mia/la tua/la sua/la nostra/la vostra/la loro famiglia**. Look at the examples below:

1. **La tua famiglia** è grande.
2. **La sua famiglia** è piccola.
3. **La nostra famiglia** è problematica.

When some family members in the singular are modified by adjectives or diminutive forms, such as **sorellina** or **fratellino**, **maggiore** or **minore**, one must include the definite article. In the plural, the standard rule of possessive adjectives with family members is applied.

See the Appendix for more information about the possessive adjectives with some family members in the singular and in the plural forms.

Esercitiamoci!

Fill in the blanks with possessive adjectives in the **singular form** choosing one of the two forms in parentheses when two options are available; do not forget to include the definite articles if needed:

1. _____ (mio/a) madre si chiama Mara. Lei è simpatica.

2. _____ (tuo/a) nonno si chiama Pietro. Lui è sportivo.

3. _____ (loro) cugino si chiama Francesco; è molto bravo con il violino.

4. _____ (suo/a) sorella maggiore si chiama Giselle. Lei è un'attrice.

5. _____ (nostro/a) fratello minore si chiama Paolo. Lui è uno studente.

6. _____ (vostro/a) famiglia è piccola. Due genitori e una figlia.

Esercitiamoci di più!

Fill in the blanks with possessive adjectives in the **plural form**, choosing one of the two forms in parentheses when two options are available; do not forget the correct definite article:

1. _____ (miei/mie) zie sono sempre in giro.

2. _____ (tuoi/tue) cugini sono amanti del cinema.

3. _____ (suoi/sue) genitori si chiamano Mario e Paolo.

4. _____ (nostri/nostre) fratelli minori hanno 4 e 6 anni.

5. _____ (vostri/vostre) sorelle maggiori hanno 20 e 23 anni.

6. _____ (loro) cani sono dei barboncini bianchi.

Scriviamo!

Form three complete sentences in Italian using the possessive adjectives with some family members in the **singular** and three complete sentences in Italian using the possessive adjectives with some family members in the **plural** (see the Appendix for this).

Lavoriamo con altre studentesse o altri studenti

Check over the exercises above with another student.

Parliamo!

Ask another student the questions below, alternating roles. Take note of the answers of your classmate and share them with the class.

1. Chi sono i membri della tua famiglia?
2. Come si chiamano?
3. Quanti anni hanno?

3.7 I GIORNI DELLA SETTIMANA, I MESI E LE STAGIONI

In Italian, the days of the week, the months, and the seasons are not capitalized as they are in English, unless they are at the beginning of a sentence.

3.7.1 I GIORNI DELLA SETTIMANA

In Italian, the week starts always on Monday:

lunedì	martedì	mercoledì	giovedì	venerdì	sabato	domenica

- In most cases, the days of the week as subjects are used **without articles**.
- They are also used **without articles** when the adjectives **scorso/a** or **passato/a** [*last*] or **prossimo/a** [*this coming, next*] are included or implied in the expression, as in the examples: Sabato (scorso) mia madre è tornata [*went back*] in Italia. Domenica (prossima) la mia famiglia e io andiamo al concerto dei Måneskin.
- The days of the week **with articles** (il lunedì, il martedì, il mercoledì, il giovedì, il venerdì, il sabato, la domenica) means *every* + the name of the day.
- You can use the day of the week as a form of greetings when departing: such as **a lunedì** [*till Monday*] or **a giovedì** [*till Thursday*].
- To ask what day of the week is, one says: **Che giorno è oggi?** For example, you might answer with **oggi è lunedì** or **oggi è martedì**.

Check the Appendix for more information about the days of the week.
What do you think these expressions mean? Translate them into English.

Oggi è sabato _____

Domani è domenica _____

Dopodomani è lunedì _____

🗨️ *Parliamo!*

Talk to your closest classmate. Ask and answer these questions, alternating roles:

1. Che giorno è oggi?
2. Che giorno è domani?
3. Che giorno è dopodomani?
4. Qual è il tuo giorno preferito della settimana? [*What is your favorite day of the week?*]
5. Qual è il tuo giorno meno preferito della settimana? [*What is your least favorite day of the week?*]

3.7.2 I MESI

As with the days of the week, months of the year are not capitalized in Italian, unless they begin a sentence:

gennaio	febbraio	marzo
aprile	maggio	giugno
luglio	agosto	settembre
ottobre	novembre	dicembre

- Months are usually preceded by the preposition **a**: such as **a gennaio** [*in January*] or **a febbraio** [*in February*].
- To express the day of the month, one says for example: **Oggi è venerdì 31 luglio**.
- To ask someone when his/her/their birthday is, you ask: **Quando è il tuo compleanno?** You might answer with **Il mio compleanno è il 13 marzo**, for example. Check the Appendix for more information about the months.

Esercitiamoci!

In the left column, write the names of well-known people you like and their jobs, and in the right column write their birth dates. Both jobs and birthdays must be written in Italian as per the example below.

NOMI E LAVORI/PROFESSIONI	DATE DI NASCITA
Sophia Loren (attrice)	20 settembre

Scriviamo!

Answer these questions with full sentences in Italian based on the actual day you complete the exercise, following the example below:

Example: Che giorno è oggi? Oggi è martedì 5 agosto.

Che giorno è oggi? _____

Che giorno è domani? _____

Che giorno è dopodomani? _____

Quando è il tuo compleanno? _____

Quando è il compleanno della tua migliore amica o del tuo migliore amico?_____

_____

Lavoriamo con altre studentesse o altri studenti

Check over the exercises above with another student.

Parliamo!

Ask your classmates when their birthdays are, take notes, and then share them with the class.

Le feste italiane. In Italy, there are many civic and religious holidays that are celebrated throughout the year (those with an asterisk denote a national holiday):

A gennaio: **Capodanno*** (1° gennaio), **l'Epifania*** (6 gennaio)

A febbraio: **San Valentino** (14 febbraio)

A marzo: **la festa internazionale dei diritti delle donne** (8 marzo), **la festa del papà** (19 marzo)

A aprile: **la festa della liberazione*** (25 aprile)

A maggio: **la festa del lavoro*** (1° maggio), **la festa della mamma** (8 maggio)

A giugno: **la festa della Repubblica*** (2 giugno)

A agosto: **la festa dell'Assunzione** o **Ferragosto*** (15 agosto)

A novembre: **il giorno di tutti Santi** o **Ognissanti*** (1° novembre), **il giorno dei defunti/morti** (2 novembre)

A dicembre: **la festa dell'Immacolata Concezione*** (8 dicembre), **Natale*** (25 dicembre), **Santo Stefano*** (26 dicembre), **l'ultimo dell'anno** (31 dicembre)

Beyond the above celebrations, Italians celebrate **Pasqua** [*Easter*] and **il lunedì di Pasqua** [*Easter Monday*], which vary every year. Also, every town and city have a patron Saint called **Patrono** or **Patrona**: the day of the **Patrona/o** is a festive day.

Italians also celebrate **il carnevale** [*Carnival*] and **il martedì grasso** [*Mardi Gras*], however these holidays vary every year in relation to Easter day. Famous Carnivals are held in Venice and in Viareggio, which is famous for its **carri** [*carts*].

Italians have started to celebrate Halloween recently; however, it does not have the importance that it holds in the United States or in other parts of the world.

Note that the first day of each month is written as **1°,** which means **il primo** [*first*].

Esercitiamoci!

Che festa è? Read the **Nota culturale** above and write down what **feste** happen on the following days:

1° maggio: _____

15 agosto: _____

26 dicembre: _____

25 aprile: _____

2 giugno: _____

6 gennaio: _____

1° novembre: _____

25 dicembre: _____

 Lavoriamo con altre studentesse o altri studenti

Check over the exercise above with another student.

Parliamo!

Le feste. Ask your classmates these questions and answer them, alternating roles:

1. Quali feste sono importanti per te [*for you*]?
2. Quali sono le tue feste preferite?
3. Quali sono le tue feste meno [*least*] preferite?

3.7.3 LE STAGIONI

To simplify, one can consider the four seasons as including three months each: winter (December, January, February), spring (March, April, May), summer (June, July, August), and fall/autumn (September, October, November). In Italian, the four seasons are:

inverno	primavera	estate	autunno

- Seasons are not capitalized, unless they begin a sentence.
- Seasons are usually preceded by the preposition **in**: **in estate** [*in the summer*], **in autunno** [*in the fall*], **in inverno** [*in the winter*], and **in primavera** [*in the spring*].
- To ask what season it is, one says: **Che stagione è?** or **In che stagione siamo?** And you answer with: **È inverno** or **Siamo in inverno,** for example.

Check the Appendix for more information about the seasons.

Lavoriamo con altre studentesse o altri studenti

What holidays do you celebrate in each season in your country? Make a list of holidays with your classmates. Some Italian holidays have already been included.

Inverno: Natale; Capodanno; Epifania _____

Primavera: 25 aprile; 1° maggio; _____

Estate: Ferragosto; _____

Autunno: Ognissanti; il giorno dei defunti/morti _____

Parliamo!

Ask your classmates these questions and answer them:

1. In che stagione siamo?
2. In che stagione è il tuo compleanno?
3. Qual è la tua stagione preferita?
4. Qual è la tua stagione meno preferita?

LA PAGINA CULTURALE

L'ITALIA E LE SUE FAMIGLIE

Family for Italians is very important; Italians tend to spend much time with their families and, if away, they remain in contact with them daily/weekly. Many families and extended families also tend to live close by constituting a network of support. Moreover, the idea of family in Italy goes beyond parents and children; grandparents are very important, as well as cousins, aunts and uncles, friends, and pets. Grandparents often play a key role in raising their grand-children

and spending time with them while their parents are at work, especially during the early years and then after school when they get older.

Until recently adult children welcomed their parents into their own homes to live once they started to get older. This trend has changed in the last 40 years; often, elderly parents live near their children and, if necessary, are being taken care of by **badanti** [*caregivers*] within their homes, however many also live in nursing homes.

Badanti have generally been mostly women from Eastern European countries as well as other parts of the world such as India and the Philippines, however there are also an increasing number of men performing this job. (For a report in Italian about **badanti**, the challenging aspects of their cultural integration in Italy, the socio-cultural controversy related to their jobs, yet their fundamental role in present-day Italian society, see the data from the Fondazione Leone Moressa: http://www.fondazioneleonemoressa.org/newsite/wp-content/uploads/2012/06/Quali-badanti-per-quali-famiglie_completo.pdf)

As in the rest of the world, in Italy there are many different types of families: small, medium, and large! In the past few decades, Italians have tended to form small or medium families with one or two children, very rarely three. This is very different from the first half of the twentieth century when society was highly influenced by the Catholic church as well as the fascist ideology, and peasant families were usually characterized by many children who helped parents and grandparents in the fields. With the Economic Boom (1958–1963) many socio-cultural changes occurred; in particular, women, who had replaced men temporarily in many jobs during WWII, entered the workforce, attended high schools and universities in large numbers, further contributing to shaping their new socio-cultural roles and thereby changing the traditional and patriarchal family structure. Thinking of Italy today as a Catholic country with large families is one of the continuing stereotypes rooted in the past about the so-called **Belpaese**, yet circumstances have changed profoundly. Further changes in the family structure started in the 1970s, thanks to strong mobilization on socio-cultural issues, as in the rest of Europe, with a leading role played by the feminist movement. Divorce was introduced in 1970, while legal equality within the marriage relationship was introduced in 1975 with the reform of the Family Code. However, divorce is still a relatively long process which includes a period of legal separation before the actual divorce. Yet, divorce can currently be achieved in two years. The contraception pill became legal in 1978, and in the same year also, abortion rights were attained.

In Italy, women do not change their family name if they get married, and a proposal was passed in 2016 to allow children to be given double surnames (from both parents), as is the case in Spain.

In 2022, the Italian constitutional court ruled that children can be given the surnames of both parents since the practice of naming a child after the father only is "discriminatory and harmful." The engagement proposal is not a common tradition (as already stated, the term **fidanzato/a** is perceived as old-fashioned) and is very rarely identified with a (diamond) ring as per the American tradition or that of other countries. Italians tend to officially recognize their relationships by inviting their significant others to family gatherings, such as holidays and parents' birthday parties. This introduction means that the significant others have become part of the family and their relationship is therefore stable and official.

Many Italians tend to form a **unione civile** or **matrimonio** after having secured a career path; therefore, the median age for having a family has been increasing since the 1970s and the 1980s. Moreover, today, marriages have decreased in favor of partnership, and birth rates have also dropped; immigrant families, however, are those having the most children. Updated data by ISTAT, *Istituto Nazionale di Statistica*, can be found here: https://www.istat.it/it/popolazione-e-famiglie; here you will find the most recent report about marriages and partnerships: https://www.istat.it/it/files/2021/02/Report-matrimoni-unioni-civili-separazioni-divorzi_anno-2019.pdf. Thanks to the so-called **legge** [*law*] (Monica) Cirinnà, opposite-sex couples have legal recognition, therefore most of the same legal protections as same-sex married-couples, although same-sex couples are still facing societal challenges; for example, single and same-sex partners cannot adopt children, however this law and attitude are being questioned.

The traditional notion of family compose of heterosexual parents and children

has changed over the years; therefore, while the majority of families (of all sexual orientation) follow this structure, there are many single parent families, grandparents looking after grandsons and granddaughters, child-free couples, single people with pets, and other options. **Tutte le famiglie sono belle!**

LE PAROLE CONTANO

In Italy, so-called **honor killing** (the murder of a family member whose perpetrator believes that the victim has dishonored the family) was abolished in 1981; today, however, **femminicidio** [*femicide*], its modern version, is on the rise in Italy, as in many other countries. Femicide is not simply the killing of a woman, but the killing of a female motivated by misogyny, the feeling of superiority over women, including a sense of ownership. **Femminicidi** are very often perpetrated by (ex) husbands, partners, and people who know the victim very well. This is a global emergency and one of the family issues related to gendered violence that need to be addressed extensively by society and governments at all levels. For further information and for updated statistics and initiatives, see the English-language website of the European Institute for Gender Equality (EIGE), https://eige.europa.eu/gender-equality-index/2019/violence, as well as the website of ISTAT in Italian for the Italian scenario: https://www.istat.it/it/archivio/violenza.

During the COVID-19 pandemic, femicides have risen exponentially in Italy and other countries around the world. It is very important to use the appropriate terminology to address this issue and raise awareness about it; therefore, one should use the word **femminicidio** rather than **omicidio** [*homicide*] when the killing of a woman happens in the conditions described above. To raise awareness against gendered violence, on November 25 every year, Italian squares host thousands of red shoes. The color red symbolizes the blood lost by victims of **femminicidi**; however, it is also the color associated with the (cultural) revolution necessary to end violence against women.

ESERCITIAMOCI CON LA CULTURA

A. Le nonne e i nonni. In Italy, grandparents are part of everyday life. The so-called **nidi** [*nurseries*] in most cases are not run by the state, but by private institutions; therefore, families might encounter challenges in terms of finding spaces for their children in a nursery in their area, as well as financial constraints. First, research stories about Italian grandparents on reputable sources online and then write below your findings in English:

I NONNI E LE NONNE

Finally, describe with full sentences in Italian **i nonni** and **le nonne** below, including their physical and personality traits. Be creative!

B. Le famiglie italiane. First, research more about Italian families on reputable sources online and then write down your findings in English:

LE FAMIGLIE ITALIANE

Finally, describe with full sentences in Italian **le famiglie italiane** below, including their physical and personality traits. Be creative!

GLOSSARIO

I numeri

zero [zero]

uno [one]

due [two]

tre [three]

quattro [four]

cinque [five]

sei [six]

sette [seven]

otto [eight]

nove [nine]

dieci [ten]

undici [eleven]

dodici [twelve]

tredici [thirteen]

quattordici [fourteen]

quindici [fifteen]

sedici [sixteen]

diciassette [seventeen]

diciotto [eighteen]

diciannove [nineteen]

venti [twenty]

ventuno [twenty-one]

ventidue [twenty-two]

ventitré [twenty-three]

ventiquattro [twenty-four]

venticinque [twenty-five]

ventisei [twenty-six]

ventisette [twenty-seven]

ventotto [twenty-eight]

ventinove [twenty-nine]

trenta [thirty]

quaranta [fourty]

cinquanta [fifty]

sessanta [sixty]

settanta [seventy]

ottanta [eighty]

novanta [ninety]

cento [one hundred]

I nomi

baffi [moustache]

bandiera arcobaleno [rainbow flag]

barba [beard]

bocca [mouth]

capelli [hair]

centesimo [cent]

ciglia [f.pl.: eyelashes]

collo [neck]

euro [Euro/s]

faccia [face]

guance [f.pl.: cheeks]

labbra [f.pl.: lips]

lenti a contatto/lenti [contact lenses]

mento [chin]

naso [nose]

occhi [eyes]

occhiali [glasses]

orecchie [f.pl.: ears]

sopracciglia [f.pl.: eyebrows]

tatuaggio [tatoo]

viso [face]

volto [face]

Gli aggettivi: tratti fisici e caratteristiche fisiche

alta/o [tall]

anziana/o [elderly]

bassa/o [short for people and things]

bionda/o [blond]

buona/o [good]

calda/o [*hot*]

cattiva/o [*bad*]

corta/o [*short* for things]

dura/o [*hard*]

fredda/o [*cold*]

giovane [*young* (for people)]

grande [*big*]

liscia/o [*straight*]

lunga/o [*long* for things]

morbida/o [*soft*]

nuova/o [*new*]

piccola/o [*small, little*]

riccia/o [*curly*]

ruvida/o [*rough*]

vecchia/o [*old*]

Gli aggettivi: tratti e altri tratti caratteriali

allegra/o [*cheerful*]

altruista [*altruist, unselfish*]

annoiata/o [*bored*]

antipatica/o [*unpleasant*]

arrabbiata/o [*angry*]

attiva/o [*active*]

brava/o [*bravo*]

buona/o [*good*]

calma/o [*calm*]

cattiva/o [*bad*]

contenta/o [*happy*]

disordinata/o [*untidy*]

divertente [*funny*]

egoista [*egotistic, selfish*]

entusiasta [*enthusiastic*]

estroversa/o [*extroverted, outgoing*]

famosa/o [*famous*]

felice [*happy*]

femminista [*feminist*]

generosa/o [*generous*]

gentile [*kind*]

infelice [*unhappy*]

insensibile [*insensitive*]

intelligente [*smart*]

interessante [*interesting*]

introversa/o [*introverted, shy*]

noiosa/o [*boring*]

ordinata/o [tidy]

ottimista [*optimistic*]

pessimista [*pessimistic*)

pigra/o [*lazy*]

scontenta/o [*unhappy*]

scortese [*rude*]

sensibile [*sensitive*]

simpatica/o [*pleasant*]

timida/o [*shy*]

triste [*sad*]

Orientamento religioso

atea/o [*atheist*]

buddista [*buddhist*]

cattolica/o [*catholic*]

cristiana/o [*christian*]

ebrea/o [*jewish*]

evangelica/o [*evangelical*]

induista [*hindu*]

musulmana/o [*muslim*]

protestante [*protestant*]

testimone di Geova [*Jehovah's witness*]

Orientamento sessuale

bisessuale [*bisexual*]

eterosessuale [*heterosexual*]

gay [*gay*]

lesbica [*lesbian*]

omosessuale [*homosexual*]

queer [*queer*]

transgender [*transgender*]

Orientamento politico

centrista [*centrist*]

conservatrice/conservatore/ [*conservative*]

liberale [*liberal*]

progressista [*progressive*]

radicale [*radical*]

I colori

arancione [*orange*]

azzurra/o [*light blue; sky blue*]

bianca/o [*white*]

blu [*blue*]

castana/o [*light brown*]

chiara/o [*light*]

celeste [*light blue*]

fucsia [*fuchsia*]

gialla/o [*yellow*]

grigia/o [*gray*]

marrone [*brown*]

nera/o [*black*]

nocciola [*hazelnut*]

rosa [*pink*]

rossa/o [*red*]

scura/o [*dark*]

verde [*green*]

viola [*purple; violet*]

Le famiglie

babbo [*dad, regional*]

bisnonna [*great grandmother*]

bisnonno [*great grandfather*]

cognata [*sister-in-law*]

cognato [*brother-in-law*]

compagna/o [*partner*]

cugina [*female cousin*]

cugino [*male cousin*]

fidanzata/o [*fiancé*]

figlia [*daughter*]

figlia adottiva [*adopted daughter*]

figlia in affido [*daughter in foster care*]

figlio [*son*]

figlio adottivo [*adopted son*]

figlio in affido [*son in foster care*]

fratello [*brother*]

genitrice/genitore [*parent*]

genitrice/genitore adottiva/o [*adoptive parent*]

madre [*mother*]

mamma [*mom*]

marito [*husband*]

moglie [*wife*]

nipote [*nephew/niece*]

nonna [*grandmother*]

nonno [*grandfather*]

padre [*father*]

papà [*dad, regional*]

ragazza [*girlfriend*]

ragazzo [*boyfriend*]

sorella [*sister*]

suocera [*mother-in-law*]

suocero [*father-in-law*]

zia [*aunt*]

zio [*uncle*]

Gli aggettivi possessivi

il mio, la mia, i miei, le mie [*my*]

il tuo, la tua, i tuoi, le tue [*your*]

il suo, la sua, i suoi, le sue [*his, her*]

il nostro, la nostra, i nostri, le nostre [*our*]

il vostro, la vostra, i vostri, le vostre [*your*]

il loro, la loro, i loro, le loro [*their*]

I pronomi possessivi

(il) mio, (la) mia, (i) miei, (le) mie [*mine*]

(il) tuo, (la) tua, (i) tuoi, (le) tue [*yours*]

(il) suo, (la) sua, (i) suoi, (le) sue [*his, hers*]

(il) nostro, (la) nostra, (i) nostri, (le) nostre [*ours*]

(il) vostro, (la) vostra, (i) vostri, (le) vostre [*yours*]

(il) loro, (la) loro, (i) loro, (le) loro [*theirs*]

I giorni della settimana

lunedì [*Monday*]

martedì [*Tuesday*]

mercoledì [*Wednesday*]

giovedì [*Thursday*]

venerdì [*Friday*]

sabato [*Saturday*]

domenica [*Sunday*]

I mesi dell'anno

gennaio [*January*]

febbraio [*February*]

marzo [*March*]

aprile [*April*]

maggio [*May*]

giugno [*June*]

luglio [*July*]

agosto [*August*]

settembre [*September*]

ottobre [*October*]

novembre [*November*]

dicembre [*December*]

Le stagioni

primavera [*spring*]

estate [*summer*]

autunno [*autumn; fall*]

inverno [*winter*]

Le espressioni idiomatiche con *avere*

avere x anni [*to be x years old*]

avere fame [*to be hungry*]

avere sete [*to be thirsty*]

avere sonno [*to be sleepy*]

avere paura [*to be scared*]

avere caldo [*to be/to feel hot*]

avere freddo [*to be/to feel cold*]

avere torto [*to be wrong*]

avere ragione [*to be right*]

avere fretta [*to be in a hurry*]

avere voglia di [*to feel like*]

avere bisogno di [*to need*]

Le espressioni e le domande utili

c'è [*there is*]

ci sono [*there are*]

non c'è [*there is not*]

non ci sono [*there are not*]

Qual è il tuo numero di telefono? [*What is your phone number?*]

Chi è? [*Who is he/she?*]

Chi sono? [*Who are they?*]

Com'è? [*How is he/she/it?*]

Come sono? [*How are they?*]

Cosa c'è? [*What is there?*] [literal translation]

Che giorno è oggi? [*What day of the week is today?*]

Che giorno è domani? [*What day of the week is tomorrow?*]

Che giorno è dopodomani? [*What day of the week is the day after tomorrow?*]

Che mese è? [*What month is it?*]

Che stagione è? [*What season is it?*]

In che mese siamo? [*In what month are we?*]

In che stagione siamo? [*In what season are we?*]

Che festa è? [*What holiday is it?*]

Qual è la tua stagione preferita? [*What is your favorite season?*]

Qual è la tua stagione meno preferita? [*What is your least favorite season?*]

Quando è il tuo compleanno? [*When is your birthday?*]

APPENDICE

I NUMERI

How can one remember the numbers from **undici** (11) to **sedici** (16)? If you think that **undici** is formed by **uno+dici** (**dici** is close enough to **dieci**), you can understand all the other additions: **dodici** (due+dieci), **tredici** (tre+dieci), **quattordici** (quattro+dieci), **quindici** (cinque+dieci), and **sedici** (sei+dieci). The *quatt* and *quin* respectively in **quattordici** and **quindici**, trace back to Latin, from which Italian retains a lot, including the numbers *quattuor* and *quinque* in **quattordici** and **quindici**.

How can one remember the numbers from **diciassette** (17) to **diciannove** (19)? The concept is very similar to that explained above; however, the difference is that now **dici** (as **dieci**) is placed at the beginning of the number: **diciassette** (dieci+sette), **diciotto** (dieci+otto), and **diciannove** (dieci+nove).

I COLORI

While basic colors are rather fixed, there also are nuances and gradients. One can use at least two adjectives to describe something that is light or dark: **chiara/o** [*light, clear*] and **scura/o** [*dark*]. Look at the examples below:

1. Il tavolo è marrone scuro/chiaro.
2. I tavoli sono marrone scuro/chiaro.
3. La tovaglia è rossa, BUT La tovaglia è rosso scuro/chiaro.
4. Le tovaglie sono rosso scuro/chiaro.

When one adds **chiaro** or **scuro** to a color, the adjectives are in the masculine singular. Why is this? Because **di colore** is omitted before the adjectives **scuro/chiaro**: *La tovaglia è (**di colore**) rosso scuro/chiaro*. **Colore** is masculine singular, therefore the adjectives following it agree in gender and number with it, even though it is not included overtly like in the example above with **di colore** in parentheses.

IL VOLTO

If one wants to describe a person's face, these adjectives can be useful:

- **capelli** [*hair*]: corti, lunghi, lisci, ricci, ondulati.
- **volto/viso/faccia** [*face*]: allungato/a, ovale, rotondo/a, lentigginoso/a.
- **orecchie** [*ears*]: rotonde, a punta.
- **occhi** [*eyes*]: grandi, piccoli, allungati, rotondi.
- **ciglia** [*eyelashes*] and **sopracciglia** [*eyebrows*]: grandi, piccole, allungate, folte, rade.
- **naso** [*nose*]: piccolo, grande, grosso, appuntito, aquilino, a patatina, alla francese.
- **guance** [*cheeks*]: rosee.
- **bocca** [*mouth*]: grande, piccola, carnosa, sottile.
- **labbra** [*lips*]: grandi, piccole, carnose, sottili.
- **mento** [*chin*]: allungato, rotondo.
- **collo** [*neck*]: grande, piccolo, allungato, corto.

I PRONOMI POSSESSIVI

In English, **i pronomi possessivi** [*possessive pronouns*] are **mine**, **yours**, **hers/his/its**, **ours**, **yours**, and **theirs**. In Italian, one uses the possessive pronouns in the same way as in English: *questo non è il mio libro, è (il) tuo* [*this is not my book, it is yours*]. The possessive pronouns must agree in gender and number with the possessed item they are substituting. Look at the examples below:

1. È il mio <u>zaino</u>, non **(il) tuo**.
2. Non è **la sua** <u>valigia</u>, è **(la) mia**.
3. Sono **i vostri** <u>libri</u>, non sono **(i) nostri**.
4. Sono **le loro** <u>amiche</u>, non **(le) sue**.

Note that, when in the presence of an adjective pronoun, the definite article can be omitted, which is why they are in parentheses in the examples above.

GLI AGGETTIVI POSSESSIVI CON ALCUNI MEMBRI DELLA FAMIGLIA AL SINGOLARE E AL PLURALE

As said, if words that describe some family members in the singular are altered or modified—in other words if they are used in their diminutive forms (for instance, **fratellino** or **sorellina**) or if they are paired with adjectives (for instance, **sorella maggiore** o **fratello minore**) or further information (**il mio zio di New York**)—always include the definite articles. However, if you add just the name of the relative, you keep the possessive adjective without the article: Mio zio Giovanni ē Simpatico. Look at the examples below:

1. **La mia sorellina** si chiama Patrizia e **il mio fratellino** si chiama Giacomo.
2. **Il mio fratello maggiore** è bravo con il violino.
3. **La mia sorella minore** è intelligente, ma ha poca voglia di studiare.
4. **La mia zia preferita** è giovane e simpatica.
5. **La mia cugina di Sydney** ha 25 anni.

In the **plural**, all family members follow the standard rule of possessive adjectives. Look at the examples below:

1. **I miei genitori** si chiamano Claudio and Pino.
2. **I loro fratelli adottivi** sono Jack e Michael e **le loro sorelle adottive** sono Alice, Mary e Margaret.
3. **Le sue zie** sono Carla e Giovanna e **i suoi zii** sono Michele e Carlo Alberto.
4. **I vostri cugini** sono simpatici e **le vostre cugine** sono creative.

I GIORNI DELLA SETTIMANA

The days of the week in Italian are based on the names of the planets in Latin:

lunedì	martedì	mercoeldì	giovedì	venerdì	sabato	domenica
È il giorno della luna	È il giorno di Marte	È il giorno di Mercurio	È il giorno di Giove	È il giorno di Venere	È il giorno del riposo*	È il giorno del Signore**

* Sabato: from the Latin *sabbātum*, from the Greek σάββατον, and this from the Hebrew *shabbāt* «(giorno di) riposo» [(day of) rest] (translated from http://www.treccani.it/vocabolario/sabato/)

** Domenica: lat. tardo domǐnǐca (dies) «(giorno) del Signore»
(source: http://www.treccani.it/vocabolario/ricerca/domenica/)

Be aware that:

- The days of the week from **lunedì** to **venerdì** have graphic accents that are compulsory.
- The days of the week from **lunedì** to **sabato** are masculine singular. When one pluralizes them, the days from **lunedì** to **venerdì** do not change in the plural because of the accent, while **sabato** becomes **sabati** (m.pl.).
- **Domenica** is feminine singular, and its plural is **domeniche**.
- Below are some useful expressions of time:

  ieri [*yesterday*]

  oggi [*today*]

  domani [*tomorrow*]

  dopodomani [*the day after tomorrow*]

  tutti i giorni [*everyday*]

  ogni giorno [*everyday*]

  mai [*never*]

  sempre [*always*]

  qualche volta [*sometimes*]

  spesso [*often*]

I MESI

Be aware that:

- The months are all masculine singular. In certain circumstances, they can be pluralized and they follow the standard rule.
- Months never require an article, unless you say for instance *the month of January*: **il mese di gennaio**.
- To ask someone when she/he was born, one can ask: **In quale mese sei nata/o?** The answer would be: **Sono nata/o a...**
- To ask what month it is, one says: **Che mese è?** And you answer with: **È luglio**. To ask what month we are in, one says: **In che mese siamo?** And you answer with: **Siamo a settembre**.

LE STAGIONI

What you need to remember:

- **La primavera** and **l'estate** are feminine, while **l'autunno** and **l'inverno** are masculine singular.
- For the pluralization, they follow the standard rule. Plurals are usually found in expressions such as **tutte le primavere** (*all springs*), **tutte le estati** (*all summers*).
- To ask what season we are in, one says: **In che stagione siamo?** And you answer with: **Siamo in primavera**, for example.

I SEGNI ZODIACALI

ARIES   TAURUS   GEMINI   CANCER

LEO   VIRGO   LIBRA   SCORPIO

SAGITTARIUS   CAPRICORN   AQUARIUS   PISCES

Many Italians enjoy reading about their horoscopes. What do you think these Zodiac signs in Italian might be? Write their English version next to them, and pay attention because they are not in order!

Leone _____   Gemelli _____

Bilancia _____   Vergine _____

Toro _____   Ariete _____

Sagittario _____   Capricorno _____

Scorpione _____   Cancro _____

Acquario _____   Pesci _____

To ask someone for his/her Zodiac sign, one says: **Di che segno sei?** The answer to this question would be: **Sono del leone** or **Sono della bilancia,** for example.

LA CUCINA ITALIANA

4

CAPITOLO

By the end of this chapter, you will be able to use the verbs ending in **-are** in the present tense. You will learn both regular and the most common irregular verbs, such as *andare* [*to go*], *dare* [*to give*], *fare* [*to do*], and *stare* [*to stay*]. You will also be able to use interrogatives, demonstrative pronouns, simple prepositions, and to ask questions. You will also learn about time and how to ask what time it is. In terms of cultural elements, you will learn about the renowned Italian cuisine.

INIZIAMO

Read the dialogue below with another student, alternating roles:

Marina:	Ciao, Giovanni!
Giovanni:	Ciao, Marina! Tutto bene al corso da chef? Oggi hai lezione?
Marina:	Sì, oggi ho lezione dalle 16 alle 19. Impariamo a fare il risotto alla pescatora.
Giovanni:	Che buono! Quanto dura il corso?
Marina:	Due anni. Questo mese abbiamo tanti esami.
Giovanni:	Ogni volta fate una ricetta nuova?
Marina:	Sì, ogni lezione cuciniamo un piatto della tradizione italiana nazionale o regionale. Impariamo anche ricette internazionali.
Giovanni:	Qual è la tua ricetta preferita?
Marina:	Non so... ma sono brava con gli gnocchi alla crema di scampi!
Giovanni:	Allora perché non invitiamo Alessandro, Paolo e Gianluca a cena?
Marina:	Ma sì! Sabato facciamo una bella cena a casa mia! Io faccio il primo e tu il secondo! E gli invitati portano il dolce e il prosecco!

Work with another student to understand the content of this short dialogue. Do you know what the words mean? Look up their meanings if you do not know them.

4.1 VERBI IN -ARE

The infinitive is the basic form of a verb. In English, the infinitive is introduced by **to**, such as in **to** *speak*, **to** *travel*, or **to** *cook*. In Italian, the infinitive is made up of a stem and one of the following endings: **-are**, **-ere**, and **-ire**. In this chapter, we will study the verbs that belong to the category of the verbs in **-are**, defined as **prima coniugazione** [*first conjugation*], which includes verbs such as **parlare**, **viaggiare**, and **cucinare**. Most verbs belong to this group; when a new verb is coined, it is formed with **-are**, such as **googolare** [*to google*].

To conjugate the regular verbs in **-are**, you must drop the ending **-are** and add the appropriate endings (a specific one for each subject pronoun). Each ending corresponds to the subject(s) performing the action:

PARLARE	TO SPEAK
IO PARLI—**O**	I SPEAK
TU PARL—**I**	YOU SPEAK
LEI/LUI PARL—**A**	SHE/HE SPEAKS
NOI PARL—**IAMO**	WE SPEAK
VOI PARL—**ATE**	YOU ALL SPEAK
LORO PARL–**ANO**	THEY SPEAK

As learned in the previous chapters, to negate a verb, we place **non** before its conjugated form. Look at the following examples:

1. Francesco e Stefania parlano italiano, ma **non** parlano francese.
2. Suad parla arabo e italiano, ma **non** parla portoghese.
3. Yoon-Hwa e Hiromi parlano italiano, coreano e giapponese, ma **non** parlano inglese.

Below, write in Italian what languages do you speak and what languages you do **not** speak (list at least two):

_____

_____

Now conjugate the verb **lavorare** [*to work*]:

IO _____   NOI _____

TU _____   VOI _____

LUI/LEI _____   LORO _____

Parliamo!

First, respond to the questions below on your own; then ask the questions to your classmate(s), exchanging roles:

1. Quante [*how many*] lingue parli? _____

2. Quali [*which/what*] lingue parli? _____

3. Quali lingue non parli? _____

4. Lavori? _____

NOTA CULTURALE

L'esterofilia italiana. Many Italians are fascinated by what is coming from other countries: one can hear people saying that Italians are **esterofile/i** (from **esterofilia**, which means a magnified preference for what is coming from abroad). This is also true for words coming from abroad. Over the past few decades, Italian has borrowed many expressions from English. Expressions related to technology are very often untranslated into Italian such as **computer**, **smartphone**, **social media**, **tablet**, and **wi-fi**. However, while some Italians love to write on social media in English, many others have also tried to Italianize some English expressions: this is the case for some verbs such as **bannare** from a social media platform. **Schedulare** is also widely used in Italian aviation to refer to flight schedules. These verbs come from the English verbs *to ban* and *to schedule*, and the ending **-are** has been added to create a word that recalls the English meaning, consequently respecting the Italian grammar. As mentioned previously, if a new verb is coined (as in the examples of **twittare**, **bloggare**, and **googlare** that can be also found in the forms of **gugolare** and **googolare**), it is conjugated using the first conjugation in **-are**. Even though Italian verbs exist for all these terms, such as **programmare** for **schedulare** or **eliminare** for **bannare**, you might still hear these hybrid, anglicized expressions.

4.1.1 I VERBI REGOLARI IN -ARE

Since you have already learned how to conjugate **parlare** and **lavorare**, now add the endings to each subject pronoun in the table below:

CUCIN-ARE	TO COOK
IO CUCIN-	I COOK
TU CUCIN-	YOU COOK
LEI/LUI CUCIN-	SHE/HE COOKS
NOI CUCIN-	WE COOK
VOI CUCIN-	YOU ALL COOK
LORO CUCIN-	THEY COOK

Look at the examples below:

1. Mara non cucina i piselli con il tonno, ma la pasta allo scoglio.
2. Simone e Daniele cucinano le patate al forno.
3. Giuseppe cucina la frittata con la cicoria.

4. Mabel e Carla non cucinano il pollo arrosto, ma la bistecca ai ferri.

E tu cosa cucini? Below, write in a full sentence in Italian what you usually cook:

_____

Parliamo!

First, respond to the questions below, then ask the questions to your classmate(s), exchanging roles:

1. Che cosa [*what*] cucini per cena stasera? _____

2. Che cosa cucini per pranzo domani? _____

3. Quali piatti [*dishes*] non cucini spesso [*often*]? _____

REGULAR VERBS IN -ARE		
Abitare (a/in)	Disegnare	Portare *
Amare	Diventare	Pranzare (a/con)
Arrivare (a/da/in)	Frequentare	Praticare
Aspettare	Guidare	Ricordare *
Cambiare	Imparare	Ritornare (a/da)
Cenare (a/con)	Incontrare	Spiegare *
Cercare	Iniziare	Studiare
Chiamare	Insegnare *	Suonare
Cominciare/Incominciare	Inviare *	Telefonare (a)
Comprare	Lavorare	Tornare (a/da)
Cucinare	Mandare *	Trovare
Decolonizzare	Mangiare	Usare
Desiderare	Pagare	Volare (a/da)
Dimenticare	Pensare (a/di)	Viaggiare (in/da)

TRANSITIVE VERBS VERSUS INTRANSITIVE VERBS

Most of the verbs listed above are **transitive**, which means that they are **followed by direct objects** responding to the questions **What?** or **Whom?** A direct object is not preceded by a preposition. Think about the English grammar through a couple of examples:

- *I eat an apple*: To eat is a transitive verb followed by a direct object. In fact, you can ask yourself: **What** do I eat? The answer to the question would be: *an apple*.
- *I call Yoji*: To call is a transitive verb followed by a direct object. In fact, you can ask yourself: **Whom** do I call? The answer to the question would be: *Yoji*.

However, some of the verbs listed in the table above are **intransitive** and require a preposition afterward, like in English when one says *I look at* the map (the verb *to look* is followed by the preposition *at*). Below is a non-exhaustive list of verbs in **-are** that are intransitive:

ABITARE A + city/town/village: Io abito **a** New York [*I live in New York*]

ABITARE IN + country: Io abito **in** Italia [*I live in Italy*]

ARRIVARE A + destination (city/town/village): Io arrivo **a** Firenze [*I arrive in Florence*]

ARRIVARE IN + destination (country): Io arrivo **in** Italia [*I arrive in Italy*]

ARRIVARE DA + origin (city/town/village): Io arrivo **da** Firenze [*I arrive from Florence*]

TORNARE A + place: Io torno **a** casa [*I come back home*]

(RI)TORNARE DA + place: Io torno/ritorno **da** Roma [*I come back from Rome*]

VOLARE A + destination (city): Volo **a** Parigi [*I fly to Paris*]

VOLARE IN + destination (country): Volo **in** Italia [*I fly to Italy*]

VOLARE DA + origin (country/city): Volo **da** Roma [*I fly from Rome*]

PENSARE A + someone/something: Io penso **a** Marco e Sheila [*I think of Marco and Stella*]

PENSARE DI + someone/something: Io penso molto bene **di** lei [*I think very well of her*]

TELEFONARE A + person/people you phone to: Io telefono **a** Marat [*I call Marat*]

*The verbs **insegnare** [*to teach*], **inviare/mandare** [*to send*], **portare** [*to bring*], **ricordare** [*to remember, to remind*], **spiegare** [*to explain*] represent actions directed at/to someone such as in the following examples: *La professoressa insegna l'italiano* (direct object) *agli studenti e alle studentesse* (indirect object); *io invio un'email* (direct object) *a mia madre* (indirect object) *ogni giorno.*

Look at the examples below:

1. Chiara **telefona a** Shaila.
2. Khalid e Giuseppe **tornano da** Stoccolma in auto.
3. Francesca **pensa** molto spesso **a** Wellington in Nuova Zelanda.

Esercitiamoci!

Fill in the blanks with the verbs in **-are** in parentheses and complete the last sentence based on what you do:

1. La scrittrice italiana di origini somale, Igiaba Scego, _____ (*volare*) a New York per presentare il suo nuovo libro.

2. Noi non _____ (*usare*) la macchina da Firenze a Bologna per andare [*to go*] al lavoro: andiamo in treno.

3. Marcello _____ (*incontrare*) il suo amico Roberto e la sua amica Adalgisa a Londra.

4. Voi _____ (*telefonare*) a vostro cugino Edoardo.

5. Tu non _____ (*cucinare*) le trofie al pesto, ma le linguine ai funghi.

6. Tu e Maria _____ (*parlare*) con la chef del ristorante.

7. Fred, Nicoletta e io non _____ (*cenare*) con Luigi in pizzeria, ma in trattoria.

8. Io _____

LE PAROLE CONTANO

As Francesca Calamita has suggested in various publications, a dichotomy has long characterized the relationship between Western women and food: on the one hand, women have been identified as those responsible for feeding their families, but on the other hand, throughout history they have not been allowed to eat qualitatively and quantitatively like men in many circumstances. In recent times, for example, we have been bombarded by advertisements that target women for low-calorie foods and men for meat products. Furthermore, cooking is traditionally considered a woman's duty, while food preparation by men always problematically includes an artistic or artisanal element. Indeed, women have been perceived as the essential cooks for the family but not as chefs, a title often reserved in the past only for men. The language reflects these dichotomies, and this happens in Italian as well. In the past,

the word **cuoca** [*cook*] often replaced the word **chef** if a woman was in charge of a kitchen restaurant. Furthermore, if you think about male chefs versus female chefs on global platforms, you will realize that the former outnumbers the latter. Visibility for women chefs has been limited and, therefore, for a long time, their talent has remained hidden behind the scenes. However, this sexist practice has changed; with many women chefs, one now uses this word for them also in Italian. In Montemerano, a little town in the Maremma area in Tuscany, the chef of the restaurant *Da Caino*, Valeria Piccini, addresses herself as **Shef** (she + chef) to give visibility to women in the profession.

Nadia Santini and Massimo Bottura are two famous Italian chefs: she works at the restaurant *Dal Pescatore* and he works at the *Osteria Francescana*. Santini has been **la prima chef** [*the first female chef*] whose restaurant received the prestigious **tre stelle Michelin** [*three Michelin stars*], while Valeria Piccini's restaurant receives **due stelle Michelin** [*two Michelin stars*].

Scriviamo!

Form six complete sentences in Italian (one for each subject: **io**, **tu**, **lui/lei**, **noi**, **voi**, **loro**) using six different verbs in **-are**.

Lavoriamo con altre studentesse o altri studenti

Check over the exercises above with another student.

Parliamo!

Ask another student the questions below, alternating roles. Pay attention to the prepositions.

1. Dove abiti? [*Where do you live?*]
2. Cosa cucini per cena? [*What do you cook for dinner?*]
3. Chi incontri all'università? [*Who do you meet at the university?*]
4. Chi chiami tutti i giorni? [*Who do you call every day?*]

Before starting to ask and answer questions, take notes.

- To answer the question #1: do not forget the rule which applies to **abitare a + city**.
- To answer the questions #2: read **La pagina culturale** at the end of this chapter and the **Nota Culturale** below.

NOTA CULTURALE

I piatti italiani (esempi di antipasti, primi, secondi, contorni e dolci). Below you will find examples of what Italians eat: **gli antipasti** [*the appetizers*], **i primi** [*the first courses*], **i secondi** [*the second courses*], **i contorni** [*the side dishes*], **la frutta** [*fruit*], and **i dolci** [*the desserts*].

Esempi di antipasti:	**Esempi di primi:**
Antipasto di mare	Pasta al pomodoro
Antipasto di terra	Pasta al pesto
Prosciutto e melone	Pasta al ragù
Caprese	Pasta in bianco
Bruschetta al pomodoro	Pasta all'amatriciana
Bruschetta ai funghi porcini	Pasta alla Norma
Crostini misti	Pasta all'arrabbiata
Formaggi misti	Spaghetti alla carbonara
Burrata	Spaghetti allo scoglio
Affettati misti	Risotto alla pescatora
Alici marinate	Risotto alla milanese
Olive all'ascolana	Lasagne/pasta al forno
Arancini	Melanzane alla parmigiana *
Esempi di secondi:	**Esempi di contorni:**
Arrosto misto	Piselli alla salvia
Bistecca ai ferri	Zucchine trifolate
Pollo alla cacciatora	Melanzane grigliate
Cinghiale in umido	Peperoni in agrodolce
Frittata	Pomodori fritti
Uova in carrozza	Insalata verde
Pesce al forno	Insalata mista
Frittura di pesce	Patate lesse
Scampi e mazzancolle alla griglia	Patatine fritte
Esempi di dolci:	**La verdura e le erbe:**
Crostata di frutta o ricotta	Aglio
Tiramisù	Cipolla
Gelato	Prezzemolo
Panna cotta	Basilico
Profiteroles	Carota
Paste fresche	Zucchina
Crème brûlée	Melanzana

Crema catalana	Pomodoro
Pasticceria mignon	Patata
Torta della nonna	Bietola
Diplomatico	Funghi
Torta alla frutta	Cavolo/Cavolfiore
Torta mimosa	Fagiolini
Salame al cioccolato	Piselli
Rotolo alla crema	Spinaci

La frutta:	Esempi di bevande:
Arancia	Acqua
Mandarino	Vino (bianco, rosso, rosé)
Pompelmo	Birra
Pesca	Caffè
Susina	Tè (caldo e freddo)
Banana	Latte
Pera	Aranciata
Mela	Limonata
Fragole	Prosecco
Ciliegie	Spumante
Anguria	Ammazzacaffè
Melone	Grappa
Kiwi	Limoncello

*Una curiosità: on the web it has been debated whether *melanzane alla parmigiana* is a first or a second course. Many Italians consider it a first course, others a second course and *contorno* (together), others think that it is simply *un piatto unico* [*a single dish*], and others think that it is *un piatto di mezzo* [*a middle dish*] that cannot be categorized.

4.1.2 ALTRI VERBI IN -ARE

With the conjugations of regular verbs in **-are**, one needs to pay attention to some peculiarities. For verbs whose stems end in **-iare**, like **studiare** [*to study*] and **cambiare** [*to change*], you need to drop the vowel **i** of the stem in the conjugated forms of **tu** and **noi,** to ensure using only one **i**.

Tu stud-**i**	Tu camb-**i**
Noi stud-**iamo**	Noi camb-**iamo**

Now conjugate the verb **studiare**:

IO   _____   NOI   _____

TU   _____   VOI   _____

LUI/LEI   _____   LORO   _____

Cosa studi? Below, respond to this question with a full sentence in Italian:

_____

Verbs whose stems end in -**ciare** and -**giare**, like **incominciare** [_to begin, to start_] and **mangiare** [_to eat_], also drop the vowel **i** in the conjugated forms of **tu** and **noi**:

Tu incominc-**i**	Tu mang-**i**
Noi incominc-**iamo**	Noi mang-**iamo**

Now conjugate the verb **mangiare**:

IO   _____   NOI   _____

TU   _____   VOI   _____

LUI/LEI   _____   LORO   _____

Cosa mangi a merenda? Below, respond to this question with a full sentence in Italian.

_____

Verbs whose stems end in -**care** and -**gare**, like **giocare** [_to play_] and **spiegare** [_to explain_], require a spelling change in the forms **tu** and **noi** to keep the hard sound [k]. You need to add an **h** to the regular endings to maintain this hard sound, as in the examples below:

Tu gioc-**hi**	Tu spieg-**hi**
Noi gioc-**hiamo**	Noi spieg-**hiamo**

Giocare means _to play_ (like **suonare**) and holds a precise meaning:

GIOCARE versus SUONARE

Giocare and **suonare** both mean _to play_, but in Italian they are used to express different actions. **Suonare** means _to play an instrument_, while **giocare** means _to play a sport_: Io suono la viola e gioco a calcio.
GIOCARE A + **sport**: Annalisa e Marco giocano a tennis [_Annalisa e Marco play tennis_]
SUONARE + **instrument**: Julia suona il flauto e Sofia il contrabbasso [Julia _plays the flute and Sofia the double bass_]
While **giocare** is an intransitive verb being followed by a preposition, **suonare** is a transitive one requiring a direct object.

Now conjugate the verb **giocare**:

IO _____   NOI _____

TU _____   VOI _____

LUI/LEI _____   LORO _____

A cosa giochi? Below, respond to this question with a full sentence in Italian:

_____

Esercitiamoci!

Fill in the blanks with verbs in **-iare**, **-ciare**, **-giare**, **-care**, and **-gare**, conjugating the verbs in parentheses:

1. Le mie amiche e io non _____ (*giocare*) a pallavolo ogni giorno.

2. Tu e i tuoi compagni di classe _____ (*spiegare*) la lezione al vostro amico Giulio.

3. Tu _____ (*cercare*) il libro di italiano, ma non lo trovi da nessuna parte.

4. Per pranzo José _____ (*mangiare*) l'insalata con il tonno e i pomodori.

5. Claudia _____ (*litigare*) spesso con sua madre, ma poi fanno subito pace [*make peace*].

6. Shazad, tu _____ (*cambiare*) spesso il telefonino?

7. Mohammed e Maddalena non _____ (*pagare*) il conto al ristorante con la nuova carta di credito: pagano in contanti [*cash*].

8. Bob, Kate, Alex e io _____ (*incominciare*) a leggere il nuovo libro per la nostra associazione culturale: siamo parte del loro Club del Libro.

9. Tu e Carmela _____ (*indicare*) la strada a Patrizia per andare [*to go*] a piedi in centro [*downtown*].

10. Mi piace [*I like*] studiare l'italiano! Tu _____ (*studiare*) questa lingua? Da quanto?

Scriviamo!

Write six sentences in Italian with the following verbs—**studiare**, **cambiare**, **giocare**, **spiegare**, **incominciare**, and **mangiare**—and using the six different subject pronouns (**io**, **tu**, **lui/lei**, **noi**, **voi**, **loro**).

Lavoriamo con altre studentesse o altri studenti

Check over the exercises above with another student.

Parliamo!

Ask your classmates what they study and say what you study. Do the same with what they eat and what you eat for breakfast, lunch, and dinner. To answer this question, check the **Nota culturale** below about widely studied subjects at the university level. Do not forget to add the definite articles before the subjects (**il**, **lo**, **l'**, **la**, **l'**, **i**, **gli**, **le**).

1. Cosa studi all'università?
2. Cosa mangi a colazione?
3. Cosa mangi a pranzo?
4. Cosa mangi a cena?

Before starting to ask and answer questions, take notes.

- To answer the question #1: read the **Nota culturale** below.
- To answer the questions #2, 3, and 4: read the **Nota culturale** about the *Cucina italiana* in the previous pages and **La pagina culturale** in the *Appendix*.

NOTA CULTURALE

Le discipline universitarie. Below is a list of subjects commonly offered at university level in Italy and in other parts of the world:

Agraria [*Agriculture*]	Lingue straniere [*Foreign Languages*]
Amministrazione [*Administration*]	Matematica [*Mathematics*]
Antropologia [*Anthropology*]	Medicina [*Medical Sciences*]
Architettura [*Architecture*]	Musica [*Music*]
Arte [*Arts*]	Orticoltura [*Horticulture*]
Biologia [*Biology*]	Pedagogia [*Pedagogy*]
Botanica [*Botany*]	Psicologia [*Psychology*]
Chimica [*Chemistry*]	Scienza della comunicazione [*Communication*]
Economia e commercio [*Economics and Business*]	Scienze ambientali [*Environmental Sciences*]
Filosofia [*Philosophy*]	Scienze infermieristiche [*Nursing*]
Fisica [*Physics*]	Scienze informatiche [*Computer Science*]
Geografia/Scienze geografiche [*Geography/Geographical Sciences*]	Scienze motorie e sportive [*Sports Sciences*]
Giornalismo [*Journalism*]	Scienze naturali [*Natural Sciences*]
Igiene dentale [*Dental Hygiene*]	Scienze politiche [*Political Science*]
Ingegneria [*Engineering*]	Storia [*History*]
Legge [*Law*]	Teatro [*Theater*]
Letteratura [*Literature*]	

The list is not exhaustive; however, it is a good start to know subjects and disciplines in Italian. If your field of study is not included in the list, check with your professor and write it below:

LE PAROLE CONTANO

Reading the chart above, you might wonder about **Studi di genere** [*Gender Studies*]: in Italy, this discipline has generally been perceived only as an interdisciplinary field, and there is not yet a specific **corso di laurea triennale** (equivalent to a bachelor of arts), as seen more commonly in many anglophone universities. Specific courses or modules with gender-oriented perspectives can be found in almost all disciplines in the humanities and social sciences, yet it largely depends on the professor. However, some universities, like the University of Bologna, offer options to specialize in gender studies at the master's level (**corso di laurea magistrale**). GEMMA is the first Erasmus Mundus master´s degree in Women's and Gender Studies in Europe. https://masteres.ugr.es/gemma/

In Italian, the word **gender** sometimes is used in its English variation, since this subject was first formally established in anglophone universities and studied by anglophone scholars; therefore, you might hear Italians say **Studi di Genere** or **Gender Studies** as well. At times, when used in English, it might take a derogatory meaning, particularly in the expressions "la teoria del gender" or "ideologia gender" which discredit the importance of gender studies, and which experts in the field do not use. A similar phenomenon is common in France and Spain.

4.2 I VERBI IRREGOLARI IN -ARE: ANDARE, DARE, FARE E STARE

Some verbs do not follow the rules introduced in 4.1, and therefore they are called **verbi irregolari** [*irregular verbs*]. Below, you will find the most common irregular verbs in **-are**:

ANDARE [*to go*]	DARE [*to give*]	FARE [*to do/to make*]	STARE [*to stay/to be/to feel*]
IO VADO	IO DO	IO FACCIO	IO STO
TU VAI	TU DAI	TU FAI	TU STAI
LEI/LUI VA	LEI/LUI DÀ	LEI/LUI FA	LUI/LEI STA
NOI ANDIAMO	NOI DIAMO	NOI FACCIAMO	NOI STIAMO
VOI ANDATE	VOI DATE	VOI FATE	VOI STATE
LORO VANNO	LORO DANNO	LORO FANNO	LORO STANNO

Please note that to negate a verb, you need to place **non** before its conjugated form: *Carlo **non** fa la pasta in casa*.

Look at the examples below:

1. Questo fine settimana vado a Roma, ma la mia amica Maria Isabel e suo cugino Marcello vanno a Firenze.

2. Le studentesse e gli studenti fanno bene l'esame.
3. — Che bello vederti [*How nice to see you*], Carla! Come stai?
   — Sto bene, grazie! E tu, Jen?

Respond to the following questions with full sentences in Italian:

Dove vai ogni mattina?

_____

A chi dai *il buongiorno* ogni mattina?

_____

Cosa fai tutte le settimane?

_____

Come stai in questo momento?

_____

Esercitiamoci!

Fill in the blanks, conjugating the verbs in parentheses in the present tense (pay attention to the subjects):

1. Gina e Luca non _____ (*andare*) al cinema domani perché lavorano fino a tardi.
2. Giorgio e Khalid _____ (*fare*) la pasta al forno per il pranzo di domenica. È molto buona!
3. Io _____ (*dare*) il libro di italiano a tua sorella Teresa perché ha bisogno di ripassare i verbi.
4. Alessia, Piero e io _____ (*stare*) a casa stasera perché fa brutto tempo.
5. Tu _____ (*andare*) in vacanza a casa di tua nonna a Firenze in estate?
6. La Professoressa Elisa Dorati _____ (*dare*) i compiti alle sue studentesse e ai suoi studenti della classe di italiano. Sono tutte e tutti molto brave e bravi!
7. Come _____ (*stare*), Angelo? Sembri stanco!
8. Tu, Guia ed Eleonora non _____ (*fare*) i compiti prima [*before*] del compleanno di Monica, non avete tempo.

Scriviamo!

Write six sentences (two sentences for each verb: **andare**, **dare**, and **stare**) using different subject pronouns (**io**, **tu**, **lui/lei**, **noi**, **voi**, **loro**) and/or names.

Lavoriamo con altre studentesse o altri studenti

Check over the exercises above with another student.

ESPRESSIONI IDIOMATICHE CON *FARE*	

In Italian, the verb **fare** expresses the basic idea of doing or making something, as in **fare i compiti** [*to do homeworks*] and **fare la pasta** [*to make pasta*], but it is also used in many idiomatic expressions, such as:

IL TEMPO	LA VITA QUOTIDIANA
■ **FARE BEL TEMPO** [*to have good weather*] ■ **FARE BRUTTO TEMPO** [*to have bad weather*] ■ **FARE FREDDO** [*to have cold weather*] ■ **FARE FRESCO** [*to have cool weather*] ■ **FARE CALDO** [*to have hot weather*] *These expressions are only used in the third person singular: **fa bel tempo**, **fa brutto tempo**, **fa freddo**, **fa fresco**, and **fa caldo**. To ask what kind of weather it is, one asks: **Che tempo fa?**	■ **FARE MALE** [*to hurt*] ■ **FARE COLAZIONE** [*to have/eat breakfast*] ■ **FARE MERENDA** [*to have/eat a mid-afternoon snack*] ■ **FARE LA DOCCIA/IL BAGNO** [*to take a shower/a bath*] ■ **FARE GLI AUGURI A** [*to congratulate someone*] ■ **FARE UNA TELEFONATA A** [*to give (someone) a call*] ■ **FARE UNA SORPRESA A QUALCUNO** [*to surprise someone*] ■ **FARE UN FAVORE A QUALCUNO** [to do someone a favour] ■ **FARE UNA DOMANDA A** [*to ask someone a question*] ■ **FARE UNA FOTOGRAFIA A** [*to take a picture of (someone or something)*]
IL VIAGGIO	GLI ACQUISTI
■ **FARE LE VALIGIE** [*to pack a suitcase(s)*] ■ **FARE IL BIGLIETTO** [*to purchase/to get a ticket*] ■ **FARE UN VIAGGIO** [*to travel*] ■ **FARE BUON VIAGGIO** [*to have a good trip*] ■ **FARE UN GIRO** [*to take a tour*] ■ **FARE UN SALTO** [*to drop by*] ■ **FARE UNA PASSEGGIATA** [*to take a walk*]	■ **FARE LA SPESA** [*to go grocery shopping*] ■ **FARE LE SPESE** [*to go shopping*] ■ **FARE UN REGALO A QUALCUNO** [*to give a gift*] ■ **FARE LA FILA** [*to queue/to stand in line*] ■ **FARE IL PIENO** [*to refuel/ fill up the gas tank*] ■ **FARE LA BENZINA** [*to get fuel/gas*] ■ **FARE ALLA ROMANA** [*to split the bill*]

Note that *fare gli auguri/una telefonata/una sorpresa/un favore/una domanda/una fotografia/un regalo* are followed by the preposition **A** to indicate who is the target of the action:

1. Fabio fa gli auguri **a** suo nonno.
2. Nadir e Carolina fanno una telefonata **a** Daniele e Silvia.
3. I genitori fanno una sorpresa **a** Lucio.
4. Sofia, Julia e io facciamo un favore **ad** Alex.
5. Tu e Marcella fate una domanda **a** Salvatore e Chiara.
6. Io non faccio una fotografia **a** Samuele.
7. Tu fai un regalo **a** Caroline.

📝 *Esercitiamoci!*

Fill in the blanks, conjugating the verb **fare** in the present tense (pay attention to subjects):

1. Noi _____ merenda tutti i giorni alle quattro con il gelato.

2. Renzo e Lucia _____ una sorpresa a Don Abbondio, ma lui non è affatto contento.

3. Quest'anno tu non _____ un viaggio alle Maldive a causa della pandemia. Che peccato!

4. Io _____ la doccia tutti i giorni, ma lavo i capelli soltanto un paio di volte a settimana.

5. Oggi non _____ bel tempo! È perfetto per stare a casa e studiare per l'esame di scienze.

6. Tu, Mabel, Claudia, Qing e io _____ alla romana al ristorante. Per noi è una tradizione!

7. Tu, Rheba e Shazad _____ le fotografie con il cellulare, ma non le stampate mai.

8. Sara non _____ la spesa al supermercato, ma al mercato ogni venerdì mattina.

✍️ *Scriviamo!*

Write eight full sentences in Italian (two sentences from each category of the table above: **il tempo**, **la vita quotidiana**, **il viaggio**, and **gli acquisti**) using the idiomatic expressions with the verb **fare** and using different subject pronouns (**io**, **tu**, **lui/lei**, **noi**, **voi**, **loro**) and/or names.

✺ *Lavoriamo con altre studentesse o altri studenti*

Check over the exercises above with another student.

💬 *Parliamo!*

Ask another student the questions below, alternating roles. Pay attention to the prepositions.

1. Che tempo fa oggi?
2. Come stai?
3. Cosa fai dopo le lezioni all'università?
4. Se lavori, cosa fai di lavoro?
5. Dove vai in vacanza?
6. Quando fai un viaggio?
7. A chi dai un libro?
8. Quando fai colazione, cosa mangi?
9. Fai la doccia o il bagno?
10. Dove fai la spesa?
11. A chi fai una telefonata ogni giorno?
12. A chi fai il prossimo [*next*] regalo?

Ask two more questions that are not listed above using a formal register:

1. _____

2. _____

4.3 GLI INTERROGATIVI

Interrogatives are question words such as **what**, **where**, **when**, **why**, and **how**. In Italian, like in English, interrogatives are placed at the beginning of the questions, and they are necessary in everyday communication. Below you will find a list of the most common interrogatives:

GLI INTERROGATIVI	
CHE COSA/COSA/CHE	WHAT
CHI	WHO/WHOM
QUALE/QUAL/QUALI	WHICH/WHAT
COME	HOW
DOVE	WHERE
PERCHÉ	WHY/BECAUSE
QUANTO/QUANTA/QUANTI/QUANTE	HOW MUCH/HOW MANY/HOW LONG
QUANDO	WHEN

Note that **CHE COSA/COSA/CHE, CHI, COME, DOVE, PERCHÉ**, and **QUANDO** are unchangeable, namely they cannot be modified. **PERCHÉ** means both *why* and *because*. Look at the examples below:

1. **Perché** fai la doccia? **Perché** è comoda.
2. **Perché** mangi le melanzane alla parmigiana? **Perché** sono buone.

In addition, note that, when followed by the verb **è** [*is*], **COME, DOVE, CHE COSA**, and **COSA** drop the final -**e** and add an apostrophe. Moreover, one uses **QUAL** (instead of **QUALE**) before **è** [*is*]. Look at the examples below:

1. — **Com'**è la ricetta di Marta?
   — Buona!
2. — **Dov'**è Nicoletta?
   — A scuola.
3. — **Che cos'**è/**Cos'**è il gusto di colore verde?
   — È il gelato al pistacchio.

4. — **Qual** è il tuo nome?
— Mi chiamo Ernesto.

Note that **CHE COSA** is the most formal and polite of the three forms, while **CHE** is the most colloquial. **COSA** is somewhere in the middle between the two. Look at the examples below:

1. — **Che cosa/Cosa** mangi?
— Mangio la crostata al cacao.

2. — **Che** guardi in TV?
— Guardo *Bake Off Italia*!

QUANTO/QUANTA/QUANTI/QUANTE and **QUALE/QUALI** can be adjectives or pronouns. Their ending depends on the gender and number of the noun they refer to if used as adjectives, or that they replace, if used as pronouns. Look at the examples below:

1. **Quanti pezzi** di pizza mangi per cena? [*How many slices of pizza do you eat for dinner?*] (**adjective**)

2. **Quali biscotti** mangi a colazione? [*Which cookies/biscuits do you eat for breakfast?*] (**adjective**)

3. — Domani faccio una festa con **le mie amiche**.
— **Quante** e **quali** sono? [–*Tomorrow, I will throw a party with my female friends. – How many of them and who are they?*] (**pronouns**)

In questions starting with an interrogative, the subject is often placed at the end of the sentence. Look at the examples below:

1. — **Dove** va in vacanza Miao-Fen?
— Va in Italia, a Palermo.

2. — **Che cosa** mangiano Giulio e Alessandro?
— La pizza caprese con i pomodori freschi, la mozzarella di bufala e il basilico.

Chi sono? Dove lavorano? Cosa fanno? Che cos'è?

Match the questions on the left numbered from one to nine with the answers on the right

1. Chi è Nadia Santini?	a. Al ristorante *Signum* a Salina Eolie.
2. Dove lavora Massimo Bottura?	b. Un reality-show.
3. Cosa fa Giada De Laurentiis?	c. Fa lo chef.
4. Chi è Pellegrino Artusi?	d. Fa la chef in televisione.
5. Che cos'è *Fatto in casa da Benedetta*?	e. All'*Osteria Francescana* a Modena.
6. Dove lavora Martina Caruso?	f. L'autore de *L'arte in cucina e la scienza di mangiar bene* (1891).
7. Che cos'è *Bake off Italia*?	g. Al ristorante *Al Sorriso* vicino [*near*] a Novara.
8. Cosa fa Carlo Cracco?	h. È un blog di cucina.
9. Dove lavora Luisa Marelli Valazza?	i. La prima chef con tre stelle Michelin.

Esercitiamoci!

Fill in the blanks with the correct interrogatives:

1. — _____ gioca a pallavolo? – Pamela, Gemma e io!

2. — _____ studi all'università? – Studio scienze politiche e italiano.

3. — _____ Carlo e Paolo non mangiano la frittata? – Sono allergici alle uova!

4. — _____ è Giuliana? – È al bar.

5. — _____ vai in vacanza? – Vado in vacanza a giugno.

6. — _____ amici e amiche avete in classe tu e Alessia? – Cinque!

7. — _____ amiche e amici vanno a lezione con Ahmed e Carlos? – Otto!

8. — _____ è? – È Michela Marzano, una filosofa italiana famosa.

9. — Ragazzi e ragazze, _____ state oggi? – Stiamo bene, grazie.

10. — _____ vestito compri? – Compro il vestito verde!

11. — _____ pollo cucina Martina? – Solo mezzo.

12. — _____ torta mangiamo? – Tutta!

Scriviamo!

Write eight full sentences in Italian, one sentence for each interrogative (1. **che cosa/cosa/che**, 2. **chi**, 3. **quale/qual/quali**, 4. **come**, 5. **dove**, 6. **perché**, 7. **quanto/quanta/quanti/quante**, 8. **quando**), using different subject pronouns (**io**, **tu**, **lui/lei**, **noi**, **voi**, **loro**) and/or names.

Lavoriamo con altre studentesse o altri studenti

Check over the exercises above with another student.

💬 Parliamo!

Ask another student the questions below, alternating roles.

1. Che giorno è oggi?
2. Come ti chiami?
3. Di dove sei?
4. Dove abiti?
5. Quanti anni hai?
6. Quando è il tuo compleanno?
7. Qual è il tuo numero di telefono?
8. Come sei? Descrivi le tue caratteristiche fisiche e psicologiche.
9. Come stai?
10. Che cosa studi?
11. Quali materie studi questo semestre?
12. Perché studi italiano?
13. Dove studi?
14. Quando vai all'università?
15. Quando è la tua laurea?
16. Qual è il tuo cibo preferito?
17. Quando fai colazione, pranzo e cena?
18. Quanti amici hai?
19. Quante amiche hai?
20. Chi è il tuo migliore amico o la tua migliore amica?
21. Cosa guardi alla TV?
22. Se lavori, dove lavori?

Ask two more questions that are not listed above using a formal register:

1. _____

2. _____

4.4 I PRONOMI E GLI AGGETTIVI DIMOSTRATIVI

Demonstrative pronouns and adjectives in English are **this**, **that**, **these**, and **those**: they help to identify spatial relationships. As demonstrative pronouns, they are used instead of a noun to point out people, pets, or things, while the adjectives help to qualify things, people, or pets. More specifically, demonstrative adjectives add more information about people, pets, or things, especially their location with respect to who is speaking. The distinction between **questo/a** and **quello/a** is the same as in English with **this** versus **that**. In Italian, the demonstrative pronouns and adjectives (**questo/a/i/e, quello/a/i/e**) must agree in gender and number with the noun they are replacing or are referring to. As demonstrative adjectives, they must be placed before a noun. Moreover, in Italian, one often uses **qui** [*here*] to express a place close to the one who is speaking, and **là** [*there*] when the place is far from the speaker.

4.4.1 QUESTA/O AS *THIS/THIS ONE*

In Italian (like in English), one uses **questo/a/i/e** when something or someone is **close** to the speaker:

THIS/THIS ONE/THESE/THESE ONES		
	Femminile	Maschile
Singolare	**QUESTA/QUEST'**	**QUESTO/QUEST'**
Plurale	**QUESTE**	**QUESTI**

— **Queste** farfalle [*butterflies*] sono colorate!
— Come sono belle!

As **demonstrative pronouns**, use the following forms only: **questo**, **questa**, **questi**, and **queste** (without elision). Look at the example below for their use:

1. — Quale penna usi, Giorgio?
    — **Questa**, grazie!

2. — Quale libro leggi, Michele?
    — **Questo**!

Esercitiamoci!

Fill in the blanks with demonstrative pronouns or adjectives **questo/a/i/e** and indicate if they are adjectives or pronouns.

1. — Non mangio _____ pasta!

   — È cattiva?

   Adjective _____   Pronoun _____

2. — _____ sono le tue compagne di corso?

   — Sì, sono loro. Sono veramente simpatiche.

   Adjective _____   Pronoun _____

3. — Scusi, _____ posto è libero?

   — Certo!

   Adjective _____   Pronoun _____

4. — Ginevra, _____ è il vestito che cerchi
   [*to look for*]?

   — Esatto!

   Adjective _____   Pronoun _____

5. — _____ scarpe rosse sono di Valentino
   o di Alberta Ferretti?

   — Ferragamo!

   Adjective _____   Pronoun _____

6. — _____ sono i libri di Michela Murgia,
   una scrittrice italiana.

   — Sono belli!

   Adjective _____   Pronoun _____

7. — _____ ricetta sembra buona. La provo
   [*I will try it out*]!

   — Brava!

   Adjective _____   Pronoun _____

8. — _____ amico di Andrea è simpatico.

   — Davvero?

   Adjective _____   Pronoun _____

Scriviamo!

Write four mini dialogues in Italian, one sentence for each demonstrative used as an adjective or a pronoun (for each sentence specify what kind of demonstrative it is: whether it is a pronoun or an adjective): 1. **questo/quest'**, 2. **questa/quest'**, 3. **questi**, 4. **queste**.

Lavoriamo con altre studentesse o altri studenti

Check over the exercises above with another student.

Parliamo!

With another student, look at the picture below, asking each other what the other student would eat among the dishes presented at this Italian table. Do not forget to use demonstrative pronouns and adjectives (**questa/o/e/i**) and to pay attention to the agreement in terms of gender (m./s.) and number (s./pl.):

Esempio: — Che cosa mangi?
— Io mangio **questo** formaggio.

4.4.2 QUELLA/O AS *THAT/THAT ONE*

In Italian (like in English), one uses **quella/o/e/i** (and other forms) when something or someone is **far** from the speaker:

THAT/THAT ONE/THOSE/THOSE ONES		
	Femminile	Maschile
Singolare	**QUELLA/QUELL'**	**QUEL/QUELLO/QUELL'**
Plurale	**QUELLE**	**QUEI/QUEGLI/QUELLI**

Quel (m.s.), **quello** (m.s.), **quell'** (m.s.), **quella** (f.s.), **quell'** (f.s.), **quei** (m.pl.), **quelli** (m.pl.), **quegli** (m.pl.), and **quelle** (f.pl.) follow the rule of the definite articles **il, lo, l', la, l', i, gli**, and **le**. Do you remember the rule? If not, go back to Chapter 2.

Based on the rule of definite articles, what do you think are the rules for the above demonstrative adjectives and pronouns?

GLI USI DI QUELLO E QUELLA

As mentioned, **quello** and **quella** have several forms, like the definite article:
- use **QUEL** (m.s.) with a masculine noun in the singular starting with a consonant (*quel libro*).
- use **QUELLO** (m.s.) with a masculine noun in the singular starting with **z** (*quello zio*) or with **s** + another consonant (*quello studente*), and in certain cases with two consonants (*quello psicologo*).
- use **QUELL'** (m.s./f.s.) with masculine or feminine nouns in the singular starting with a vowel (*quell'amico, quell'amica*).
- use **QUEI** (m.pl.) with a masculine plural noun starting with a consonant (*quei libri*).
- use **QUEGLI** (m.pl.) with a masculine plural noun starting with a vowel (*quegli amici*), with **z** (*quegli zii*) or with **s** + another consonant (*quegli studenti*), and in certain cases with two consonants (*quegli psicologi*).
- use **QUELLI** (m.pl.) only as a pronoun: *Chi sono quelli? Quelli sono i nostri amici.*
- use **QUELLE** (f.pl.) with a feminine plural noun starting with a vowel or with a consonant, and never elide (even in front of vowels): *quelle ragazze, quelle amiche.*

Like the **demonstrative adjectives**, you can use all of the forms introduced above (except **quelli**). Look at the examples below for their proper usage:

1. — **Quella** bambina è brava a suonare il pianoforte.
   — Davvero! Hai ragione!

2. — **Quel** ragazzo è bravo a scuola.
   — È bravo davvero!

Like the **demonstrative pronouns**, use the following forms only: **quello, quella, quelli,** and **quelle**. Look at the examples below for their proper usage:

1. — Quale gelato vuoi [*want*], Martina?
   — **Quello**, mamma!

2. — Quale pizza mangi, Giorgio?
   — **Quella**!

Esercitiamoci!

Fill in the blanks with demonstrative pronouns or adjectives **quella/o** in all its forms and determine if they are adjectives or pronouns:

1. — Guarda [*Look*]! C'è la chef!

   — _____ è Antonia Klugmann! È molto famosa!

   Adjective _____   Pronoun _____

2. — Li conosci [*Do you know them*]?

   — Sì, _____ studenti sono i miei compagni di classe!

   Adjective _____   Pronoun _____

3. — Quali sono gli amici di Omar?

   — _____! Giocano a pallacanestro per Farmingdale.

   Adjective _____   Pronoun _____

4. — _____ trattoria fa una pasta all'arrabbiata molto buona.

   — Bene!

   Adjective _____   Pronoun _____

5. — _____ studente va a lezione ogni giorno.

   — È vero! Simone è molto studioso.

   Adjective _____   Pronoun _____

6. — Chi sono?

   — _____ sono le mie amiche Hiromi e Marina!

   Adjective _____   Pronoun _____

7. — _____ studentesse suonano il pianoforte.

   — Sono proprio brave!

   Adjective _____   Pronoun _____

8. — _____ ragazzi giocano a football americano per l'Università della Virginia.

   — Complimenti! Sono proprio bravi!

   Adjective _____   Pronoun _____

Scriviamo!

Write four mini dialogues in Italian, one sentence for each demonstrative used as an adjective or as a pronoun (for each sentence, specify what kind of demonstrative it is: if it is a pronoun or an adjective): 1. **quel/quello/quell'**, 2. **quella/quell'**, 3. **quei/quegli/quelli**, and 4. **quelle.**

Lavoriamo con altre studentesse o altri studenti

Check over the exercises above with another student.

Parliamo!

With another student, look at the picture below, asking what the other student would **not** eat among the dishes presented at this Italian table. Do not forget to use demonstratives (**quello/a/i/e**) and to pay attention to the agreement in terms of gender (m./s.) and number (s./pl.):

Esempio: — Che cosa **non** mangi?
          — Io **non** mangio **quel** formaggio.

4.5 LE PREPOSIZIONI SEMPLICI

Like in English, prepositions are invariable and in most cases cannot be literally translated from English into Italian. Prepositions can be followed by nouns (including articles and adjectives), pronouns, and verbs in their infinitive forms.

In Italian, prepositions are of two types: simple and articulated. The **preposizioni semplici** [*simple prepositions*] are prepositions that stand by themselves and are not constructed with articles (in English, the equivalent are the prepositions not followed by articles), while the **preposizioni articolate** [*articulated prepositions*] include definite articles (in most cases, they are merged with articles). As we will introduce **le preposizioni articolate** later in the textbook, in this chapter we focus on **le preposizioni semplici**:

Preposizioni semplici	
DI	OF, FROM
A	TO, AT, IN
DA	FROM, SINCE, BY, AT
IN	IN, TO, AT
SU	ON, ABOUT, IN
PER	FOR, THROUGH, IN ORDER TO
CON	WITH
TRA/FRA	BETWEEN, AMONG, IN

As pointed out, one cannot translate prepositions literally from English into Italian; however, some do match. Look at the examples below:

1. La ricetta **di** Carla è buona!
2. Oggi David e Marco vanno **a** Roma.
3. **Da** lunedì Mohammed inizia le lezioni **di** tennis.
4. Chiara va **in** Italia **a** giugno.

5. Il pizzaiolo Salim fa le pizze solo **su** ordinazione.

6. Questo regalo è **per** Martina.

7. Il sabato esco **con** le mie amiche e i miei amici.

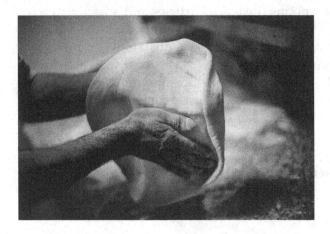

8. La mia famiglia e io andiamo in Nuova Zelanda **tra/fra** due mesi.

The prepositions **A** and **IN** are used with the verb **ANDARE** (see 4.2):

ANDARE + IN or A
ANDARE A + city/town/village: Io vado **a** New York [*I go to New York*] **ANDARE IN** + country: Io vado **in** Italia [*I go to Italy*]

However, there are more idiomatic expressions with the prepositions **A** and **IN** that are used with the verbs **andare** and **stare**. In the chart below, you will find the most common ones.

ESPRESSIONI IDIOMATICHE CON *ANDARE* E *STARE* E LE PREPOSIZIONE IN & A	
Locations (IN)	**Miscellaneous (A)**
In casa	A casa
In montagna	A scuola
In campagna	A lezione
In città/paese	A una festa
In piazza	A tavola
In centro	A colazione
In biblioteca	A pranzo

In palestra	A merenda
In piscina	A cena
In banca	A letto
In chiesa	A teatro
In ufficio	A piedi
In farmacia	A cavallo
In ospedale	A + infinitive verbs
In prigione	A + gennaio/febbraio/marzo/aprile...
In cucina/salotto/camera/bagno	
In classe	
In pizzeria/birreria/cartoleria	
In vacanza	
In + estate/autunno/inverno/primavera	

Means of transportations (IN)
In macchina/auto
In treno
In aereo
In barca
In moto
In bicicletta/bici
In motorino
In autobus

In the table devoted to **transitive verbs versus intransitive verbs** (4.1.1), you will find more examples of verbs constructed with prepositions.

LE PAROLE CONTANO

In sedia a rotelle is translated into English as *in a wheelchair*, while **difficoltà di apprendimento** is the expression used for *learning disabilities*. **Disabile** [*disabled*] is the correct terminology to describe any kind of physical and mental disability; however, sometimes you might also hear **diversamente abile** [literally: *differently abled*]. Especially in recent years, campaigns to support people with disabilities and raise awareness have been promoted in Italy, although there is still a long way to go, as in many other countries. Furthermore, structures have been created to support **disabili**, including a variety of measures facilitating disabled access to buildings and installing bathrooms that accommodate those in wheelchairs. Italian athletes with physical disabilities participate in the **Paralimpiadi** and have been paramount in championing respect for the cause. Among those, **Alex Zanardi** and **Bebe Vio**. Alex Zanardi (born in 1966) is a professional racing driver, **pilota da corsa**, who lost his legs in a car accident in 2001. He is currently a paralympic champion who had another traumatic accident in 2020 while he was cycling in Tuscany.

Bebe Vio (born in 1997) is a professional Italian fencer, **schermitrice**, in a wheelchair. She lost her arms and legs when she was 11 years old because of meningitis. She also inspires many teenagers to pursue their dreams.

Esercitiamoci!

Fill in the blanks with the simple prepositions and make sure to review the table with **transitive verbs versus intransitive verbs** (4.1.1):

1. Viaggio sempre _____ aereo!

2. Adriana telefona _____ Luigi.

3. Oggi mia madre e io andiamo _____ libreria.

4. Oggi studio _____ il mio amico Mohammed.

5. Sydney va _____ scuola _____ bicicletta.

6. Il compleanno _____ Giulio è venerdì.

7. il nuovo libro _____ Elena Ferrante è disponibile _____ libreria.

8. Domani Alessandro e Gianluca vanno _____ montagna.

9. Tu e Cornelia andate _____ studiare _____ Charlotte.

10. _____ cinque minuti siamo pronti!

11. _____ cucinare, la chef ha bisogno _____ tempo.

Esercitiamoci di più!

Which ingredients would you need to prepare *l'insalata caprese*? Fill in the blanks with the simple prepositions:

1. I pomodori rossi.

2. La mozzarella _____ bufala campana.

3. Le foglie _____ basilico _____ guarnire [*garnish*].

4. Un pizzico [*a pinch*] _____ sale. Quanto basta!

5. Un po' [*a bit*] _____ olio extravergine di oliva.

6. Accompagna la ricetta _____ fette [*slices*] _____ pane.

7. Mangia la caprese _____ pranzo o _____ cena, _____ gli amici e _____ le amiche _____ estate!

Buon appetito!

Scriviamo!

With another student, write a dialogue in Italian using all the simple prepositions (**di**, **a**, **da**, **in**, **su**, **per**, **con**, **tra/fra**) and the following words: **ricetta**, **chef** (m. or f., s. or pl.), **ristorante preferito** or **pizzeria preferita**, and **cibo italiano**. For ideas about dishes, see **La nota culturale** in 4.1.1 and **La pagina culturale**.

Lavoriamo con altre studentesse o altri studenti

Check over the exercises above with another student.

Parliamo!

Ask another student the questions below (some or all of them), alternating roles.

1. Di dove sei?
2. Dove abiti?
3. Dove vai in vacanza?
4. Come viaggi? Con quale mezzo viaggi?
5. Dove vai a scuola?
6. Come vai a scuola?
7. Quando vai a lezione?
8. Con chi studi?
9. Da chi vai a studiare?
10. Per passare un esame, quanto studi?
11. Vai piscina o in palestra?
12. Vai a teatro?
13. Cosa mangi a colazione?
14. Cosa mangi a pranzo?
15. Cosa mangi a cena?
16. Vai spesso in pizzeria?
17. Vai spesso in birreria?
18. Tra quanto vai a casa?

Ask two more questions that are not listed above using a formal register:

1. _____

2. _____

4.6 CHE ORA È? CHE ORE SONO?

To know what time it is, in Italian one asks: **Che ora è?** or **Che ore sono?**, in either the singular or plural form. Answering these questions and expressing the time with **è** or **sono** depends on the actual hour. Use **è** with **mezzogiorno** [*noon*], **mezzanotte** [*midnight*], and **l'una** [*one o'clock*], as in the examples below:

È mezzogiorno

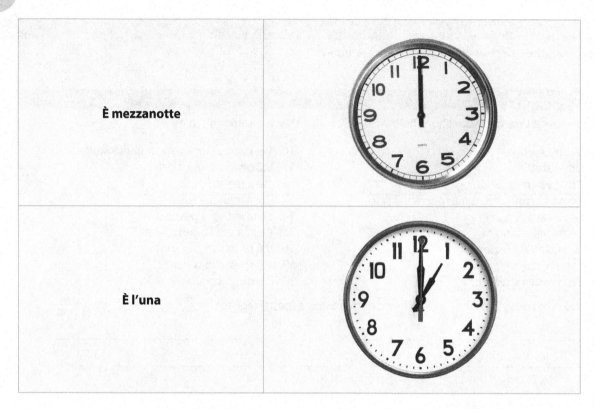

| È mezzanotte | |
| È l'una | |

ATTENZIONE: For one o'clock, do not forget the article **l'**.

Express all the other hours with **sono le...,** as in the examples below:

| Sono le quattro | |
| Sono le cinque | |

Sono le otto

To express the minutes of an hour, use **e** followed by numbers of expressions of time:

Sono le cinque e un quarto
Sono le cinque e quindici

Sono le otto e mezzo/a
Sono le otto e trenta

Sono le quattro e quarantacinque
Sono le quattro e tre quarti

People also use **meno** after the half hour up to the next hour, as in the example below:

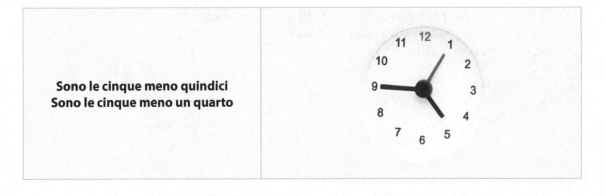

Sono le cinque meno quindici
Sono le cinque meno un quarto

Usually, one tends to use **meno** followed by minutes when there are less than 20 minutes to the next hour: *Sono le cinque meno venti*. Otherwise, if it is twenty-five or more, one says *Sono le quattro e trentacinque*.

To express at what time something is happening, like in the example *We meet at 3 p.m.*, one uses the expressions below:

ESATTAMENTE, QUANDO...?

Use **ALLE** [*at*] followed by hours from two to 24:
- Faccio colazione **alle** nove.
- Ho la lezione di italiano **alle** quattro.

Use **ALL'** [*at*] with **una** (at 1 a.m./1 p.m.):
- Pranzo **all'**una.

Use **A** [*at*] followed by **mezzogiorno** or **mezzanotte**:
- **A** mezzogiorno studio in biblioteca.
- Il sabato **a** mezzanotte ballo in discoteca.

If one wants to express a time period that goes from a certain time to another (from… to…), in Italian, one uses a mix of simple and articulated prepositions (that will be introduced in the next chapter) such as **dalle… alle…, dall'… all'**, or **da… a…**

QUANDO...?

Use **DALLE... ALLE...** [*from… to...*] followed by hours from two to 24:
- Faccio colazione **dalle** otto **alle** nove.
- Ho la lezione di italiano **dalle** quattro **alle** cinque.

Use **DALL'... ALL'...** [*from… to...*] with **una** (at 1 a.m./1 p.m.):
- **Dall'**una **all'**una e trenta pranziamo.

Use **DA... A...** [*from… to...*] followed by **mezzogiorno** or **mezzanotte**:
- **Da** mezzogiorno **a** mezzogiorno e quarantacinque studio in biblioteca.

You can mix them, like in the examples below:

1. — Cosa fa Alì il lunedì **dalle** dieci **a** mezzogiorno?
   — Studia in biblioteca.

2. — Quando è la lezione di italiano?
   — **Da** mezzogiorno **all'**una e trenta.
   — No! È **da** mezzogiorno **alle** due!

3. — Quando pranzano gli studenti?
   — Mangiano **dall'**una **all'**una e quarantacinque.

4. — Quando lavorate in pizzeria tu e Maria?
   — **Dalle** sei **a** mezzanotte.

5. — Quando siete a casa?
   — **Da** mezzanotte **alle** otto.

6. — Dov'è il tuo negozio preferito di libri antichi e quando è aperto?
   — Il mio negozio di libri antichi preferito è a Roma ed è aperto **dalle** otto e mezzo **a** mezzogiorno, e poi **dall'**una **alle** sei.

La giornata con le 24 ore. Italians sometimes use military time, also known as the **24h clock**.

1 p.m. → 13:00

2 p.m. → 14:00

3 p.m. → 15:00

8 p.m. → 20:00

12 a.m. → 24:00

For example, you might hear **sono le quindici** or **sono le venti**. Italians use the 24h clock for schedules, appointments and, more generally, to avoid confusion, as one sees in aviation. In the picture you can see **l'orario dei voli all'aeroporto "Leonardo Da Vinci" di Roma-Fiumicino**.

In everyday life and to carry out interpersonal communication, Italians tend not to use military time since they understand from the context what time (of the day) it is. To distinguish between **a.m.** and **p.m.**, Italians use **di mattina** and **di sera** preceded by the time from 1 to 11 (**mezzogiorno** and **mezzanotte** do not need to be specified with these Terms): however, you might also hear **di pomeriggio** and **di notte**; it depends on habits and on regional attitudes toward time. In fact, the perception of morning and evening times in Italy are different from their understanding in other countries such as the anglophones.

Usually, one uses **buongiorno** since we wake up until lunch time; however, lunch time can vary from region to region and among people (based on jobs, family's habits, etc.). Generally, Italians tend to refer to mornings up to 1 p.m. (yet some might also push it to 2 p.m.), while **il pomeriggio** [*afternoon*] is not well defined: for instance, many Italians do not use **buon pomeriggio** [*good afternoon*] too often; in case they meet someone in the afternoon, they can say also **salve** or **ciao** (however, they use **ciao** only if they are familiar with the people they meet). The use of **buonasera** [*good evening*] varies from region to region. Many Italians use it from 5 to 6 p.m. (sometimes 7 p.m.) onward until they go to sleep (though right before going to sleep, they wish **buonanotte**); however, in some parts of Tuscany, one may hear people saying **buonasera** already at 2-3 p.m. in the afternoon. Finally, Italians usually identify the concept of night time beginning after dinner, from 10-11 p.m. onwards. You might hear **l'una di mattina** or **l'una di notte**, they both mean 1 a.m.

Esercitiamoci!

Look at the picture below and write what time it is around the world

Che ora è a New York? _____

Che ora è a Hong Kong? _____

Che ora è a Tokyo? _____

Che ora è a Sydney? _____

Che ora è a Parigi, Berlino e Roma? _____

Che ora è a Londra? _____

Che ora è a Kiev? _____

 Scriviamo!

Write seven full sentences in Italian saying what you usually do: (1) **alle otto di mattina**, (2) **a mezzogiorno**, (3) **all'una e mezzo del pomeriggio**, (4) **alle quattro del pomeriggio**, (5) **alle otto di sera**, (6) **a mezzanotte**, (7) **alle tre di mattina**.

 Lavoriamo con altre studentesse o altri studenti

Check over the exercises above with another student.

🗨️ *Parliamo!*

Ask another student the questions below (some or all of them) using the time expressions and making sure to alternate roles.

1. Che ore sono?
2. Quando fai colazione? A che ora fai colazione?
3. Quando pranzi? A che ora pranzi?

4. Quando ceni? A che ora ceni?
5. Quando vai a letto? A che ora vai a letto?

With the following questions, use the expressions **dalle... alle...**

1. Quando hai la lezione di italiano?
2. Quando studi italiano?
3. Quando sei all'università?

4. Se lavori, quando lavori?
5. Se fai sport, quando fai sport?

Ask two more questions that are not listed above using a formal register:

1. _____

2. _____

LA PAGINA CULTURALE

MANGIARE ALL'ITALIANA

Mangiare all'italiana means eating the Italian way. Italians usually have three meals per day: **la colazione** [*breakfast*], **il pranzo** [*lunch*], and **la cena** [*dinner*]. There are also **lo spuntino** [*snack*] and **la merenda** [*mid-afternoon snack*], which is mostly for children, and it is light and sweet. Before dinner, sometimes Italians enjoy **l'aperitivo** [*aperitif*]: in some circumstances, the latter has become almost like a dinner, to the extent that very often it is called **l'apericena**, mixing the words aperitif and dinner.

Per colazione [*for breakfast*], Italians might drink **un espresso,** very often prepared in a **moka, il latte** [*milk*], **il caffellatte** [*milk with espresso*], or **il tè** [*tea*], with **i biscotti da colazione** [*light breakfast cookie*s] or **il pane tostato** [*toasted bread*] con **la marmellata** [*jam or marmalade*] or **la cioccolata spalmabile** [spreadable *chocolate*].

If Italians have breakfast at a **bar** [*cafè*] in the morning or **a metà mattinata** [*mid-morning*], they usually have **un espresso** or **un cappuccino** [*an espresso with milk foam*] with **un cornetto** (similar to a croissant) or **una pasta** [*pastry*].

In Italy, **il latte** is plain white milk, and it does not contain any coffee: if you want an American latte, you would need to ask for a **caffellatte**. Moreover, if you want to drink a tall coffee as it is common in many other parts of the world, in Italy you should ask for **un caffè americano** [*an American coffee*].

La colazione and **lo spuntino di metà mattina** are always rather light and sweet. Italians do not drink **il cappuccino** after lunch or dinner.

Italians tend to see lunch as the most important meal of the day; therefore, when it is possible, they return home for it. However, during **i giorni feriali** [*weekdays*], if they work outside of their home or they have a short lunch break, many tend to eat a light lunch, such as a quick bowl of pasta, a salad, or a sandwich; sometimes, a quick lunch might include **tramezzini**, which entails two slices of bread cut in triangles often filled with **prosciutto cotto e sottiletta** [*ham and cheese*], **tonno e pomodoro** [*tuna and tomatoes*], **rucola e gamberetti** [*rucola and shrimp*], or other combinations.

During **il fine settimana** [*weekend*], many Italians eat out and usually have more time to cook. A full dinner or lunch might include **gli antipasti** [*appetizers*], **i primi** [*first courses*], **i secondi** [*second courses*], **i contorni** [*side dishes*], **la frutta** [*fruit*], and **i dolci** [*desserts*]. In Italy, **l'insalata** [*salad*] is never eaten at the

beginning of a meal, and **la pasta** and **il riso** [*rice*] are first courses. There are Italians who eat **i formaggi** [*cheese*] before, or instead of, a dessert; **i formaggi** are also often eaten as **antipasti** or **secondi**. **Il pane** [*bread*] **italiano** tends to have a hard crust and, in most Italian regions, it is salted, but not in Tuscany, which is famous for baking unsalted bread. Italians usually eat **il pane** with **gli antipasti** and with **i secondi**, not with **i primi**. In most cases, Italians do not eat bread as a starter with extra virgin olive oil, as in many restaurants in anglophone countries.

La pizza follows a different practice: it might be eaten alone or enjoyed together with an appetizer and a dessert.

In Italy, **la pizza con i peperoni** (not pepperoni) comes with green, red, or yellow peppers, and not with **salame** [*salami*]! In many **pizzerie** [*pizzerias*] in Italy, pizza is baked in a woodfired oven and it is served on round plates. The thickness of the crust varies, based on the different regional traditions.

With pizza, many Italians love to drink **una birra** [*beer*], while with other meals they prefer to have **l'acqua** [*water*] and **il vino** [*wine*]. **L'acqua** can be **naturale** [*still*] or **gassata** [*sparkling*]; **il vino** can be **rosso** [*red*], **bianco** [*white*], or **rosé** [*rosé*]. **Le bevande** [*drinks*] can be **a temperatura ambiente** [*room temperature*] or **fredde** [*cold*], however Italians do not frequently add **il ghiaccio** [*ice*] to drinks (including **l'acqua**), nor do many of them often drink **le bevande gassate** [*soft drinks*], although some might enjoy **l'aranciata** [*orange soda*], **la limonata** [*lemon soda*], or **il tè freddo** [*ice tea*] during the summer time. With appetizers, many Italians like to drink **il prosecco** [*sparkling wine*], and if they celebrate something important, they might likely toast with **lo spumante** [*sparkling wine*] while eating certain desserts. After **i dolci**, many Italians may have

un espresso and sometimes **un ammazza-caffè** [*after-meal liquor*], such as **la grappa** or **il limoncello**.

Finally, if you are wondering about **il gelato**, you can find **le gelaterie** [*ice cream parlors*] almost everywhere, and in most cases, **il gelato** is **artigianale** [*artisanal*]. You can also find industrially-made **gelato** by producers such as Sammontana, Algida, or Motta, however Italians prefer the handmade option. Gelateria Dondoli in San Gimignano is well known by tourists who visit the towered town in Tuscany, and if you go there, do not forget to try the numerous **gusti** [*flavors*] that they offer, including **la crema di Santa Fina** [*the cream of Saint Fina*].

L'ITALIA E LE SUE CUCINE REGIONALI

Italy is a young country. In fact, as we know it today, with its 20 regions, it is only 160 years old. Before 1861 (the year of Italian unification), Italy was formed of states, including the Papal ones that were annexed by Italy in 1870. Not only was Italy formed by many states, but it was also characterized by many different languages (the so-called dialects), traditions, and diverse cuisines. Therefore, when Italy was unified, Italians spoke different languages and cooked differently. It is told that after the Unification of Italy, Massimo D'Azeglio (1798–1866), an Italian politician of the time, said that **Fatta l'Italia, dobbiamo fare gli italiani** [*Now that Italy is made, we must make the Italians*]: note that at that time there was no inclusive language and **le italiane** and **gli italiani** were referred together in masculine plural. D'Azeglio's sentence summarized the goals: national political unification must be followed by linguistic and also cultural unification. Standard Italian was chosen (based on the Tuscan language) and taught in school: all the Italians from the Alps to Sicily had to learn a new language in both its written and oral forms.

After 1861, Italian cuisine also started to be unified. Before then, there were cookbooks dating back to the Middle Ages and the Renaissance that can be seen as forebears of modern Italian cuisine. These include Platina's *Respectable Pleasure and Good Health* (circa 1465), a cookbook written in Latin (*De honesta voluptate et valetudine*), which was a revised version of Master Martino of Como's cookbook (circa 1465), or *The Art of Cooking*, written in vernacular (*Libro de arte coquinaria*). Another well-known cookbook is Bartolomeo Scappi's *Opera dell'arte del cucinare* (1570). However, Italy's fragmented cuisine began to be unified after 1861.

Pellegrino Artusi (1820–1911) is considered one of the founding figures of modern Italian cuisine. In 1891, he published a cookbook, which has become a classic: ***La scienza in cucina e l'arte di mangiar bene***, translated into English as *Science in the Kitchen and the Art of Eating Well*. The cookbook is also known as simply ***L'Artusi*** by generations of Italians. Pellegrino Artusi simply collected recipes from different regions (even if most were from Tuscany and Emilia Romagna) and published a book at his expense. This work is also considered important from a linguistic perspective because it helped to disseminate the newly chosen Italian language. Indeed, his recipes were very popular across Italy. At the same time, writers also published works where food takes center stage, as in the narrative production of **Matilde Serao** (1856–1927), who sprinkles references to Neapolitan and Roman recipes in her novels and short stories, such as *La virtù di Checchina* [*Checchina's virtue*] (1884).

Nowadays, Italian cuisine is characterized by dishes informed by regional traditions that have been modified over time and adapted to a more modern palate. Among the many examples, **la pasta alla carbonara** from Lazio, **gli spaghetti all'amatriciana** from Amatrice, **il pesto** from Liguria, **i tortellini** from Emilia Romagna, **il risotto alla milanese** from Milan, **la pizza** from Naples, and **i cannoli** from Sicily. Such recipes were created in the different regions, however they have also passed beyond the regional borders to become the heritage of Italy and the world.

If you are interested in the history of Italian cuisine, we recommend, among others, *Delizia: The Epic History of the Italians and their Food* (New York: Free Press, 2008) by John Dickie; *Al Dente: A History of Food in Italy* (London: Reaktion Books, 2014) by Fabio Parasecoli; and also *Women and Food in Italian Literature, Culture and Society: Eve's Sinful Bite* (London: Bloosmbury, 2020) edited by Claudia Bernardi, Francesca Calamita, and Daniele DeFeo, for the intersections between Italian food, literature, and cinema.

ESERCITIAMOCI CON LA CULTURA

A1. Lo Slow Food. Do some research online (reputable sources) on the Slow Food movement and write ten full sentences in Italian about it, using only verbs and tenses studied up to now.

A2. La dieta mediterranea. Do some research online (reputable sources) on the Mediterranean Diet and write ten full sentences in Italian about it, using only verbs and tenses studied up to now.

B. Inventa una ricetta. Invent a recipe using as many new nouns, articles, and verbs as you can, and try to be original!

PAROLE UTILI (look up more words if you need)

Acqua	Limone	Pecorino	Salmone
Aglio	Mandorla	Pepe	Sedano
Arancia	Mela	Peperoncino	Tacchino
Basilico	Melanzana	Pesce	Tonno
Burro	Mirtilli	Pollo	Uova
Carota	Mortadella	Pomodoro	Vino bianco/rosso
Cioccolato	Olio di oliva	Prezzemolo	Zenzero
Cipolla	Pane	Prosciutto	Zucchero
Farina	Panna	Ricotta	Zucchina
Fragola	Parmigiano	Riso	
Latte	Pasta	Sale	

VERBI (For more verbs look here: https://www.granconsigliodellaforchetta.it/tecniche-di-cucina /i-verbi-della-cucina/):

Affumicare	Dorare	Incorporare	Montare
Amalgamare	Foderare	Infornare	Pelare
Bagnare	Frullare	Legare	Rosolare
Brasare	Glassare	Lessare	Saltare
Caramellare	Gratinare	Macellare	Scottare
Crogiolare	Imburrare	Marinare	Tagliare
Decantare	Impanare	Mescolare	Tritare

For the **RICETTA,** conjugate the verbs in the second person plural: **voi.**

---

[3]Activity primarily contributed by Stella Mattioli. Copyright © Kendall Hunt Publishing Company.

GLOSSARIO

Verbi in -are

Abitare (a/in) [*to live*]

Amare [*to love*]

Arrivare (a/da/in) [*to arrive, to get*]

Aspettare [*to wait*]

Cambiare [*to change*]

Camminare [*to walk*]

Cenare [*to dine, to eat dinner*]

Cercare [*to look for*]

Chiamare [*to call*]

Cominciare/Incominciare [*to start, to begin*]

Comprare [*to buy*]

Cucinare [*to cook*]

Desiderare [*to wish*]

Dimenticare [*to forget*]

Disegnare [*to draw*]

Diventare [*to become*]

Frequentare [*to attend*]

Giocare [*to play*]

Guidare [*to drive*]

Imparare (a) [*to learn*]

Incontrare [*to meet*]

Iniziare [*to begin, to start*]

Insegnare [*to teach*]

Inviare [*to send, to ship*]

Lavorare [*to work*]

Mandare [*to send, to ship*]

Mangiare [*to eat*]

Pagare [*to pay*]

Parlare [*to speak, to talk*]

Pensare (a/di) [*to think*]

Portare [*to bring, to carry*]

Pranzare [*to eat lunch*]

Praticare [*to practice*]

Ricordare [*to remember*]

Ritornare [*to come back, to return*]

Spiegare [*to explain*]

Studiare [*to study*]

Suonare [*to play an instrument*]

Telefonare (a) [*to call*]

Tornare [*to return, to come back*]

Trovare [*to find*]

Usare [*to use*]

Volare [*to fly*]

Viaggiare [*to travel*]

Verbi irregolari in -are

Andare [*to go*]

Dare [*to give*]

Fare [*to do, to make*]

Stare [*to stay, to be, to feel*]

Espressioni idiomatiche con *fare*

Fare bel tempo [*to have good weather*]

Fare brutto tempo [*to have bad weather*]

Fare freddo [*to have cold weather*]

Fare fresco [*to have cool weather*]

Fare caldo [*to have hot weather*]

Fare le valigie [*to pack a suitcase*]

Fare il biglietto [*to purchase, to get a ticket*]

Fare un viaggio [*to travel*]

Fare buon viaggio [*to have a good trip*]

Fare un giro [*to take a tour*]

Fare un salto [*to drop by*]

Fare una passeggiata [*to take a walk*]

Fare male [*to hurt, to feel bad*]

Fare colazione [*to have/eat breakfast*]

Fare merenda [*to have/eat snack*]

Fare la doccia/il bagno [*to take a shower/a bath*]

Fare gli auguri a [*to give best wishes to someone, to congratulate*]

Fare una telefonata a [*to give a call*]

Fare una sorpresa a [*to surprise*]

Fare un favore a [*to do a favor*]

Fare una domanda a [*to ask a question*]

Fare una fotografia a [*to take a picture*]

Fare la spesa [*to go grocery shopping*]

Fare le spese [*to go shopping*]

Fare un regalo a [*to give a gift*]

Fare la fila [*to queue, to stand in line*]

Fare il pieno [*to refuel, to fill up the gas tank*]

Fare la benzina [*to get fuel/gas*]

Fare alla romana [*to split the bill*]

Gli interrogativi

Che cosa/cosa/che [*what*]

Chi [*who, whom*]

Quale/quali/qual [*which, what*]

Come [*how*]

Dove [*where*]

Perché [*why, because*]

Quanta/o/e/i [*how much, how many, how long*]

Quando [*when*]

I dimostrativi

Questa/o/quest' [*this, this one*]

Queste/i [*these, these ones*]

Quella/o/quell' [*that, that one*]

Quelle/quelli/quegli [*those, those ones*]

Le preposizioni

Di [*of, from*]

A [*to, at, in*]

Da [*from, since, by, at*]

In [*in, to, at*]

Su [*on, about, in*]

Per [*for, through, in order to*]

Con [*with*]

Tra/fra [*between, among, in*]

Le espressioni con IN

In casa [*at home*]

In montagna [*in the mountains*]

In campagna [*to/in the countryside*]

In città/paese [*to/in the city, to/in the town/village*]

In piazza [*to/in the square*]

In centro [*downtown*]

In biblioteca [*to/in the library*]

In palestra [*to/in the gym*]

In piscina [*to/in the swimming pool*]

In banca [*to/in the bank*]

In chiesa [*to/in the church*]

In ufficio [*to/in the office*]

In farmacia [*to/in the pharmacy*]

In ospedale [*to/in the hospital*]

In prigione [*to/in the prison/jail*]

In cucina/salotto/camera/bagno [*to/in the kitchen/sitting room/bedroom/bathroom*]

In classe [*to/in the classroom*]

In pizzeria/birreria/cartoleria [*to/in the pizzeria/pub/stationery store*]

In vacanza [*on vacation*]

In + estate/autunno/inverno/primavera [*in summer/fall/winter/spring*]

In macchina/auto [*by car*]

In treno [*by train*]

In aereo [*by plane*]

In barca [*by boat*]

In moto [*by motorcycle*]

In bicicletta/bici [*by bicycle/bike*]

In motorino [*by scooter*]

In autobus [*by bus*]

In sedia a rotelle [*in a wheelchair*]

Le espressioni con A

A casa [*at home*]

A scuola [*at school*]

A lezione [*at the lesson*]

A una festa [*at a party*]

A tavola [*at the table*]

A colazione [*at breakfast*]

A pranzo [*at lunch*]

A merenda [*at snack time*]

A cena [*at dinner*]

A letto [*to bed*]

A teatro [*at the theater*]

A piedi [*by foot*]

A cavallo [*by horse*]

A + gennaio/febbraio/marzo/aprile/maggio… [*in January/February/March/April/May...*]

Il tempo

Che ora è? [*What time is it?*]

Che ore sono? [*What time is it?*]

ANDARE, DARE, FARE E STARE

The verbs **DARE** and **FARE** are built in the same way, with their constructions being similar to that in English:

- Io do qualcosa a qualcuno [*I give something to someone*]
- Io faccio qualcosa a qualcuno [*I do something to/for someone*]

One can use the verb **FARE** to express a profession (see Chapter 2):

- Cosa fai? [*What do you do?*]
- Faccio l'avvocata, l'astrofisica, l'architetto, l'operatore ecologico, l'insegnante, la direttrice d'orchestra, ecc.

Regarding the verb **ANDARE**, it is very important to remember that it is followed by the preposition **A** or **IN**:

ANDARE A + city/town/village: Io vado **a** New York [*I go to New York*]
ANDARE IN + country: Io vado **in** Italia [*I go to Italy*]

Regarding the usage of the verb **STARE**, see the examples below:

- — Come stai? – Sto bene [– *How are you? – I am well; – How do you feel? – I feel well*]
- — Dove stai? – Sto a Pisa [– *Where are you? – I am in Pisa; – Where do you live? – I live in Pisa*]
- — Stai a cena? – Sì, grazie! [– *Will you stay/remain for dinner? – Yes, I will! Thank you!*]

To ask someone how she/he is doing, you can say **Come stai?**, but also **Come va?** [*How are you?*]

GLI INTERROGATIVI: QUALE/I

To be specific in terms of structures, **QUALE/QUALI** has two forms: **QUALE** for m.s. and f.s., and **QUALI** for m.pl. and f.pl. They must agree in gender and number with the noun(s) they refer to. As mentioned in 4.3, **QUAL** (dropping the **e** at the end and without apostrophe) is used with the verb **essere** in the third person singular: **QUAL È...** Look at the examples below:

1. **Qual è** l'università dove studi?
2. **Qual è** il tuo numero di telefono?
3. **Quali** studi fai?
4. **Quale** piatto cucini?
5. **Quali** piatti di pesce cucini?

GLI INTERROGATIVI: QUANTO/A/I/E

As you know, **QUANTO/QUANTA/ QUANTI/QUANTE** has four forms: **QUANTO** for m.s., **QUANTA** for f.s., **QUANTI** for m.pl., and **QUANTE** for f.pl. They must agree in gender and number with the noun(s) they refer to. **QUANTO** is also an adverb (which also means it is invariable) and it is often used with the verb **costare** [*to cost*]. Look at the examples below:

1. **Quanto** costa il libro di italiano?
2. **Quanto** freddo hai?
3. **Quanta** voglia hai di studiare?
4. **Quanti** anni hai?
5. **Quante** studentesse ci sono in classe?
6. — **Quanti** savoiardi usi per fare il tiramisù?
   — Un pacco per un tiramisù piccolo!

LE PREPOSIZIONI

Regarding **A** + infinitive verbs, **DA** + at someone's place, and **A** + months, look at the examples below:

1. Bilal e Marcella vanno **con** Silvio **a** <u>studiare</u> **da** Aureliana.
2. La mia famiglia e io stiamo a casa **a** giugno e **a** luglio.

In the first example, when one wants to express going to do something at someone's place, the verb **andare** is followed by **a + infinitive** of the action verb; moreover, to express the action taking place at someone's house, **da** is followed by a name.

In the second example, the preposition **a** followed by a month expresses in which month an action takes place.

When a **preposition** is used with **an interrogative** such as **chi** or **dove** (see the examples below), the preposition must precede the interrogative like in the examples below:

1. — **Con chi** vai a pranzo?
   — Vado a pranzo con i miei cugini Carlo e Mohammed.
2. — **Da dove** viene la pasta all'amatriciana?
   — Viene da Amatrice.

Do you remember a similar case learned earlier in this textbook? We use this construction when we ask someone where he/she is from:

— **Di dove** sei?
— Sono di Lecce, una città della Puglia.

CHE ORA È? CHE ORE SONO?

Sometimes people also say **alle** after the half hour point to the next hour, as in the example below:

Sono un quarto **alle** cinque [*It is 4:45*]	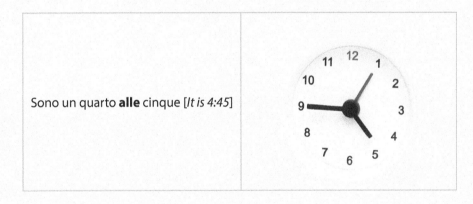

Another example is: **Sono venti alle cinque** [*It is 4:40*].

VIAGGIO NELLE ARTI ITALIANE

5

CAPITOLO

By the end of this chapter, you will be able to use the verbs ending in **-ere** and **-ire** in the present tense, including some specific verbs such as **sapere** and **conoscere** [*to know*], and also **piacere** [*to like*]. Moreover, you will be able to use articulated prepositions and the partitive. You will learn about numbers from 100 onwards, ordinal numbers, and how to express dates. In terms of cultural elements, you will learn about the world-famous Italian art.

Grammar Structures

5.0 Iniziamo
5.1 Verbs in **-ere** in the present tense
5.2 Verbs **sapere** and **conoscere**
5.3 Verb **piacere**
5.4 Verbs in **-ire** in the present tense
5.5 Articulated prepositions
5.6 Verbs **andare** vs. **venire**
5.7 Partitives
5.8 Numbers from 100 onward, ordinal numbers, and dates

GLOSSARIO
APPENDICE
 Verbi regolari in **-are**, **-ere** e **-ire**
 Piacere
 Le preposizioni articolate
 I numeri ordinali

Culture

Note culturali
 Gli alcolici in Italia
 Le operazioni matematiche e le frazioni
 Il mercato italiano

La pagina culturale
 L'arte in Italia

Le parole contano
 Breaking the glass ceiling
 Mi piace la lingua italiana inclusiva!

INIZIAMO

Read the dialogue below with another student, alternating roles:

Abrar:	Ecco Safia, finalmente!
Safia:	Ciao, Abrar! Aspettiamo Virginia e Matteo e poi andiamo al museo.
Abrar:	Sì, ma ho fame! Prendiamo da mangiare e anche da bere.
Safia:	Cosa vuoi mangiare? E bere?
Abrar:	Prendo un po' di patatine e un succo di frutta. Tu cosa prendi?
Safia:	Io ho bisogno di un caffè altrimenti [*otherwise*] dormo al museo.
Abrar:	Ecco Virginia e Matteo. Andiamo tutti insieme al bar.
Matteo:	Ciao! Scusate il ritardo. Dove andate?
Safia:	Andiamo a prendere qualcosa al bar. Venite con noi?
Virginia:	Certo!

Al bar

Safia:	Io prendo un caffè.
Matteo:	Anch'io prendo un caffè, ma decaffeinato.
Virginia:	Io invece prendo un cappuccino.
Safia:	Un cappuccino?? Ma sono le cinque! Il cappuccino è da colazione!
Abrar:	Ha ragione Safia: adesso è tempo di fare merenda, non colazione!
Matteo:	Adesso basta, eh! E se prende il cappuccino, prende il cappuccino!
Virginia:	Grazie, ma so difendermi [*I can defend myself*] da sola! Tu cosa prendi, Matteo?
Matteo:	Io prendo un bignè alla crema.

Al museo degli Uffizi a Firenze

Abrar:	Questo museo è enorme! C'è anche un'opera famosa di Artemisia Gentileschi.
Safia:	Sai chi è Artemisia Gentileschi?
Matteo:	Certo che lo sappiamo: è un'artista del 1600!
Virginia:	Un quadro famoso di Artemisia Gentileschi è quello di Giuditta che [*who*] decapita Oloferne.
Abrar:	È un quadro del 1612 o 1613.
Safia:	L'originale è al Museo Nazionale di Capodimonte a Napoli. Agli Uffizi c'è un'altra versione.
Matteo:	È un quadro molto bello e anche molto significativo per parlare di violenza di genere. Lo ha detto [*said*] la professoressa a lezione.
Abrar:	Davvero?
Virginia:	Sì, è collegato [*is linked*] allo stupro [*rape*] di Artemisia Gentileschi da parte di un aiutante [*aid*] del padre. Poi ti [*to you*] dico la storia quando siamo lì.
Safia:	Andiamo a vedere il quadro!
Matteo:	Sì, andiamo subito!

Work with another student to understand the content of this dialogue. Do you know what the words mean?

5.1 VERBI IN -ERE

All the verbs ending in **-ere** in the infinitive belong to the **seconda coniugazione** [*second conjugation*], while those ending in **-ire** belong to the **terza coniugazione** [*third conjugation*]. Therefore, verbs such as **scrivere** [*to write*] and **leggere** [*to read*] belong to the second conjugation, while verbs such as **aprire** [*to open*] and **finire** [*to finish, to end*] belong to the third conjugation.

As explained in the previous chapters, to negate a verb, place **non** before its conjugated form: *Bilal legge i libri in italiano, ma **non** scrive in questa lingua.*

5.1.1 VERBI REGOLARI IN -ERE

To conjugate the regular verbs in **-ere**, drop the ending **-ere** from the infinitive and add the endings below based on the subject pronouns. As you know by now, each ending corresponds to the subject(s) performing the action:

SCRIV–ERE	TO WRITE
IO SCRIV–**O**	I WRITE
TU SCRIV–**I**	YOU WRITE
LEI/LUI SCRIV–**E**	SHE/HE WRITES
NOI SCRIV–**IAMO**	WE WRITE
VOI SCRIV–**ETE**	YOU ALL WRITE
LORO SCRIV–**ONO**	THEY WRITE

Now, look at the examples below:

1. Ayesha scrive un'e-mail a Giulio.
2. Carlos e Andrea scrivono un biglietto di auguri per il compleanno di Cristina.
3. Tu, Marco e Giovanna scrivete un messaggio su WhatsApp.
4. Ogni giorno scrivi un post su Facebook e metti una foto su Instagram.

E tu, quanti messaggi [*how many*] scrivi al giorno? Answer the question below with a complete sentence:

Unlike verbs in **-are**, most verbs in **-ere** follow the regular pattern when the stem ends in **-c** or **-g**. Verbs in **-cere** such as **vincere** [*to win*], in **-gere** such as **scorgere** [*to see, to sight, to notice*] and **dipingere** [*to paint*], and in **-scere** such as **conoscere** [*to know*], **nascere** [*to be born*], and **crescere** [*to grow*] follow the regular pattern.

Conjugate below the verb **VINCERE:**

Io _____   Noi _____

Tu _____   Voi _____

Lui/Lei _____   Loro _____

E tu, vinci spesso qualcosa? Answer the question below with a complete sentence:

_____

And now conjugate the verb **DIPINGERE:**

Io _____   Noi _____

Tu _____   Voi _____

Lui/Lei _____   Loro _____

E tu, dipingi nel tempo libero? Answer the question below with a complete sentence:

_____

And finally, conjugate the verb **CRESCERE**:

Io _____   Noi _____

Tu _____   Voi _____

Lui/Lei _____   Loro _____

REGULAR VERBS IN -ERE		
Chiedere (a)	Dipingere	Ripetere
Chiudere	Eleggere	Rispondere (a)
Conoscere	Leggere	Sapere
Correggere	Mettere	Scrivere (a)
Correre	Nascere	Sorprendere
Credere (a, in)	Perdere	Sorridere
Crescere	Piangere	Spendere
Cuocere	Prendere	Vedere
Decidere	Proteggere	Vendere
Deludere	Ricevere	Vincere
Difendere	Ridere	Vivere

As you have already learned, **transitive verbs** are **followed by direct objects** responding to questions such as **what?** and **whom?**; intransitive verbs require a preposition afterward. In Italian, we use **qualcosa** [*something*] or **qualcuno/a** [*someone*] to express transitiveness and **a qualcuno/a** [*to someone*] to express intransitivity. Most of the verbs listed in the table above are transitive, while those followed by the preposition **a** are intransitive; note that there are also verbs of movement (such as **correre**), verbs such as **piangere**, **sorridere**, or **ridere**, and verbs expressing state of life (**nascere**, **crescere**, or **vivere**). Look at the expressions below:

1. Chiedere qualcosa **a** qualcuno/a
2. Chiudere qualcosa
3. Conoscere qualcuno/a
4. Cuocere qualcosa
5. Decidere qualcosa
6. Difendere qualcuno/a
7. Eleggere qualcuno/a
8. Leggere qualcosa
9. Perdere qualcosa
10. Proteggere qualcuno/a
11. Ricevere qualcosa
12. Rispondere qualcosa **a** qualcuno/a
13. Sapere qualcosa
14. Scrivere qualcosa **a** qualcuno/a
15. Vedere qualcosa
16. Vendere qualcosa **a** qualcuno/a

There are several idiomatic expressions commonly used in everyday conversation that are built with the verb **prendere**:

ESPRESSIONI CON *PRENDERE*

- **prendere una decisione** [*to make a decision*]
- **prendere un caffè**, un cappuccino, una pasta, una pizza [*to have a coffee, a cappuccino, a pastry, a pizza, etc.*]
- **prendere gli appunti** [*to take notes*]
- **prendere + mezzo di trasporto**: prendere l'autobus, il treno, la metro, l'aereo, la bici, la moto, il motorino, il taxi [*to take + means of transportation: to take the bus, the train, the subway, the plane, the bike, the motorcycle, the scooter, the taxi*]

- **prendere il sole** [*to sunbathe*]
- **prendere lezioni di italiano** [*to get Italian lessons*]

Read the short dialogue below in an Italian bar:

— Cosa prendi?
— Prendo uno spritz*, e tu?
— Anch'io!

* A **spritz** is an alcoholic drink prepared with white wine, very often prosecco, and a bitter liqueur such as Aperol or Campari. It is typically served with an orange slice to garnish it.

LE PAROLE CONTANO

Breaking the glass ceiling is an expression used to refer to the barriers preventing women from rising to senior leading positions, once they are broken or overcome. It is often used in politics, as well as in other contexts. In Italian, this expression (literally translated with **rompere il soffitto di cristallo**) can be also read as **abbattere i muri** or **abbattere una barriera**. Over the course of history, social and cultural progress happened because people were able to overcome barriers, whether more or less visible. In the past two centuries, women have been able to break the glass ceiling regularly in many fields. Among the many achievements, the right to vote is central. In 1893, New Zealand was the first country world-wide to allow women to vote in parliamentary elections. The efforts were led by **Kate Sheppard**, one of the leaders of the women's suffrage movement. Other countries followed over the course of the twentieth century. In Italy, women gained the right to vote in 1945 (voting for the first time on June 2, 1946, in the referendum that sanctioned Italy as a Republic), similar to other European countries, such as France (1944). In the United States in 1920, some states passed legislation to allow women to vote in certain elections, such as municipal ones, while others required women to own property to vote. However, it is very important to note that African American, Asian American, Latinx, and Native American women were only granted the right to vote significantly after 1920. For example, African American women were not allowed to vote in several Southern states until 1965, the first year when *all* women could vote in the United States.

World-wide, the first woman to be democratically elected as a prime minister was **Sirimavo Bandaranaike** of Ceylon (present-day Sri Lanka), in 1960. The first woman serving in the position of president was **Isabel Martínez de Perón** of Argentina, in 1974. The first woman to be elected as president was Iceland's **Vigdís Finnbogadóttir**, in 1980, who led the country for 16 years. To date, Italy has never had a female **Presidente del Consiglio** [*Prime Minister*] or **Presidente della Repubblica** [*President of the Republic*], yet in September 2022 **Giorgia Meloni's** party won the election, which would lead to her likely selection as Italian Prime Minister. Examples of prominent women in positions of power include **Laura Boldrini**, the former **Presidente della Camera**, **Emma Bonino**, the former leader of the **Partito Radicale**, as well as **Monica Cirinnà**, a well-known **senatrice** who fought for the approval of same-sex unions (2016). Just recently several glass ceilings were broken worldwide: **Jacinda Arden**, the Prime Minister of New Zealand, has been praised internationally for the response to the COVID-19 pandemic, with a list of other women in top-leading positions, such as **Angela Merkel**, the former Chancellor of Germany, and **Ursula Von der Leyen**, the President of the European Commission since 2019. In 2020, **Kamala Harris** was elected vice-president of the USA, thus being the first woman to reach this position, as well as the first black woman of South Asian origin; and since June 30, 2022, **Ketanji Brown Jackson** serves in the U.S. Supreme Court, making her the first black woman to hold such a position.

(Jacinda Arden, la prima ministra neozelandese)

(Emma Bonino, la capa del partito radicale)

(Kamala Harris, la vice-presidente statunitense)

 Esercitiamoci!

Look at the pictures and write down when you do these activities; use the days of the week you have already learned in Chapter 3 as in the example below and do not forget the articles when it is a repeated activity.

Example:

scrivere al computer

Sentence: <u>Io scrivo al computer il lunedì, il martedì e il venerdì</u>

leggere un libro

_____

spendere i soldi e per cosa [_for what_]

_____

cuocere qualcosa

_____

vedere le amiche e gli amici

_____

Lavoriamo con altre studentesse o altri studenti

Check over the exercise above with another student.

5.1.2 VERBI IRREGOLARI IN -ERE

As you learned, irregular verbs deviate from the regular pattern, and among verbs in **-ere**, there are also some; for instance, with the verb **cuocere** [*to cook*] and other similar verbs such as **stracuocere** [*to overcook*], you must add an **i** to the endings of the conjugated forms of subjects **io** and **loro**, to keep the soft sound:

CUOCERE
IO CUOC–**I**–**O**
TU CUOC–**I**
LEI/LUI CUOC–**E**
NOI CUOC–**IAMO**
VOI CUOC–**ETE**
LORO CUOC–**I**–**ONO**

Among verbs in **-ere**, there are some others that are irregular, such as **tacere** [*to keep quiet*], **giacere** [*to lay*], **nuocere** [*to harm*], **dispiacere** [*to displease*], or **piacere** [*to like, to please*], which will be introduced later in the chapter. These verbs add a **c** to the endings of the conjugated forms of subjects **io**, **noi**, and **loro**, beyond adding an **i** to subjects **io** and **loro** to keep the soft sound, as in the example below:

TACERE
IO TAC–**C**–**IO**
TU TAC–**I**
LEI/LUI TAC–**E**
NOI TAC–**C**–-**IAMO**
VOI TAC–**ETE**
LORO TAC–**C**–**IONO**

Another irregular verb is **bere** [*to drink*], which originates from the ancient popular form of **bevere** (coming from the Latin verb **bibere**); **bere** is conjugated following the regular pattern of **bevere**:

BERE
IO BEV–**O**
TU BEV–**I**
LEI/LUI BEV–**E**
NOI BEV–**IAMO**
VOI BEV–**ETE**
LORO BEV–**ONO**

It is important to remember that the verb **prendere**, when it is used in relation to food and drink, implies that one is going to have something to eat or to drink: *Laura prende un caffè* means, in that she has the intention to drink a coffee and she will have one.

NOTA CULTURALE

Gli alcolici in Italia. In Italy, people can buy and drink alcoholic beverages from the age of 18 (this was raised in 2012, before which the legal age to buy and drink alcohol was 16). You might be asked to show your ID card to check your age. Although in the past young people could not buy alcohol, there were no sanctions if they consumed alcohol before turning 18 years; the situation has changed, since both buying and drinking are now prohibited be-

fore the legal age. Things might be different in a family context, as it might be customary for young Italians to be allowed to taste a sip of **spumante** for special family occasions. Howe-ver, while in the past Italy was not plagued by underage drinking, young people suffering problems with alcoholism is a concern nowadays.

On the website of the **Ministero della Salute** [*Ministry of Health*], one can find this reference to the law and a general consideration: "In Italia con la Legge 8 novembre 2012 n. 189 vige [*is in force*] il **divieto di somministrazione e vendita di bevande alcoliche ai minori di 18 anni**, da ciò [*from this*] si deduce [*one infers*] che i giovani di età inferiore ai 18 anni che con-sumano anche una sola bevanda alcolica durante l'anno presentano un comportamento a rischio [*risky behavior*] nel consumo di alcol" (Source: http://www.salute.gov.it/portale/temi/p2_6.jsp?lingua=italiano&id=2351&area=alcol&menu=vuot).

Esercitiamoci!

Conjugate the verbs in **-ere** in parentheses, paying attention to the subject pronouns, and complete the last sentence based on something you do:

1. Gisella _____ (*scrivere*) un messaggio su Whatsapp al suo amico Gianluca. Lui è sempre molto contento di ricevere i suoi messaggi!

2. Heidi e Alessandro _____ (*bere*) un tè freddo al bar. Oggi fa proprio caldo!

3. Carlo _____ (*prendere*) un espresso macchiato senza zucchero tutte le mattine alle 8. È un'abitudine!

4. Io _____ (*chiedere*) sempre i consigli alla mia migliore amica. Mi fido [*I trust*] di lei!

5. Oggi tu e tua sorella Marina _____ (*ricevere*) un pacco dall'Italia. C'è l'olio di oliva fatto da [*made by*] vostro nonno!

6. Sara e Juan Antonio _____ (*ridere*) mentre guardano il loro film preferito. È un film co-mico, ma non ricordo il nome.

7. Tu che _____ (*vincere*) alla lotteria è un sogno! Cosa fai con tutti quei soldi?

8. Io _____.

Lavoriamo con altre studentesse o altri studenti

Conjugate the infinitive forms of the verbs, creating complete sentences in Italian. Put the scrambled words and the correctly conjugated verbs in the right order.

da Maria/io/un regalo/**ricevere**	
la maratona/**correre**/New York/non/tu/di	
al bar/un cornetto e un cappuccino/**prendere**/Giulia	
di/*L'amica geniale*/**leggere**/Elena Ferrante/noi	
alle domande/**rispondere**/voi	
a Torino/**vendere**/Giancarlo e AnnaMaria/la casa di famiglia	

 Scriviamo!

Form six complete sentences in Italian (one for each subject: **io, tu, lui/lei, noi, voi, loro**) using six different verbs in **-ere**. Do not forget to conjugate the infinitives based on the subject pronouns.

 Lavoriamo con altre studentesse o altri studenti

Check over the exercises above with another student.

 Parliamo!

Ask another student the questions below, alternating roles. Pay attention to the prepositions. Ask your classmate one last question not listed below using a formal register. Take note of your classmate's answers and share them with the class.

1. Dove vivi?

2. A chi scrivi ogni giorno?

3. Da chi ricevi email?

4. Prendi appunti alezione?

5. Prendi lezioni di italiano?

6. Cosa prendi per andare all'università? L'autobus, la macchina, il treno…?

7. A chi chiedi aiuto quando hai bisogno?

8. Cosa leggi di solito?

9. Cosa prendi di solito al bar?

10. Cosa prendi di solito al ristorante o in pizzeria?

11. Cosa prendi di solito quando sei all'università con gli amici o le amiche?

12. Cosa bevi a colazione?

13. Cosa bevi a pranzo e a cena?

14. Cosa bevi nelle occasioni speciali?

15. _____

5.2 SAPERE E CONOSCERE

At the beginning of section 5.1, we learned that verbs in **-scere** such as **conoscere** [*to know*] follow the regular pattern. The verbs **sapere** and **conoscere** both mean *to know*, yet they are used differently. **Conoscere** means to be familiar with something or someone (a topic, a person, a place, or a subject); **sapere** means to have knowledge of something, such as a fact, an event or a piece of information. One uses **sapere** also to describe an ability or a skill, and it is usually followed by an infinitive. Complete the conjugations of verb **conoscere** in the table below:

SAPERE	CONOSCERE
IO SO	IO
TU SAI	TU
LEI/LUI SA	LEI/LUI
NOI SAPPIAMO	NOI
VOI SAPETE	VOI
LORO SANNO	LORO

Look at the examples below with **conoscere**:

1. Conosco la storia dell'arte italiana molto bene. E adoro la Cappella Sistina! **(topic)**

2. Conosco Vincent Van Gogh: è un pittore olandese molto famoso. **(person)**
Autoritratto di Van Gogh (1889):

3. Conosco una galleria d'arte contemporanea a Milano. **(place)**

Look at the examples below with **sapere**:

1. Non lo so! *[I do not know it]* / Lo so *[I know it].* **(have knowledge of, or not)**

2. Sai a che ora apre *[opens]* il museo Nazionale di Capodimonte a Napoli? **(information)**

3. Sai che il pittore messicano Diego Rivera era *[was]* il marito della famosa pittrice messicana Frida Kahlo? **(fact)**

Murales di Diego Rivera, *Sueño de una tarde dominical en la Alameda Central* (1946-1947, Città del Messico):

As we have stated above, **sapere** works as a modal verb indicating an ability when it is followed by an infinitive. In this case it means that one is able to do or perform something. Look at the examples below:

1. Simran e Simanti sanno parlare bene l'hindi.

2. Noemi sa dipingere con i piedi.

3. Federica Pellegrini è una famosa nuotatrice italiana. Sa nuotare molto bene! [*very well*].

Esercitiamoci!

Fill in the blanks with the properly conjugated verbs in parentheses and complete the last two sentences based on what you know:

1. Giada _____ (*conoscere*) una galleria molto d'arte moderna e contemporanea famosa. Andiamo!

2. Alessandro e Paolo non _____ (*sapere*) che il quadro *Guernica* è di Pablo Picasso!

3. Michael, Selma e io non _____ (*conoscere*) i genitori di Matteo.

4. Giovanni, _____ (*sapere*) se Claudia dipinge nel tempo libero?

5. Stefano e Francesca _____ (*sapere*) parlare bene il francese.

6. Tu, Cesar e Christiana _____ (*sapere*) dov'è la casa di Omar.

7. Riccardo _____ (*conoscere*) una scultrice famosa.

8. Io _____ (*conoscere*)

9. Io _____ (*sapere*)

Scriviamo!

Form six complete sentences in Italian using **conoscere** and **sapere** (three for each verb). Do not forget to conjugate the infinitives based on the subject pronouns.

Lavoriamo con altre studentesse o altri studenti

Check over the exercises above with another student.

Parliamo!

Ask another student the questions below, alternating roles. Ask two final questions (one with **sapere** and one with **conoscere**) not listed below with a formal register. Take note of your classmate's answers and share them with the class.

1. Sai parlare italiano?
2. Sai parlare altre lingue straniere? Quante e quali lingue sai parlare?
3. Sai suonare uno strumento?
4. Sai giocare a tennis?
5. Cosa sai fare bene?
6. Cosa non sai fare o non sai fare bene?
7. Sai che molte persone parlano italiano a New York?
8. Sai quando c'è l'esame di italiano?
9. Conosci la storia dell'arte italiana?
10. Conosci la storia e la letteratura italiane?
11. Conosci persone italiane?
12. Conosci un buon ristorante italiano?
13. Conosci una gelateria italiana?
14. Conosci l'Italia?
15. _____
16. _____

5.3 PIACERE

The verb **piacere** [*to like*] belongs to the **seconda coniugazione**, and it is an irregular verb conjugated like the verbe **tacere** (see 5.1.2). In Italian, one uses the verb **piacere** to express what or whom someone likes. Look at the construction of this verb below. What do you notice?

PIACERE	TO LIKE
MI PIACE/PIACCIONO	I LIKE
TI PIACE/PIACCIONO	YOU LIKE (informal)
LE PIACE/PIACCIONO	YOU LIKE (formal)

PIACERE	TO LIKE
LE/GLI PIACCIONO	SHE/HE LIKES
CI PIACE/PIACCIONO	WE LIKE
VI PIACE/PIACCIONO	YOU ALL LIKE
GLI PIACCIONO	THEY LIKE

1. There are only two conjugated verbal forms to express what one likes: **piace** and **piacciono**. Literally, in English the expressions are translated with *It pleases me* [**piace**], and *They please me* [**piacciono**].

   ■ **PIACE** is followed by a noun in the singular (*mi piace la scultura*), by a verb in the infinitive (*le piace correre*), or by a list of verbs in the infinitive (*gli piace cucinare e mangiare*).

   ■ **PIACCIONO** is followed by a noun in the plural (*ti piacciono gli spaghetti*) or by a list of nouns in the singular, in the plural, or a mix of the two: *Ci piacciono il gelato e la pizza; Mi piacciono le lasagne e le fettuccine; Vi piacciono le vongole e il merluzzo*.

2. Instead of the subject pronouns **io, tu, lui/lei, noi, voi**, and **loro**, with this construction of **piacere** one uses other pronouns called indirect pronouns such as **mi, ti, gli** (for **lui**), **le** (for **lei**), **ci, vi**, and **gli**. Because **mi** stands for **a me**, **ti** for **a te**, ecc. (see the Appendix at the end of this chapter for further examples and explanations), one can construct the verb **piacere** with first names: in this case, you use the preposition **A** followed by a name or a list of names: *a Chiara; a Luigi; a Paola e Giordano*.

   Now, review the examples below:

   ■ *A Tania e a Tom piace la campagna.*
   ■ *A Sofia piace leggere.*
   ■ *A Julia e a nonna Sandra piacciono i dolci.*

3. To negate the verb **piacere** in its conjugated forms, one adds **non** before the indirect pronouns: *non mi piace andare in ascensore; non mi piacciono i serpenti*. However, if there is a name or a list of names, **non** is placed before the verb: *A Christiana e a Cesar **non** piace il mare; A Natasha **non** piacciono i quadri astratti*.

4. In an informal context, to ask someone what she/he likes or what she/he likes to do, you ask **Cosa ti piace?** [*What do you like?*] or **Cosa ti piace fare?** [*What do you like to do?*]. In a formal context, to ask someone what she/he likes or what she/he likes to do, you ask **Cosa Le piace?** [*What do you like?*] or **Cosa Le piace fare?** [*What do you like to do?*]. Check the Appendix at the end of this chapter for further information.

The chart below will help you to recap:

MI TI/LE LE GLI CI VI GLI	**PIACE**	■ nouns in the singular (just one) ■ verb in the infinitive (just one) ■ a list of verbs in the infinitive
	PIACCIONO	■ nouns in the plural ■ a list of nouns in the singular ■ a list of nouns in the plural ■ a list of mix nouns in the singular and in the plural

The construction with **mi piace/piacciono** expresses what people like or like to do, and it is preferable to **amo** [*I love*]: saying *mi piace il caffè* is what a native speaker would say, while *amo il caffè* sounds like a direct translation from English. Check the Appendix to find out more about these expressions.

LE PAROLE CONTANO

Mi piace la lingua italiana inclusiva! In Chapter 3, we learned how to address a group of people in an inclusive way; one could start, for instance, with **Care tutte e cari tutti; Care/i tutte/i; Cari/e tutti/e; Car* tutt*** as well as **Carə tuttə.** In this chapter, we learn more about the symbol ə (**schwa**), when we address a group of people. The **schwa** is an unstressed mid-central vowel that some Italians already use in the Neapolitan dialect. Feminist linguist Vera Gheno, who collaborated for many years with *Accademia della crusca*, suggests that it might be one of the possible solutions to forge a more inclusive Italian. You might not find the **schwa** in traditional newspapers yet, but you might come across it in progressive blogs on the net as a way to address their audience with inclusivity. In writing, the salutation formula **Ciao ragazzə!** is widely used, for example. In 2021, Michela Murgia and Chiara Tagliaferri published *Morgana. L'uomo ricco sono io* with the use of the **schwa**; in the same year the audiobook of *Femminili plurali* by Gheno also came out featuring it. In April 2021, the administration of Castelfranco, a little town in Emilia Romagna, declared that the **schwa** will be used in all communications to be more inclusive. You can learn more about it on *Il fatto quotidiano: https://www.ilfattoquotidiano. it/2021/04/14/il-comune-di-castelfranco-emilia-inizie-ra-a-usare-lo-schwa-%C9%99-nelle-comunicazioni-isti-tuzionali-vogliamo-essere-piu-inclusivi/6165783/*

Esercitiamoci!

Translate the following sentences from English into Italian:

1. I like Italian paintings and sculptures.
2. Yinan, do you like gelato?
3. Professor Gheno, do you like the book by Murgia and Tagliaferri?
4. You like to go out [*uscire*] with friends.
5. Peyton and Emma do not like swimming and playing tennis.
6. You all like spaghetti and espresso!
7. Monica, Stefano, and I like Italian contemporary art.
8. He likes Jonathan, but Jonathan does not like him.
9. Martha does not like lies.
10. Miranda and Steve like an inclusive world.
11. I like tattoos! Do you like them?
12. Juditta likes writing and drawing: she is an artist!
13. My mother, my sister, and I like watching Studio Ghibli's films.
14. My family likes modern art.

Scriviamo!

Write four complete sentences in Italian stating what you like and/or what you like to do using **piace** and **piacciono** (two per each). Furthermore, write other four complete sentences stating what you do **not** like and/or what you do **not** like to do using **piace** and **piacciono** (two per each).

Lavoriamo con altre studentesse o altri studenti

Check over the exercises above with another student.

Parliamo!

Talk to another classmate asking what she/he likes (or does not like) or he/she likes to do (or does not like to do), and respond to the questions posed by your classmate. Ask as many questions as possible alternating roles. You must ask the questions 1 through 4 first to be able to complete the second part of the exercise. Furthermore, all the questions below are for an informal context: how would you change them if you were in a formal context?

1. **Cosa ti piace?**

2. **Cosa non ti piace?**

3. **Cosa ti piace fare?**

4. **Cosa non ti piace fare?**

5. Cosa ti piace mangiare?

6. Cosa non ti piace mangiare?

7. Ti piace andare al cinema?

8. Quali film ti piacciono?

9. Ti piace viaggiare? Se sì, dove ti piace andare?

10. Ti piace guardare la televisione? Se sì, quali programmi ti piacciono?

11. Ti piacciono le serie televisive? Se sì, quali in particolare?

12. Ti piace l'arte? Se sì, quale tipo di arte ti piace?

13. Cosa ti piace fare nel tempo libero?

14. Ti piace studiare l'italiano? E quali altre materie ti piace studiare?

15. Ti piace fare compere? Se sì, ti piace fare compere online o di persona?

16. Ti piacciono gli sport? Se sì quali in particolare?

Using a formal register, write down two more questions that are not listed above but that you would like to ask to your classmate:

1. _____.

2. _____.

Tell the class what your classmate likes and does not like and what he/she likes or does not like to do (four sentences in total).

5.4 VERBI IN -IRE

To conjugate the regular verbs in **-ire** belonging to the **terza coniugazione**, drop the ending **-ire** from the infinitive form and add the endings below based on the subject pronouns. Each ending corresponds to the subject(s) performing the action. To negate a verb, place **non** before its conjugate form: *Bilal apre le finestre, ma **non** pulisce i vetri.* Look at the conjugations below:

APRIRE [*to open*]	CAPIRE [*to understand*]
IO APR–**O**	IO CAP–**ISC**–**O**
TU APR–**I**	TU CAP–**ISC**–**I**
LEI/LUI APR–**E**	LEI/LUI CAP–**ISC**–**E**
NOI APR–**IAMO**	NOI CAP–**IAMO**
VOI APR—**ITE**	VOI CAP–**ITE**
LORO APR–**ONO**	LORO CAP–**ISC**–**ONO**

As you can see, there are two types of verbs in **-ire**. Those conjugated like **capire** insert **-isc-** between the stem and the ending with the subject pronouns **io**, **tu**, **lui/lei**, and **loro**, while the verbs like **dormire** only add the endings based on the subjects, following the patterns that you have already learned with **-are** and **-ere** verbs. Verbs in **-isc-** are not considered irregular verbs.

As a student, it would be useful for you to know how to say that you understand (**capisco**) or that you do not understand (**non capisco**):

Scusi, Professoressa, non capisco!

Now conjugate the verb **DORMIRE** (see **aprire**):

Io	_____	Noi	_____
Tu	_____	Voi	_____
Lui/Lei	_____	Loro	_____

And the verb **FINIRE** (see **capire**):

Io	_____	Noi	_____
Tu	_____	Voi	_____
Lui/Lei	_____	Loro	_____

VERBS CONJUGATED LIKE *APRIRE*

Aprire	Offrire
Avvertire	Partire
Bollire	Riempire
Convertire	Scoprire
Coprire	Seguire
Cucire	Sentire
Divertire	Servire
Dormire	Sfuggire
Fuggire	Smentire
Inseguire	Soffrire
Investire	Vestire
Mentire	

VERBS CONJUGATED LIKE *CAPIRE*

Abolire	Finire	Reagire
Attribuire	Fornire	Restituire
Capire	Garantire	Ricostruire
Chiarire	Gestire	Riunire
Colpire	Guarire	Sostituire
Condire	Impedire	Sparire
Contribuire	Indebolire	Spedire
Costruire	Infastidire	Stabilire
Definire	Istruire	Suggerire
Diminuire	Obbedire	Tossire
Distribuire	Percepire	Trasferire
Esaurire	Preferire	Unire
Favorire	Pulire	

Look at the examples below:

1. Stasera Timur e Valerio vanno in campeggio e dormono in tenda.
2. Noi dormiamo fino alle 8 di mattina tutti i giorni feriali.

E tu fino a che ora dormi la mattina? Scrivi la risposta sotto:

_____

Like the verb **bere** (see 5.1.2), another verb that might be useful in our everyday life is the verb **dire** [*to say, to tell*]. It derives from the Latin verb *dicere* and it is conjugated following the regular pattern; however, it is not conjugated from the infinitive **dire**, but from the Latin form. Complete the table below:

DIRE [*to say, to tell*]
IO
TU
LEI/LUI
NOI
VOI **DITE**
LORO

In Italian, the verb **dire** is constructed like the English verb *to say*: **io (non) dico qualcosa a qualcuno/a** [*I do (not) say something to someone*].

Do not forget that if you want to express *the action of talking to someone*, you need to use the verb **parlare (a qualcuno/a di qualcosa/qualcuno/a)**, while if you mean *to tell a story*, you need to use the verb **raccontare (qualcosa a qualcuno/a)**.

Here is Bebe Vio, an Italian paralympian that we have already talked about:

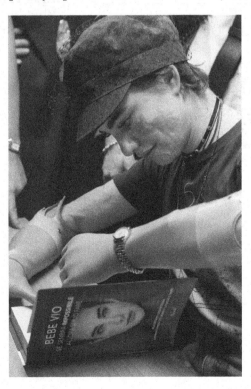

What can Bebe Vio say to a young person? Complete the sentences below:

Bebe Vio dice _____

Bebe Vio parla _____

Bebe Vio racconta _____

Esercitiamoci!

Conjugate the infinitives in parentheses paying attention to the subject pronouns:

1. Ma [io] non _____ (*capire*)!

2. Mio zio Gianluca _____ (*partire*) alle otto di sera da Roma arriva a Bologna alle undici.

3. Giuseppe e Andra _____ (*pulire*) quasi tutta la casa, ma non il bagno.

4. La mia amica Boyun _____ (*offrire*) un espresso ad Andrea, ma per lui è troppo tardi: non beve il caffè dopo le cinque del pomeriggio.

5. Tu _____ (*seguire*) la pallavolo? A me piace proprio tanto!

6. Quando _____ (*finire*) il corso di pittura?

7. Cosa fanno i tuoi amici e le tue amiche in campeggio?
   _____ (*dormire*) tutta la mattina!

8. La mia famiglia e io _____ (*aprire*) le finestre tutti i giorni per cambiare l'aria. È una sana abitudine!

9. I politici devono [*must*] _____ (*dire*) la verità, ma non sempre succede.

10. Io _____ (*preferire*) l'espresso al cappuccino, e tu?

Scriviamo!

Form six complete sentences (one for each subject: **io, tu, lui/lei, noi, voi, loro**) using six different verbs in **-ire** (at least four verbs must be from the **-isc-** verbs). Do not forget to conjugate the infinitives based on the subject pronouns.

Lavoriamo con altre studentesse o altri studenti

Check over the exercises above with another student.

Parliamo!

Talk to another classmate, asking and answering the following questions. Ask as many questions as possible alternating roles.

1. Apri le finestre? Se sì, di mattina o di sera?
2. Quante ore dormi la notte?
3. Dormi nel pomeriggio?
4. Quando parti da casa per andare all'università?
5. Quanti corsi segui ogni semestre?
6. Capisci sempre il professore o la professoressa di italiano quando parla?
7. Finisci sempre i compiti prima di andare in classe?
8. Cosa preferisci mangiare e bere a colazione?
9. Ti piace pulire la casa? Cosa pulisci più spesso [_more often_]?
10. Quante e-mail spedisci al giorno?
11. Cosa ti dice sempre il tuo migliore amico o la tua migliore amica?
12. Cosa preferisci fare nel tempo libero?
13. Preferisci il tè o il caffè?
14. Quante ore dormi la notte?
15. Finisci sempre di leggere i libri che inizi?

Ask two more questions that are not listed above using a formal register:

1. _____.

2. _____.

5.5 LE PREPOSIZIONI ARTICOLATE

In the previous chapter, we learned that the simple prepositions in Italian are: **di** [_of, than, about_], **a** [_to, at, in_], **da** [_from, by, since, to, at_], **in** [_in, inside, to, within, at_], **su** [_on, in, about_], **per** [_for, to, by_], **con** [_with_], and **tra/fra** [_between, among_]. Some of them (**di, a, da, in, su**), when preceding the definite article **the** [_il, lo, la, l', i, gli, le_], combine together to become the **preposizioni articolate** [_articulated prepositions_]. While in English they are separated (**in the, on the, from the, at the,** just to name a few combinations), in Italian they are merged to become one word.

Look at the chart below and complete it with the missing **preposizioni articolate**:

	il	lo	l'	la	i	gli	le
di	del	dello	dell'			degli	delle
a	al			alla	ai		
da				dalla		dagli	
in	nel				nei		nelle
su		sullo	sull'			sugli	

The simple prepositions **per, con,** and **tra/fra** combine with the definite articles, but they do not merge to form a single word. Look at the chart below and complete it with the missing **preposizioni articolate**:

	il	lo	l'	la	i	gli	le
per	per il		per l'		per i		
con		con lo		con la		con gli	con le
tra/fra	tra/fra il				tra/fra i		

Look at the examples below showing the articulated preposition formed with the simple preposition **a**:

1. Oggi pomeriggio Mario va **al** museo.
2. Giuseppe e Cinzia vanno **allo** stadio domenica prossima.
3. Quando è bel tempo, è meglio mangiare **all**'aperto.
4. **Alle** casse dei musei italiani ci sono sempre molte persone in fila.
5. Chiedi se il menù va bene **agli** invitati e **alle** invitate.
6. La mostra è vicino **ai** giardini di Boboli.

Look at the examples below showing the articulated preposition formed with the simple preposition **in**:

1. C'è una mosca **nel** bicchiere!
2. D'estate Preya e Martina nuotano **nello** stagno **nei** dintorni del loro paese.
3. Il vestito rosso è **nell**'armadio, mentre [*while*] quello verde è sulla sedia.
4. Cerco i biscotti **nella** credenza, e invece sono sul piano della cucina.
5. **Negli** alberghi di lusso ci sono sempre quadri famosi.
6. **Nei** teatri in Italia, come *La Scala* a Milano, c'è sempre molta gente.

Do you remember the idiomatic expressions with the simple prepositions **in** and **a**? When they are specific places and not generic ones, one needs to use the articulated prepositions, and in some cases these change:

ESPRESSIONI IDIOMATICHE CON LE PREPOSIZIONE IN & A	
Locations (IN)	**Miscellaneous (A)**
In casa → nella casa di Guia	**A casa → a casa di Filippo**
In montagna → **sulle** montagne francesi	A scuola → alla scuola di Giulia
In campagna → nella campagna toscana	A lezione → alla lezione di storia
In città → nella città natale di Renato Guttuso	A una festa → alla festa di compleanno
In paese → nel paese di Artemisia Gentileschi	A pranzo → al pranzo di laurea
In piazza → nella piazza del paese	A cena → alla cena di Claudia
In centro → nel centro cittadino	A teatro → al teatro *La Scala*
In biblioteca → nella biblioteca dell'università	
In palestra → **alla** palestra Equinox	
In piscina → **alla** piscina comunale	
In banca → **alla** Banca Toscana	
In chiesa → **alla** chiesa di Sant'Agostino	
In ufficio → nell'ufficio del direttore/della direttrice	
In farmacia → **alla** farmacia Pacini	
In ospedale → **all'**ospedale di Campostaggia	
In prigione → **alla** prigione delle Murate	
In camera → nella camera dei bambini	
In classe → nella classe della figlia	
In pizzeria/birreria/cartoleria → nella pizzeria/birreria/cartoleria di Luigi	

Do you remeber the use of **in** and **a** with countries and cities? Review the rule below:

- **IN + country/federal state/region:** Vado/Vivo/Abito **in** Italia/Francia/Germania/Virginia/Piemonte/Toscana/Puglia/Sardegna
- **A + city/town/village:** Vado/Vivo/Abito **a** Roma/New York/Parigi

When the country is a plural noun, such as the United States, one needs to use the articulated preposition:

- **NEGLI/NEI/NELLE + country in the plural:** Vado/Vivo/Abito **negli** Stati Uniti/**negli** Emirati Arabi/**nelle** Filippine.

Below are some other expressions with places that do not follow the regular patterns:

- Vado/Vivo/Abito **nel** Lazio.
- Vado/Vivo/Abito **nelle** Marche.
- Vado/Vivo/Abito **ai** Caraibi/Tropici.
- Vado/Vivo/Abito **alle** Hawaii/Samoa.
- Vado/Vivo/Abito **all'**Isola d'Elba/Isola del Giglio.
- Vado/Vivo/Abito **a** Long Island.
- Vado/Vivo/Abito **a** Cuba (but: **in** Jamaica).

ESPRESSIONI CON IL TEMPO

As stated previously, the **preposizioni articolate** are also used to define time and schedule when one needs to clarify from when to when. See below:

11:00–12:00 p.m. → **dalle undici a mezzogiorno**

1:00–4:00 → **dall'una alle quattro**

5:00–8:00 → **dalle cinque alle otto**

9:00–12:00 a.m. → **dalle nove a mezzanotte**

Esercitiamoci con il tempo e scriviamo!

Look at the schedule below and write four sentences saying when a local fluvial park is opened in the months of **febbraio**, **maggio**, **luglio**, and **novembre**. Use the expressions of time with the **preposizioni articolate**:

Parco fluviale	
Gennaio: 10:30–14:30	Luglio: 7:45–20:30
Febbraio: 10:30–14:30	Agosto: 7:45–20:30
Marzo: 10:00–15:00	Settembre: 8:30–19:00
Aprile: 10:00–15:30	Ottobre: 9:00–18:00
Maggio: 9:00–18:00	Novembre: 10:00–15:30
Giugno: 8:30–19:00	Dicembre: 10:30–14:30

Esercitiamoci!

Fill in the blanks with the correct articulated prepositions among those listed below:

AL	DELLA	AI	AGLI	SUL	ALLA	NEI	NELLA

1. In camera _____ muro ho una stampa molto bella di un'artista francese: Niki De Saint Phalle, creatrice del Giardino dei Tarocchi a Capalbio, in Toscana.

2. _____ valigia di Jasmine ci sono un libro e la brochure di una galleria d'arte.

3. _____ museo degli Uffizi a Firenze c'è un dipinto di Artemisia Gentileschi.

4. Quando ho tempo, vado spesso _____ vernissage. Sono interessanti!

5. Tra gli artisti e le artiste di tutto il mondo, preferisco Renato Guttuso; _____ dipinti di Guttuso ci sono colori molto vivi.

6. Quest'opera è _____ famosa scultrice Amalia Del Ponte.

7. Vicino _____ Uffizi c'è il David di Michelangelo, ma non ē l'originale.

8. Sei stata _____ mostra fiorentina di Marina Abramovich?

Scriviamo!

Write ten full sentences in Italian using the articulated prepositions. Five of them must be chosen from among the idiomatic expressions.

Lavoriamo con altre studentesse o altri studenti

Check over the exercises above with another student.

Parliamo!

Talk to another classmate, asking and answering the following questions. Ask as many questions as possible, alternating roles.

1. Quando vai all'università?
2. In quale biblioteca vai a studiare?
3. Se vai in palestra, in quale palestra vai?
4. Vai al cinema? Se sì, quali film vai a vedere?
5. Cosa c'è nel tuo zaino?
6. Cosa c'è nel frigorifero di casa tua?
7. Cosa c'è nella libreria in camera tua?
8. Cosa c'è sul muro della tua camera?
9. Cosa c'è nella tua camera?
10. Vai spesso a mangiare al ristorante? In quale ristorante vai?

Ask two more questions that are not listed above using a formal register:

1. _____.

2. _____.

5.6 ANDARE E VENIRE

Irregular verbs **andare** [*to go*] (which you have already learned) and **venire** [*to come*] are used regularly in everyday conversation and they have different meanings. Complete the table below with the missing conjugated forms of the two verbs:

	ANDARE	VENIRE
IO	VADO	VENGO
TU		
LEI/LUI		VIENE
NOI	ANDIAMO	
VOI		
LORO	VANNO	VENGONO

Andare is used when we want to express movement from point A to point B, even when point A is implicit:

1. Io **vado** a teatro una volta al mese.
2. Luca **va** al cinema ogni fine settimana.
3. Noi **andiamo** in Italia in estate.
4. Lara **va** in aereo da Hong Kong a Roma.

In the examples above, the perspective is that of the speaker: he/she is at point A (implicit or explicit) and wants to reach point B.

If a speaker at point A talks to someone in point B, or if the speaker at point A speaks with someone who will be at point B at a certain point in the future, we use the verb **venire**:

1. Talking to my mom who is in Italy right now: *Quest'estate **veniamo** in Italia.*
2. Talking to my classmate who is at his/her house: ***Vengo** a studiare da te alle sei del pomeriggio.*

3. Talking to my friend who is coming to visit me by train: *Vengo a prenderti alle cinque alla stazione.*

4. Talking to friends I have an appointment to go to the cinema: *Vengo al cinema in autobus.*

5. Talking about the origin of the movement (B) and going toward A (as considered the home) where there is someone waiting: *Vengo dall'università a casa a piedi.*

When you try to distinguish between **andare** and **venire**, you have to think of where the listener is located in relation to the speaker. It is about perspective, and it is different from English.

Below you will find expressions with the verbs **andare** and **venire** followed by articulated prepositions:

ESPRESSIONI CON *ANDARE* E *VENIRE* E LE PREPOSIZIONI ARTICOLATE	
ANDARE	**VENIRE**
Andare dalla dottoressa/dal dottore	Venire dalla montagna
Andare dalla medica/dal medico	Venire dalla campagna
Andare dall'avvocata/o	Venire dalla città
Andare dall'ingegnera/e	Venire dall'università
Andare dall'architetta/o	Venire dalla stazione
Andare dalla/dal commercialista	Venire dall'aeroporto
Andare dalla nonna/dal nonno/dai nonni	Venire dall'Italia
Andare al cinema	Venire dagli Stati Uniti
Andare al ristorante	Venire dal Venezuela
Andare all'edicola	Venire dalla Cina
Andare all'università	Venire dalla Nuova Zelanda

Esercitiamoci!

Choose either **andare** or **venire** and conjugate them in the first person singular (except sentence 8), paying attention to where the person you are talking to is located:

1. *Talking to a friend after Italian class*: Oggi _____ in biblioteca.

2. *Talking on the cellphone to one of my classmates who is already at the university*: Oggi _____ all'università in treno.

3. *Talking to my friend about our plans for the weekend*: Quando _____ al cinema a vedere l'ultimo film di Tarantino?

4. *Talking to someone in my household*: Ho la tosse e non passa. _____ dalla dottoressa.

5. *Talking to my friend who will come to pick me up at the airport*: L'aereo arriva alle cinque e quaranta. _____ a prendermi [*to pick me up*] alle sei?

6. *Talking to my friends to find out when they will go to a museum*: Quando _____ al museo?

7. *Talking to my friend to let her/him/them know when I would go to her/his/their house*: Domani _____ da te alle tre per studiare italiano.

8. *Talking to my friend to know when another friend of ours is going to Italy*: Quando _____ in Italia Leonard?

Scriviamo!

Dal diario di Camilla [*From Camilla's diary*]:

Lunedì: andare in banca e andare all'allenamento di pallavolo

Martedì: studiare all'università e fare shopping

Mercoledì: leggere in biblioteca e mangiare al bar

Giovedì: vedere la nonna e cuocere le lasagne

Venerdì: andare al lavoro e dormire

Sabato: andare al mare e prendere il sole con le amiche

Domenica: festeggiare il compleanno di Francesco e andare in discoteca

E tu cosa fai questa settimana? Write down the activities you are going to do this week (two activities per day) using verbs and nouns as in the example above:

Lunedì:	
Martedì:	
Mercoledì:	
Giovedì:	
Venerdì:	
Sabato:	
Domenica:	

Scriviamo!

In groups, write a dialogue between two people using the verbs **andare** and **venire**. Write at least ten lines. Choose one of the possible situations:

1. Two friends are making plans to go out.
2. Two people are making plans to take a vacation.
3. A parent and a son/daughter are talking about the plans of the day.
4. Two classmates are making plans to complete a group project together.

 Lavoriamo con altre studentesse o altri studenti

Check over the exercises above with another student.

🗨 *Parliamo!*

Talk to another classmate, asking and responding to the following questions. Ask as many questions as possible, alternating roles.

1. Quando vieni all'università?
2. Se lavori, quando vai a casa dal lavoro?
3. Di solito quando vai in vacanza? Dove vai?
4. Quando vai al cinema? Vieni con me? Andiamo insieme?

5. Vieni a studiare italiano con me in biblioteca? Se sì, quando?
6. Vieni a mangiare un gelato con me? Se sì, quando andiamo?
7. Quando vieni al corso di italiano, di solito quando arrivi?

Ask two more questions that are not listed above using a formal register:

1. _____.
2. _____.

5.7 IL PARTITIVO

The articulated prepositions **del, dello, dell', della, dei, degli, delle**, are also used to indicate a part of a totality or an undetermined quantity of something, and it corresponds to the English *some, a little bit of, a bit of*. Complete the table below with the missing **preposizioni articolate**:

	il	lo	l'	la	i	gli	le
di	del		dell'				delle

In the singular form (**del, dello, dell', della**), the partitive means *a little, a few, a little bit, a bit, some,* and it is used with nouns that indicate an unspecified quantity of something. Look at the examples below:

1. Vuoi [*would you like*] **dello** zucchero nel caffè?
2. Vuoi **del** limone nel tè?
3. Vuoi **dell'**aranciata?
4. Vuoi **della** crostata di ciliegie per merenda?

In the plural form (**dei, degli, delle**), the partitivo takes the meaning of *some* or *any*. Look at the examples below:

1. Simone legge **dei** libri.
2. Pamela scrive **delle** poesie molto belle.
3. Oggi pranzo con **delle** colleghe e **dei** colleghi di lavoro.
4. Federico, tu vai sempre al mare a Portofino con **degli** amici, mentre Michela va sempre in Spagna con **delle** amiche.

Esercitiamoci!

Fill in the blanks with the correct partitive paying attention to the gender and number of the nouns that they precede and refer to:

1. Per cena vorrei [*I would like*] _____ carne ai ferri.

2. Alla mostra Fernando e Angelo comprano _____ quadri per la loro casa al mare.

3. Durante le vacanze, la mia migliore amica e io guardiamo sempre _____ serie televisive alla TV.

4. Voi fate _____ sport (m.pl.)?

5. Preya chiede al cameriere _____ latte freddo per il caffè.

6. Quando viaggiamo, la mia famiglia e io visitiamo sempre _____ musei molto famosi.

7. Mohammed, tu hai _____ fratelli e _____ sorelle?

8. A fine mese Daniele paga sempre _____ bollette alla posta. Ma perché non paga le bollette online?

9. Giulia e Valentina pranzano al ristorante con _____ amiche e _____ amici d'infanzia.

10. Donatella fa _____ tatuaggi fantastici!

Scriviamo!

Look at the images below and describe them using as many partitives as possible. Write one complete sentence for each image.

Ai Musei Vaticani:

A Venezia:

A Milano:

A Positano:

Agli Uffizi:

Ad Alberobello (i trulli):

 Lavoriamo con altre studentesse o altri studenti

Check over the exercises above with another student.

 Parliamo!

Ask each other about your grocery list and use **il partitivo** to answer, like in the example below:

— Che cosa compri al supermercato?

— Compro della frutta, della verdura, dello zucchero e del caffè! E tu?

— Io compro del pesce, della carne e del formaggio.

5.8 I NUMERI OLTRE 100, I NUMERI ORDINALI E LE DATE

In Chapter 3, we learned numbers from 1 to 100 (**cento**). To form numbers from two hundred (**due-cento**) to nine hundred (**novecento**), the suffix **cento** is added to the multiplier digit to form your hundreds. Write the missing numbers in the chart below:

CENTO	DUECENTO			CINQUECENTO
			NOVECENTO	MILLE

From 101 to 199 (the same rule applies to the other hundreds), just add the tens and the units (if you do not recall how to form numbers from 1 to 99, go back to Chapter 3). See the examples below and note how the numbers are written in one word:

101 = centouno

205 = duecentocinque

347 = trecentoquarantasette

679 = seicentosettantanove

892 = ottocentonovantadue

933 = novecentotrentatré

As for **mille** [*thousand*], look at the examples below and note how the numbers from 1,000 to 1,999 are written and how **mille** is always a separate word:

1.005 = mille e cinque

1.545 = mille e cinquecentoquarantacinque

1.200 = mille e duecento

1.794 = mille e settecentonovantaquattro

1.452 = mille e quattrocentocinquantadue

1.873 = mille e ottocentosettantatré

Thousands are formed by adding **mila** to the digit multiplier. Write the missing numbers in the chart below:

MILLE		TREMILA		
		OTTOMILA		DIECIMILA

Look at the examples below:

2.537 = duemilacinquecentotrentasette

7.765 = settemilasettecentosessantacinque

3.055 = tremilacinquantacinque

9.999 = novemilanovecentonovantanove

One million is **un milione**, two million—**due milioni**, three million—**tre milioni**. A billion is **un miliardo**, two billion—**due miliardi**. In Italian, a millionaire is **un milionario** or **una milionaria**; a billionaire is **un miliardario** or **una miliardaria**.

When you would like to ask for the price of something, in Italian you ask **Quanto costa?** or **Quanto costano?** Look at the examples below:

— Quanto costa questo libro?
— Costa venticinque euro.

— E quanto costa questa borsa di Dolce e Gabbana?
— Costa settecentoventi dollari.

— Quanto costano questi pantaloni di Armani?
— Costano duecentosettantacinque euro.

— Quanto costano un tè e una pasta a Londra?
— Costano dieci sterline.

5.8.1 I NUMERI ORDINALI

Numbers also include **numeri ordinali** [*ordinal numbers*]: first, second, third, fourth, and so on. In Italian, ordinal numbers are adjectives, which means that they agree in gender and number with the nouns they refer to:

PRIMO/A/I/E	SECONDO/A/I/E	TERZO/A/I/E	QUARTO/A/I/E	QUINTO/A/I/E
SESTO/A/I/E	SETTIMO/A/I/E	OTTAVO/A/I/E	NONO/A/I/E	DECIMO/A/I/E

From eleventh onward, in Italian we add **-esimo/a/i/e** to the cardinal number once the ending vowel is dropped: **undicesimo/a/i/e** (11th), **dodicesimo/a/i/e** (12th), …, **ventesimo/a/i/e** (20th). Pay attention to the two **E**'s in **ventitreesimo/a/i/e** (23rd). Look at the examples below:

1. **La Ferrari** arriva spesso **prima** nelle gare di Formula 1. Questi sono Michael Schumacher e Jean Todt nel 2006.

2. Questa è la **terza volta** che telefono: perché non rispondi?

3. L'ufficio della rettrice dell'università è al **quarto piano**.

4. I **primi semestri** all'università sono difficili.

The Appendix contains more information about ordinal numbers.

NOTA CULTURALE

Le operazioni matematiche e le frazioni. Also related to numbers are mathematical operations such as **l'addizione** [*addition*], **la sottrazione** [*subtraction*], **la divisione** [*division*], and **la moltiplicazione** [*multiplication*]. Below, you will see how we express them in Italian:

$2 + 2 = 4 \rightarrow$ due più due uguale/fa quattro

$10 - 3 = 7 \rightarrow$ dieci meno tre uguale/fa sette

$55 : 5 = 11 \rightarrow$ cinquantacinque diviso cinque uguale/fa undici

$8 \times 5 = 40 \rightarrow$ otto per cinque uguale/fa quaranta

Regarding **le frazioni** [*fractions*], below you see how we express them in Italian:

$\frac{1}{2} \rightarrow$ un mezzo

$\frac{1}{3} \rightarrow$ un terzo

$\frac{1}{4} \rightarrow$ un quarto

$\frac{3}{5} \rightarrow$ tre quinti

We use a mix of cardinal and ordinal numbers to express fractions, exactly like in English.

Esercitiamoci!

Write the following numbers in words:

133 _____

248 _____

367 _____

5.410 _____

581 _____

1.677 _____

721 _____

3.899 _____

920 _____

8.104.062 _____

Scriviamo!

Quanto costa? Quanto costano? Look at the images below, guessing how much they could cost, forming complete sentences in Italian, and writing the numbers in words, such as: *La penna costa due euro*. Be creative!

 Lavoriamo con altre studentesse o altri studenti

Check over the exercises above with another student.

Parliamo!

Imagine you are shopping in an Italian market alone or with your friends. Working in pairs or in small groups of 3–4 students, create a skit in Italian: one of you is the vendor and the other student(s) is/are the customer(s). Be creative!

Mercato di San Lorenzo a Firenze:

NOTA CULTURALE

Il mercato italiano. I mercati italiani can be fascinating spots for tourists, while for Italians they are part of their everyday life, and they are considered an "institution." **Il mercato** is usually held on the streets or in the main square of a city or a town once a week, often on a weekday, or in some locations everyday (like **il mercato di San Lorenzo a Firenze**). The stalls are assembled very early in the morning (between six and seven) and dismantled around 12:30 and 1:00 o'clock. **Al mercato** you can find many things that you can also find in stores such as fruit and vegetables, cheese and cold cuts, meat, fish, candy, clothes, undergarments and pajamas, shoes, linen, purses, pottery, make-up, toys, etc. Every stall is highly specialized, selling only one category of items. Locals go to these markets regularly.

Palermo:

Venezia:

While in many locations one can find a mix of different stalls, there also are **mercati** that sell specialized items, such as **il mercato di San Lorenzo a Firenze** that mostly sell leather items (jackets, purses, wallets), clothes (dresses and shirts), hats, scarfs, and foulards, and Florentine paper stationery (see the picture above in the exercise ***Parliamo!***). Markets are also held inside. An example is the mercato **il mercato centrale di San Lorenzo a Firenze** held inside a historical building that is right in the middle of the market held **all'aperto** [*in the open space*].

Here, one can buy products or produce:

Or you can eat lunch:

Il mercato centrale di San Lorenzo a Firenze opened for the first time in 1874, and nowadays it is up and running: **dal lunedì al venerdì dalle 7:00 alle 14:00, il sabato dalle 7:00 alle 17:00 (escluso da metà giugno a settembre) e la domenica chiuso.**

5.8.2 LE DATE

Dates in Italian follow the order: *giorno-mese-anno*. You can go to Chapter 3 (including the Appendix) to refresh your knowledge of numbers up to 31 and months of the year. Look at the example below:

- 13/03/2020 (tredici, marzo, duemilaventi)
- 06/05/2021 (sei, maggio, duemilaventuno)

If this seems confusing, you might use this trick:

- 13/marzo/2020
- 06/maggio/2021

If you need to say dates in Italian, you read it by adding the article. Look at the examples below:

▶ 04/09/2022= Oggi è il quattro settembre duemilaventidue
▶ 07/10/2023= Domani è il sette ottobre duemilaventitré
▶ 03/08/2020= Ieri era [*was*] il tre agosto duemilaventi

If you would like to ask someone when they were born, you could say: **Quando sei nata/o?** or **Quando è il tuo compleanno?** Look at the examples below:

— Quando sei nato, Mario?
— Sono nato il 5 maggio (del) 1987.

— Quando è il tuo compleanno, Carla?
— Il 9 febbraio.

Esercitiamoci!

Write the dates like in the example:

Example: 14/05/1947—quattordici maggio millenovecentoquarantasette

14/02/1955 _____

25/04/1968 _____

18/06/1974 _____

17/07/1988 _____

23/09/1999 _____

7/12/2009 _____

28/03/2013 _____

3/11/2020 _____

Scriviamo!

Write down when you were born as a complete sentence:

_____

Write full sentences in Italian saying when these famous artists were born and where (use the prepositions) like in the example:

Caravaggio 29/09/1571—Milano, Italia 	Caravaggio è nato il ventinove settembre millecinquecentosettantuno a Milano, in Italia.

Write the sentences in the column on the right:

Artemisia Gentileschi 08/07/1593—Roma, Lazio 	
Michelangelo Buonarroti 6/03/1475—Toscana, Italia 	

Georgia O'Keeffe
15/11/1887—Sun Prairie, Wisconsin

Salvador Dalì
11/05/1904—Figueres, Spagna

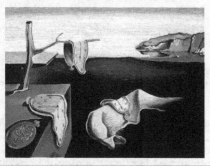

Renato Guttuso
26/12/1911—Bagheria, Sicilia, Italia

Marina Abramoviç
30/11/1946—Belgrado, Serbia

Look for the date and the place of birth of two further famous people and write them down, forming full sentences in Italian:

1. _____

2. _____

Lavoriamo con altre studentesse o altri studenti

Check over the exercises above with another student.

 Parliamo!

Go around the class and ask when the other students were born. Take notes to share them later with the whole class. Examples:

— **Quando sei nato/nata?**
— **Sono nato/nata il 10 ottobre.**

If you want to use the expression with **compleanno**, see above in this section for how to ask for it.

LA PAGINA CULTURALE

L'ARTE IN ITALIA

Italy is synonymous with art. Each era, from Etruscan and Roman times to modern and contemporary ones, has a long list of artists spanning a variety of genres. If you think about Italy, you can think about it as an open-air museum with buildings and churches, monuments, and statues that remind both visitors and inhabitants about Italian history and its multifaceted artistic representations dating back to the Etruscans and the Romans and spanning up to the 21st century.

I Fori Imperiali a Roma:

La Basilica di San Marco a Venezia:

La Cupola del Duomo di Firenze del Brunelleschi:

La Cattedrale Normanna dell'Assunzione della Vergine Maria a Palermo:

Certainly, Italy is also home to many public museums, such the Uffizi in Florence:

It is well known that Italians were at the forefront of art during the renaissance, with some of the most prominent artists being **Brunelleschi** (1377–1446), **Botticelli** (1445–1510), **Leonardo Da Vinci** (1452–1519), **Michelangelo** (1475–1564), and **Raffaello** (1483–1520), a list which is male-dominated. However, at that time women were already active in the field. **Iaia of Cyzicus** was a well-known Roman painter and one of the five women artists of ancient times cited in Pliny the Elder's *Natural History*. She broke the glass ceiling by earning more than her male competitors **Sopolis** and **Dionysius**. **Lucia Anguissola** (1536 or 1538–1565 or 1568) was one of five daughters of a Genoese noble; as a late mannerist, she was praised by **Giorgio Vasari** (1511–1574), and trained with **Sofonisba Anguissola** (1532–1625), one of her sisters, who worked at the Spanish court, and whose talent was recognized by Michelangelo. Feminist art historians consider the Anguissola sisters highly significant. There has never been a period in Western history in which women were absent in the visual arts, however, in most cases, they have been hidden by the traditional curriculum at all levels. The Anguissola sisters paved the way for larger numbers of women artists. For example, **Lavinia Fontana** (1552–1614) and **Irene di Spilimbergo** (1538–1559) were inspired by the works and life of Sofonisba Anguissola, as were **Barbara Longhi** (1552–1638) and **Fede Galizia** (1578–1630).

Italian art has continued to shine throughout the centuries. In the 16th century, **Pontormo** (1494–1557) and **Tintoretto** (1518–1594) should also be mentioned, and in the **Baroque** era, prominent artists include **Caravaggio** (1571–1610),

Bernini (1598–1680), **Elisabetta Sirani** (1638–1665), and **Giovanna Fratellini** (1666–1731). **Fratellini** is quoted as an example of an artist teaching other women in Baroque Florence in the documentary *Invisible Women, Forgotten Artists of Florence* (2013). Similarly, **Sirani** established an academy for women artists in Bologna, which is regarded as the first European school of painting for women artists. Though women artists could be found in convents, this was the first school to operate outside the religious context. Some of her trainees included **Veronica Fontana** (1651–1690), a top-notch wood-engraver, **Caterina Pepoli** and **Maria Elena Panzacchi**, as well as **Camelia Lanteri**, **Lucretia Forni**, **Veronica Franchi**, and **Lucrezia Scarfaglia**. **Artemisia Gentileschi** (1593–1656) was already an artist by the age of fifteen. Inspired by Caravaggio, Gentileschi became a member of the *Accademia dell'Arte del Disegno* in Florence, and her artworks focus on women in various contexts from myths to the Bible. A survivor of rape at the hands of a mediocre painter, she established herself as one of the leading painters of her time. Her famous painting, *Judith Slaying Holofernes*, is in the Uffizi, in Florence, while *Judith and Her Maidservant* hangs in Detroit's Institute of Arts. In the 1970s Linda Nochlin, an American art historian, published the well-known article "Why Have There Been No Great Women Artists?" where she suggests

Judith Slaying Holofernes, Uffizi Museum, Florence, Italy.

that society, institutions and the patriarchy have not supported women's visibility or the same level of recognition given to men. Gentileschi was no exception; however, since the 1970s she has finally been progressively recognised as one the greatest artists of her time. In 2020, an exhibition at the National Gallery in London, and one in 2021 at Palazzo Barberini Rome (alongside **Caravaggio**) are evidence of the current interest in the artist.

In the Rococò period of the 18th century, painters such as **Giambattista Tiepolo** (1696–1770), **Canaletto** (1697–1768), and **Rosalba Carriera** (1675–1575) are world-renowned. *La Reggia di Caserta*, which is now a UNESCO heritage site, is an example of this period and style:

Another example is the **Fontana di Trevi, Roma**, which was started in 1732 and completed in 1762:

Neoclassicismo is well represented by **Antonio Canova** (1757–1822) and **Vincenza Giovanna Rovisi** (1750–1824); Canova's statue of *Le tre Grazie* (1814–1817) is renowned around the world:

In the 19th century, notable mentions include **Amalia de Angelis** (active in Rome 1851–1871) and **Elisabetta Benato-Beltrami** (1813–1888). From the same period, the movement of **macchiaioli** counted **Giovanni Fattori** (1825–1908) and **Telemaco Signorini** (1835–1901) among its numbers, while **verismo** included **Giuseppe Pellizza da Volpedo** (1868–1907), whose *Quarto Stato* (1898–1901) is well-known around the world:

The twentieth century alternated between several movements, from Futurism to Metaphysics and from Pop Art to Avant-garde, just to name a few. **Amedeo Modigliani** (1884–1920), the metaphysic painters **Giorgio Morandi** (1890–1964) and **Giorgio de Chirico** (1888–1978), but also the futurists **Giacomo Balla** (1871–1958), **Umberto Boccioni** (1882–1916), and **Mario Sironi** (1885–1961) contributed to Italian art in the twentieth century, as well as **Emma Ciardi** (1879–1933), whose works were featured at the *Exposition Universelle* in Paris, the *Promotrice* in Turin, the *Esposizione Internazionale d'Arte di Venezia*, the Leicester Galleries in London, and the Howard Young Gallery in New York City.

Jeanne Hébuterne by Amedeo Modigliani (1919):

The Sicilian painter **Renato Guttuso** (1911–1987) was active until his death. Among his friends, one counts the Spanish painter **Pablo Picasso** (1881–1973) and Chilean poet **Pablo Neruda** (1904–1973).

In these two stamps, Guttuso paid homage to Picasso on his birth centenary:

Un francobollo emesso a San Marino è un omaggio di Renato Guttuso a Pablo Picasso (1881–1973) nel centenario della nascita dell'artista nel 1981:

Un francobollo emesso a San Marino mostra l'artista Pablo Picasso (1881–1973). È un omaggio di Renato Guttuso a Picasso nel centenario della nascita nel 1981:

Italy also features numerous street paintings. In the city of Orgosolo, in the province of Nuoro, Sardinia, large murals have appeared on the external building walls since the end of 1960s. Below, you can see a couple of examples:

Carla Accardi (1924–2014) was part of the second wave of Italian feminism, and together with **Carla Lonzi**, she founded *Rivolta femminile*, one of the first feminist groups of the 1970s in Rome. An abstract painter of the *Arte Informel* and *Arte Povera* movements, Accardi is regarded as a key member of the Italian Avant-Garde and has been exhibited throughout the world. Other honorable mentions should include **Bettina Werner** (born in 1965, in Milan), who is based in New York and has used a unique colorized salt technique for her works, and **Rabarama**, the pseudonym of **Paola Epifani** (born in 1969), who creates sculptures and paintings of people in eccentric poses, which have been exhibited in public spaces throughout Europe. To conclude this non-exhaustive survey of Italian art, we should not forget about an emerging artist, **Simona Atzori** (born in 1974 in Milan), who uses her feet to draw and write. She started to paint at the age of four and to dance at the age of six. In March 2006, Atzori was featured during the Opening Ceremony of the Paralympic Games in Torino with a dance performance. Italian art is rich, infinite, and has many shades of beauty, which you will continue to study over the course of the semester and beyond.

ESERCITIAMOCI CON LA CULTURA

A1. La storia dell'arte. Find the following artists online (reputable sources), and write some new information about them in Italian. What have you learned?

1. Elisabetta Sirani
2. Raffaello
3. Antonio Canova
4. Emma Ciardi
5. Carla Accardi
6. Giorgio de Chirico

A2. Scegli un'artista o un artista. Choose one artist from the ones you have learned about in this chapter or look for others that are not mentioned, search for information about them online (reputable sources, such as online newspapers and arts blogs), take notes below, and then share your findings with the class.

Il mio artista/La mia artista è _____.

B. Conosci Banksy?

Banksy (Bristol, 1973 o 1974) è un artista inglese, considerato [*considered*] uno dei maggiori [*one of the major*] esponenti della street art, la cui vera identità rimane ancora sconosciuta [*unknown*]. Le sue opere sono spesso a sfondo [*with a background*] satirico e riguardano argomenti come [*such as*] la politica, la cultura e l'etica. Banksy decide di "colpire" anche Venezia durante l'inaugurazione della 58ª Biennale e nella notte dell'8 maggio 2019 realizza *Naufrago bambino*, un murales a sostegno dei migranti che vengono bloccati [*are intercepted*] in mare da una politica di chiusura dei porti molto discussa [*debated*] dal governo italiano in carica [*in charge*] in quei mesi.

Now it is your turn! Search more about Banksy online (reputable sources, such as online newspapers and arts blogs), take notes on *Naufrago bambino* below, and then share your findings with the class.

Tutto su Banksy!

GLOSSARIO

Verbi in -ere

Bere [*to drink*]

Chiedere (a) [*to ask*]

Chiudere [*to close*]

Conoscere [*to know*]

Correggere [*to revise, to grade*]

Correre [*to run*]

Credere [*to believe*]

Crescere [*to grow, to raise*]

Cuocere [*to cook*]

Decidere [*to decide*]

Deludere [*to disappoint*]

Difendere [*to defend*]

Dipingere [*to paint*]

Dispiacere [*to displease*]

Eleggere [*to elect*]

Giacere [*to lay*]

Leggere [*to read*]

Mettere [*to place*]

Nascere [*to be born*]

Nuocere [*to harm*]

Perdere [*to lose*]

Piacere [*to like*]

Piangere [*to cry*]

Prendere [*to take*]

Proteggere [*to protect*]

Ricevere [*to receive*]

Ridere [*to laugh*]

Ripetere [*to repeat*]

Rispondere (a) [*to respond*]

Sapere [*to know*]

Scrivere (a) [*to write*]

Sorprendere [*to surprise*]

Sorridere [*to smile*]

Spendere [*to spend*]

Tacere [*to keep quiet*]

Vincere [*to win*]

Verbi in -ire

Aprire [*to open*]

Avvertire [*to inform*]

Bollire [*to boil*]

Convertire [*to convert*]

Coprire [*to cover*]

Cucire [*to sew*]

Divertire [*to entertain*]

Dormire [*to sleep*]

Fuggire [*to escape*]

Inseguire [*to chase*]

Investire [*to invest*]

Mentire [*to lie*]

Offrire [*to offer*]

Partire [*to leave*]

Riempire [*to fill up*]

Scoprire [*to discover*]

Seguire [*to follow*]

Sentire [*to feel, to hear*]

Servire [*to serve*]

Sfuggire [*to escape*]

Smentire [*to deny*]

Soffrire [*to suffer*]

Stracuocere [*to overcook*]

Vestire [*to dress*]

Verbi in -ire con il suffisso -isc

Abolire [*to abolish*]

Attribuire [*to bestow*]

Capire [*to understand*]

Chiarire [*to clarify*]

Colpire [*to hit*]

Condire [*to season*]

Contribuire [*to contribute*]

Costruire [*to build*]

Definire [*to define*]

Diminuire [*to diminish*]

Distribuire [*to distribute*]

Esaurire [*to run out of*]

Favorire [*to favor, to foster*]

Finire [*to finish, to end*]

Indebolire [*to weaken*]

Infastidire [*to bother, to annoy*]

Istruire [*to educate*]

Obbedire [*to obey*]

Percepire [*to perceive*]

Preferire [*to prefer*]

Pulire [*to clean*]

Reagire [*to react*]

Restituire [*to return, to give back*]

Ricostruire [*to rebuild*]

Riunire [*to reunite*]

Sostituire [*to substitute*]

Sparire [*to disappear*]

Spedire [*to send*]

Stabilire [*to establish*]

Suggerire [*to suggest*]

Tossire [*to cough*]

Trasferire [*to transfer*]

Unire [*to unite*]

Venire [*to come, to go*]

Espressioni con *prendere*

prendere una decisione [*to make a decision*]

prendere un caffè, un cappuccino [*to have a coffee, a cappuccino*]

prendere gli appunti [*to take notes*]

prendere l'autobus, l'aereo, etc [*to take a bus, a flight, etc.*]

prendere il sole [*to sunbathe*]

prendere lezioni [*to take lessons*]

Piacere

Mi piace/Mi piacciono [*I like*]

Ti piace/Ti piacciono [*You like*]

Gli piace/Gli piacciono [*He likes*]

Le piace/Le piacciono [*She likes*]

Ci piace/Ci piacciono [*We like*]

Vi piace/Vi piacciono [*You all like*]

Gli piace/Gli piacciono [*They like*]

Il partitivo

del, dello, della, dell', dei, degli, delle [*some, a bit of*]

I numeri oltre 100

cento [*one hundred*]

duecento [*two hundred*]

trecento [*three hundred*]

quattrocento [*four hundred*]

cinquecento [*five hundred*]

seicento [*six hundred*]

settecento [*seven hundred*]

ottocento [*eight hundred*]

novecento [*nine hundred*]

mille [*one thousand*]

due mila [*two thousand*]

un milione [*a million*]

un miliardo [*a billion*]

I numeri ordinali

primo/a/i/e [*first*]

secondo/a/i/e [*second*]

terzo/a/i/e [*third*]

quarto/a/i/e [*fourth*]

quinto/a/i/e [*fifth*]

sesto/a/i/e [*sixth*]

settimo/a/i/e [*seventh*]

ottavo/a/i/e [*eight*]

nono/a/i/e [*nineth*]

decimo/a/i/e [*tenth*]

undicesimo/a/i/e [*eleventh*]

dodicesimo/a/i/e [*twelfth*]

ventesimo/a/i/e [*twentieth*]

centesimo/a/i/e [*hundredth*]

APPENDICE

VERBI REGOLARI IN -ARE, -ERE E -IRE

You have studied the three conjugations in **-are (prima coniugazione)**, **-ere (seconda coniugazione)**, and **-ire (terza coniugazione)**. Below is a recap:

PARLARE	SCRIVERE	APRIRE
IO PARLI–**O**	IO SCRIV–**O**	IO APR–**O**
TU PARL–**I**	TU SCRIV–**I**	TU APR–**I**
LEI/LUI PARLI–**A**	LEI/LUI SCRIV–**E**	LEI/LUI APR–**E**
NOI PARL–**IAMO**	NOI SCRIV–**IAMO**	NOI APR–**IAMO**
VOI PARL–**ATE**	VOI SCRIV–**ETE**	VOI APR–**ITE**
LORO PARL–**ANO**	LORO SCRIV–**ONO**	LORO APR–**ONO**

If you look at the table above, you see that you have two ways to learn the endings (after you have dropped the last three letters of an infinitive): horizontally or vertically. This means that you can remember the endings based on the subject pronouns if you decide to go **horizontally**, or you can practice the ending based on the conjugation if you decide to go **vertically**.

PIACERE

If you like someone, you write the first name after the construction with **piacere**: *Mi piace Cosetta; Mi piacciono Marcella e Cesare.* When you like someone, you might like that person or those people not just in a romantic way, but as people.

Regarding the indirect pronouns, we have already stated that **mi** stands for **a me**, **ti** for **a te**, and below you can find all the forms:

These pronouns...	means...	that stands for
MI	**A ME**	to me
TI	**A TE**	to you (informal)
LE	**A LEI**	to you (formal)
LE	**A LEI**	to her
GLI	**A LUI**	to him
CI	**A NOI**	to us
VI	**A VOI**	to you all
GLI	**A LORO**	to them

To ask what someone likes or likes to do:

Cosa mi piace? Cosa mi piace fare?	What do I like? What do I like to do?
Cosa ti piace? Cosa ti piace fare? (informal)	What do you like? What do you like to do?
Cosa Le piace? Cosa Le piace fare? (formal)	What do you like? What do you like to do?

Cosa le piace? Cosa le piace fare?	What does she like? What does she like to do?
Cosa gli piace? Cosa gli piace fare?	What does he like? What does he like to do?
Cosa ci piace? Cosa ci piace fare?	What do we like? What do we like to do?
Cosa vi piace? Cosa vi piace fare?	What do you all like? What do you all like to do?
Cosa gli piace? Cosa gli piace fare?	What do they like? What do they like to do?

Note that verb **piacere** is also used to say that someone is liked by someone else, and in this context is conjugated in this way: **io piaccio, tu piaci, lui/lei piace, noi piacciamo, voi piacete, loro piacciono**. Check the examples below:

1. Io piaccio a Marco ⇒ *Marco likes me.*
2. Tu piaci a Carlo e a Ernesto ⇒ *Carlo and Ernesto like you.*
3. Lei piace a Marinella ⇒ *Marinella likes her.*
4. Lui piace a Zoe e a Leo ⇒ *Zoe and Leo like him.*
5. Noi piacciamo a Carmela ⇒ *Carmela likes us.*
6. Voi piacete a zio Loreno ⇒ *Uncle Loreno likes you all.*
7. Loro piacciono a Abrar e a Safia ⇒ *Abrar and Safia like them.*

Although English speakers use expressions such as *I like* and *I love* based on the intensity of the feelings, Italians mostly use the verb **amare** [*to love*] to express love between people or for someone, and it is intended to convey strong sentiment and feeling. When you want to tell someone *I love you*, you say **Ti amo**: this form expresses romantic love. If you want to tell someone that you love her/him/them, but not in a romantic way, you say **Ti voglio bene**. This expression implies that you want her/his/their good.

LE PREPOSIZIONI ARTICOLATE

To better understand how **le preposizioni articolate** are formed, see below:

di + il = del   a + il = al

di + lo = dello   a + la = alla

In speaking (but not in writing) you might hear:

con il → col   **con i → coi**

con lo → collo   **con gli → cogli**

con l' → coll'   **con le → colle**

con la → colla

If you look at the charts earlier in the chapter, you want to pay attention to both the simple prepositions and the definite articles:

- The simple prepositions follow the rule of the prepositions as studied in the previous chapter, and they are dictated by grammar rules in their uses, including what to use with certain verbs, like in English.
- Because prepositions are placed before a noun, the **gender** (masculine or feminine) and the **number** (singular or plural) of such a noun determine the articles merged into the articulated prepositions.

I NUMERI ORDINALI

In Italian, in most instances one uses the ordinal numbers written in Roman characters to indicate centuries:

1st century → I secolo

2nd century → II secolo

3rd century → III secolo

4th century → IV secolo

5th century → V secolo

6th century → VI secolo

7th century → VII secolo

8th century → VIII secolo

9th century → IX secolo

10th century → X secolo

11th century → XI secolo

12th century → XII secolo

13th century → XIII secolo

14th century → XIV secolo

15th century → XV secolo

16th century → XVI secolo

17th century → XVII secolo

18th century → XVIII secolo

19th century → XIX secolo

20th century → XX secolo

21th century → XXI secolo

Do not forget that **XX secolo** corresponds to the 1900s, **XIX secolo** to the 1800s, **XVIII secolo** to the 1700s, and so on.

The centuries are also expressed with numbers written in letters and capitalized:

1200 → il Duecento

1300 → il Trecento

1400 → il Quattrocento

1500 → il Cinquecento

1600 → il Seicento

1700 → il Settecento

1800 → l'Ottocento

1900 → il Novecento

2000 → il Duemila

CIAK SI GIRA: L'ITALIA E IL CINEMA

6

CAPITOLO

By the end of this chapter, you will be able to use the modal verbs **dovere** [*must, to have to, to need to*], **potere** [*can, may, to be able to*], and **volere** [*want*] in the present tense. You will also learn how to form and use **gli avverbi** [*adverbs*], **i participi passati** [*past participles*], and the past tense called **il passato prossimo** in all conjugations. In terms of cultural elements, you will learn about Italian cinema and its place within world cinema.

Grammar Structures

6.0 Iniziamo
6.1 Modal verbs **dovere** [*must, to have to, to need to*], **potere** [*can, may, to be able to*], and **volere** [*want*] in the present tense
6.2 Adverbs and **molto, tanto, troppo,** and **poco**
6.3 Past participles of **essere** and **avere**, and of regular and irregular verbs in **-are, -ere,** and **-ire**
6.4 Construction of the past tense **passato prossimo**
6.5 Other uses of **passato prossimo**

GLOSSARIO
APPENDICE
   Il condizionale per esprimere *I would like*
   I verbi in **-re** al presente e al passato prossimo

Culture

Note culturali
   Il movimento #Metoo

La pagina culturale
   Il cinema italiano

Le parole contano
   Asterisk and schwa in complex sentences

INIZIAMO

Read the dialogue below with another student, alternating roles:

Stefano:	Hai preso i biglietti?
Francesca:	Sì, sì! Sono nella mia borsa.
Stefano:	Per fortuna abbiamo avuto l'idea di prenotare i biglietti online. Ho saputo che la prima del film è esaurita [*sold out*].
Francesca:	Certo! *Miss Marx* di Susanna Nicchiarelli alla Mostra del Cinema di Venezia ha ricevuto ottimi giudizi, ovviamente la gente è molto curiosa.
Stefano:	Ma Susanna Nicchiarelli è anche quella regista che ha fatto la serie su Netflix? Parlo della serie che si chiama *Luna Nera*.
Francesca:	Sì, ho appena [*just*] finito di guardare *Luna Nera*! Le registe sono Francesca Comencini, Paola Randi e Susanna Nicchiarelli. Ma sai che la serie è girata a Farnese?
Stefano:	A Farnese? Davvero?
Francesca:	Sì, alla Selva del Lamone hanno girato delle scene e alcune [*some*] persone del paese hanno partecipato come comparse [*extras*]!
Stefano:	Quest'estate andiamo a vedere i posti lì intorno [*around there*]!

Stefano:	Guarda! Ci sono Omar, Hiromi e Giulio!
Francesca:	Sempre in giro [always *around*], voi, eh?!?!
Hiromi:	Che meraviglia *Miss Marx*! Non vi [*you*] abbiamo visto nella sala, però.
Francesca:	Quarta fila, davanti allo schermo! Non ci [*us*] avete visto?
Stefano:	Gli unici posti rimasti [*remaining*]!
Omar:	Avete cenato? Possiamo cercare un ristorante in zona [*in the area*] su Tripadvisor!
Francesca:	Infatti vogliamo mangiare qualcosa!
Giulio:	Perché non andiamo da *Fellini*? È vicino.
Hiromi:	Ottima idea! Però prima facciamo un aperitivo, dai [*come on*]!
Francesca:	Perfetto, da *Fellini*! Giulio, puoi chiamare? Devono avere dei posti liberi. Oggi è martedì, non deve essere pieno!
Omar:	Chiedi il tavolo "Otto e mezzo", è una meraviglia! E una bottiglia di Amarone della Valpolicella!
Stefano:	Andiamo subito!

Work with another student to understand the content of this dialogue. Do you know what the words mean?

6.1 I VERBI MODALI: DOVERE, POTERE E VOLERE

The Italian modal verbs **dovere** [*must, to have to, to need to*], **potere** [*can, may, to be able to*], and **volere** [*want*] express, respectively, **necessity** and **obligation, possibility** and **ability**, as well as **wish** and **determination**. They are used when one must do something, can do something, or wants to do something. They often precede the **infinitive** of another verb, except **volere** that can be used to express desire for something. As for all the conjugated verbs, to express a negation, place **non** before the conjugated modal verb. Look at the examples below:

1. **Devo** andare a casa: è tardi!
2. **Posso** chiudere la finestra? Fa freddo!
3. Non **voglio** andare al cinema stasera, sono stanca.
4. Non **voglio** un gelato, **voglio** una pasta alla crema.

6.1.1 DOVERE

Below, find the conjugation of the verb **dovere**, translated into English as *must, to have to, to need to*, in the present tense:

DOVERE
IO DEVO
TU DEVI
LEI/LUI DEVE
NOI DOBBIAMO
VOI DOVETE
LORO DEVONO

The verb **dovere** suggests a duty or an obligation (must/have to). It is also used to give suggestions and advice, or it expresses a necessity (need to). Look at the examples below:

1. Oggi **dobbiamo vedere** il film *Ladri di biciclette* per il corso sul cinema italiano.

2. Abrar e Pamela **devono passare** l'esame per laurearsi [*to graduate*] alla scuola di regia a Cinecittà.

3. Vanda **deve andare** dalla dentista per la pulizia dei denti.

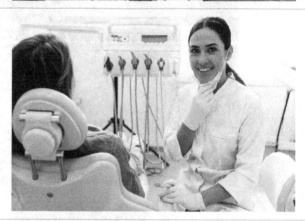

4. I bambini e le bambine **non devono fare sempre** troppi compiti durante le vacanze estive: **devono anche giocare!**

6.1.2 POTERE

Below, find the conjugation of the verb **potere**, translated into English as *can, may, to be able to*, in the present tense:

POTERE
IO POSSO
TU PUOI
LEI/LUI PUÒ
NOI POSSIAMO
VOI POTETE
LORO POSSONO

The verb **potere** is used to ask permission, to express a possibility and the ability to do something, as in English. Look at the examples below:

1. Professoressa, **posso scrivere** il saggio [*essay*] finale su *Pinocchio* di Luigi Comencini?

2. Maestro, **possiamo andare** a giocare fuori?

3. Lucas, **puoi suonare** la chitarra domenica prossima? Abbiamo bisogno di un chitarrista per il concerto.

4. Pamela, Carla e Mabel **non possono viaggiare** a causa della pandemia. Che peccato!

Regarding the ability to do something, the difference between **potere** and **sapere** [*to know*] relies on nuances: if one uses **sapere**, it means that the person has learned to do something (with this verb, we describe the ability that has been acquired by the person); if one uses **potere** to express the ability to do something, it means that the person's ability to perform an activity depends on the circumstances or on their desires and plans, or by the desires and plans of other people. Look at the examples below

1. Giorgia **sa suonare** la chitarra. (*acquired ability*)
2. Giorgia **può suonare** la chitarra domenica prossima perché è libera. (*circumstances*)

3. Mengsteab **sa parlare** il giapponese. (*acquired ability*)
4. Mengsteab **può tradurre** la lettera di Yomiko perché parla il giapponese. (*circumstances*)

6.1.3 VOLERE

Below, find the conjugations of the verb **volere**, translated into English as *want*, in the present tense:

VOLERE
IO VOGLIO
TU VUOI
LEI/LUI VUOLE
NOI VOGLIAMO
VOI VOLETE
LORO VOGLIONO

The verb *volere* expresses wishes and desires, and it is often followed by an infinitive (like the other modal verbs). One can use **volere** by itself to express the desire for something: **voglio un espresso** [*I want an espresso*]. However, as in English, in Italian it is considered a very informal way to express wishes, and it is perceived in formal contexts as not being very polite. To express the desire for something in a polite way, we use the conditional tense: **io vorrei un caffé** [*I would like a coffee*]. For the form of the conditional, see the Appendix.

Look at the examples below:

1. Giulia e Massimo **vogliono andare** in vacanza alle Isole Eolie. **Vogliono visitare** l'Isola di Lipari.

2. Aseem **vuole mangiare** qualcosa di indiano con Bijal.

3. Noi **vogliamo studiare** italiano e cinema all'università.

4. Tu, Claudia e Lodovica **non volete vedere** i film dell'orrore perché non vi piacciono.

Esercitiamoci!

Conjugate the infinitives in parentheses, paying attention to the subject pronouns:

1. Alessandro e Giancarlo _____ (*dovere*) guidare da Milano a Roma per visitare Cinecittà.

2. Mariella e io _____ (*volere*) fare un viaggio a Cape Town, in Sud Africa.

3. Florina, _____ (*potere*) chiudere la porta, per favore?

4. Mohammed _____ (*volere*) studiare scenografia [*scenography*] per diventare uno scenografo.

5. Che fortuna [*What luck*]! Anita e Carla, _____ (*potere*) vivere in Italia e negli Stati Uniti perché avete la doppia cittadinanza!

6. Viviana, sai se Fabio _____ (*dovere*) andare a lezione oggi?

Esercitiamoci di più!

Complete the following sentences with the correct modal verb (**dovere**, **potere**, or **volere**), paying attention to the subject pronouns and to the context. Sometimes, more than one option is possible.

1. Nonna Marcella e nonno Cesare, _____ guardare vostro nipote ogni giorno perché siete in pensione [*you are retired*] e avete tempo libero.

2. Noi _____ andare in vacanza ai Caraibi dopo i mesi passati [*spent*] a casa durante la pandemia da COVID-19.

3. Shazad _____ comprare la macchina per andare al lavoro perché la sua vecchia auto non va più.

4. Qing e Scott _____ guardare i film in cinese perché conoscono questa lingua: sanno parlare cinese!

5. Pierluigi, Silvia e io _____ cenare in un ristorante con almeno una stella Michelin: sabato andiamo a mangiare alla *Leggenda dei Frati* a Firenze.

6. Tu e Carmela _____ scrivere una relazione finale per l'associazione italiana di studi di genere.

7. Io _____ andare a vedere l'aurora boreale [*northern lights*] appena _____ prendere un aereo.

8. Elsa, _____ finire di studiare prima di andare a giocare fuori.

9. Voi, studentesse e studenti di italiano, non _____ passare l'esame se non studiate di più!

10. — Giuseppe, cosa _____ mangiare a cena? _____ la pasta o la carne con le verdure?
    — _____ una pizza, grazie!

Esercitiamoci ancora di più!

Conjugate the infinitive forms of the verbs, creating complete sentences in Italian. Do not forget to put the scrambled words in the correct order!

a Ginevra/io/un regalo/fare/**dovere**	
potere/in giardino/giocare/Marco e io/mamma/?	
Gisella/vedere/l'ultimo/di/Gabriele Salvatores/film/**volere**	
i/di/guardare/il/Marvel/gli/della/**dovere**/corso/film/cinema/studenti/per	
dei/bere/tu/francesi/**volere**/vini/non/bianchi/ma rossi	
potere/al/da/tu e Peyton/cinema/andare/sole	

Scriviamo!

Write three complete sentences in Italian with the verb **dovere**, three complete sentences with the verb **potere**, and three complete sentences with the verb **volere**.

Lavoriamo con altre studentesse o altri studenti

Check over the exercises above with another student.

Parliamo!

Ask another student the questions below, alternating roles. Take note of the answers of your classmate and share them with the class.

1. Cosa devi fare ogni giorno?
2. Cosa devi fare oggi?
3. Cosa devi fare per laurearti [*to graduate*]?
4. Cosa devi fare per passare gli esami?
5. Cosa puoi fare oggi senza aspettare domani?
6. Cosa puoi fare quando sei in vacanza?
7. Cosa puoi ordinare al ristorante?
8. Cosa puoi fare con l'italiano?
9. Cosa vuoi fare dopo l'università?
10. Cosa vuoi fare oggi?
11. Cosa vuoi fare nel fine settimana?
12. Cosa vuoi fare in estate?

Now ask three more questions of your choice to your classmate using the verbs **dovere**, **potere,** and **volere** in a formal register:

1. _____
2. _____
3. _____

6.2 GLI AVVERBI E *MOLTO, TANTO, TROPPO,* AND *POCO*

Adverbs help define and qualify verbs, as well as other adverbs and adjectives, and they are **unmodifiable** in Italian. Think of the English adverbs **very** and **a lot** in sentences such as: *He studies a lot*; *She is very smart*. Many English adverbs end in **-ly** and they correspond to Italian adverbs ending in **-mente** that are formed from the adjectives. Ultimately, adverbs give information about **ogni quanto** [*how often*], **quando** [*when*], and **dove** [*where*] something happens, **come** [*how*] something is, and **quanto** [*how much*] of something.

If adverbs qualify a verb, they are usually placed **after** the verb (conjugated or in the infinitive), and if they qualify or modify an adjective or another adverb, they are usually placed **before** the adjective.

6.2.1 GLI AVVERBI IN -MENTE E ALTRI USATI FREQUENTEMENTE

Many **avverbi di modo** [*adverbs of manner*] are constructed by adding **-mente** at the end of an adjective in its feminine, singular variant (for the adjectives ending in -a, -o, i, -e), such as in **chiaramente** and **onestamente**. If an adjective ends in **-e** in its singular form, simply add **-mente** at the end of the adjective, such as in **frequentemente** and **semplicemente**. However, for adjectives ending in **-le** we drop the **-e** at the end of the adjective and add **-mente** such as in **facilmente** or **debolmente**. Be aware that not every adjective can be converted into an adverb that is commonly used.

As mentioned above, adverbs respond to certain questions:

- **gli avverbi di frequenza** answer the question **ogni quanto?** [*how often?*]
- **gli avverbi di tempo** answer the question **quando?** [*when?*]
- **gli avverbi di luogo** answer the question **dove?** [*where?*]
- **gli avverbi di modo** answer the question **come?** [*how?*]
- **gli avverbi di quantità** answer the question **quanto?** [*how much?*]

Ogni quanto? [How often?]	Quando? [When?]	Dove? [Where?]	Come? [How?]	Quanto? [How much?]
sempre	ieri	qua	→ **most of adverbs in -mente**	molto
spesso	oggi	qui	bene	tanto
ogni tanto	domani	là	male	assai
mai	stamani	lì	così così	troppo
talvolta	stasera	vicino	volentieri	poco
qualche volta	stanotte	lontano	abbastanza	parecchio
di solito	stamattina	sopra	davvero	soltanto
di nuovo	domattina	sotto	soprattutto	piuttosto
già	di notte	dietro	purtroppo	abbastanza
raramente	di mattina	davanti	soltanto	più
	di pomeriggio	su		meno
	ora	giù		un po'
	adesso	dentro		appena
	prima	fuori		niente
	dopo	intorno		nulla
	poi	attorno		affatto
	presto			
	ormai			
	ancora			
	ogni giorno			
	tutti i giorni			
	recentemente			
	successivamente			

Use a dictionary to see what the adverbs in the chart above mean and take notes.

Attenzione!

The adverbs **niente** [*nothing*] and **nulla** [*nothing*], **per niente** [*by no means*], and **affatto** [*at all*] are negative and must be constructed with the double negation. Look at the examples below:

1. Il caffè **non** mi piace **per niente**.
2. Grazie, **non** voglio **niente/nulla** da mangiare o da bere.
3. Quel film **non** è **affatto** interessante.

Esercitiamoci!

Fill in the blanks with adverbs in **-mente** from the adjectives in parentheses:

1. Il tiramisù è un dolce che [*that*] possiamo fare _____ (*veloce*).

2. La ditta di costruzioni [*construction company*] ha rifatto quel teatro d'epoca molto _____ (*attento/a/i/e*).

3. Per preparare l'insalata caprese servono pochi ingredienti, ma di ottima qualità. Potete fare l'insalata _____ (*facile*).

4. Vengo a vedere quel film _____ (*solo/a/i/e*) perché ci [*there*] sei tu.

5. _____ (*recente*) Giselle è andata a vedere uno spettacolo in uno dei teatri della West End di Londra.

6. Le poltrone del nuovo cinema *Odeon* sono fatte [*designed*] per guardare i film _____ (*comodo/a/i/e*).

7. Claudio è _____ (*perenne*) in ritardo!

8. Naomi e Adelaide sono studentesse di storia e italiano in due università diverse, ma loro studiano _____ (*momentaneo/a/i/e*) insieme a Oxford per uno scambio [*exchange*].

Esercitiamoci di più!

Fill in the blanks in the story below with the adverbs provided in the chart:

qualche volta	nuovamente	oggi	di mattina	bene
tanto	sempre	soltanto	volentieri	molto

Al mercato settimanale

Carlos e Yuniko vanno al mercato _____ presto per trovare le verdure fresche. _____ gli [*to them*] è capitato [*happened*] di andare più tardi [*later*] e hanno trovato [*found*] _____ poche cose buone. Vanno al mercato perché non è _____ costoso ed è _____ divertente girare per i banchi del mercato. Però _____ non possono andare al mercato perché Yuniko non sta _____ e Carlos non va _____ al mercato da solo senza la sua migliore amica. La prossima settimana andranno [*will go*] _____ insieme al mercato!

Scriviamo!

Form ten complete sentences using the adverbs (two for each category) of (1) **frequenza** (**ogni quanto?**), (2) **tempo** (**quando?**), (3) **luogo** (**dove?**), (4) **modo** (**come?**), and (5) **quantità** (**quanto?**).

Lavoriamo con altre studentesse o altri studenti

Check over the exercises above with another student.

Parliamo!

Ask another student the questions below, alternating roles. Use adverbs in your replies. Take note of the answers of your classmate and share them with the class.

1. Come stai oggi?
2. Ti piace andare ai concerti? Se sì, ogni quanto vai ai concerti?
3. Fai qualche sport? Se sì, quando fai sport?
4. Ti piace guardare i film? Se sì, quali film guardi? Vai spesso al cinema?
5. Ti piace cucinare? Se sì, come cucini?
6. Ti piace studiare l'italiano? Se sì, quante ore al giorno studi l'italiano? Come parli l'italiano?
7. Parli altre lingue? Come parli le altre lingue?
8. Quando vai di solito all'università? Di mattina o di pomeriggio?
9. Vai volentieri all'università?
10. Abiti vicino o lontano dall'università?
11. Ti piace studiare? Se sì, quanto: molto o poco?
12. Quando vai in vacanza, quanto tempo rimani?
13. Cosa fai di solito ogni mattina? E cosa fai ogni sera?
14. Cosa sai fare bene e cosa non sai fare bene?

Ask three more questions of your choice to your classmate using a formal register and making sure that they use adverbs when responding to you:

1. _____
2. _____
3. _____

6.2.2 MOLTO, TANTO, TROPPO E POCO

Molto, tanto, troppo, and **poco** can be used as adverbs and adjectives. As **adverbs**, in Italian, they are unmodifiable, while as **adjectives** they follow the rule of the adjectives.

As adverbs, one uses them in the invariable forms of **molto** [*very*], **tanto** [*a lot, very much*], **troppo** [*too much*], and **poco** [*little*]. In some regions, **assai** often replaces **tanto.**

As adjectives, one uses them in the variable forms of **molto/a/i/e** [*much, many, a lot of, lots of*], **tanto/a/i/e** [*a lot of, many*], **troppo/a/i/e** [*too much, too many*], and **poco/a/pochi/poche** [*little, few, not many*]. As adjectives, they agree in gender and number with the noun(s) they modify and qualify.

Look at the examples below to see the difference between adjectives and adverbs:

ADJECTIVES	ADVERBS
Marcella e Alessia mangiano **molta verdura**.	Loro mangiano **molto**.
Ogni giorno faccio **tanti chilometri** in macchina per andare al lavoro.	Marco guida **tanto** ogni giorno.
Giuseppe e Anita guardano **troppa televisione**.	Voi dormite **troppo** quando siete in vacanza.
Dylan, c'è **poco latte** nel frigorifero: dobbiamo andare al supermercato.	Juan, Isabela e io leggiamo **poco**, ma scriviamo **tanto**.
Io ho **troppo poco tempo** per fare tutto.	Mia figlia studia **troppo poco** per gli esami.

Esercitiamoci!

Fill in the blanks with the adverbs **molto**, **tanto**, **troppo**, and **poco**. More than one solution is possible. Pay attention to the meanings!

1. Gigliola va _____ dal dentista ultimamente perché ha l'apparecchio.

2. Paolo e Mattia camminano _____ perché gli piace fare lunghe passeggiate.

3. L'ultimo documentario di Gianfranco Rosi è _____ bello, ma non ha vinto [*did not win*] un premio importante.

4. Tu e tua sorella mangiate _____ durante l'estate perché di solito con il caldo avete meno appetito.

5. Tu e i tuoi amici ascoltate _____ quello che dicono gli altri.

6. Quella serie che ho visto [*I watched*] su Netflix è _____ interessante.

7. Vado _____ in piscina perché vivo vicino al mare e preferisco andare in spiaggia.

8. Quel regista che ho incontrato [*I met*] al Festival del Cinema di Venezia è veramente _____ simpatico.

Esercitiamoci di più!

Fill in the blanks in the dialogue below with the adjectives **molto/a/i/e**, **tanto/a/i/e**, **troppo/a/i/e**, or **poco/a/pochi/poche** in the singular or plural forms:

Mara: Ci sono _____ persone al cinema stasera. È pieno!

Luigi: È vero, ma ci sono _____ sedie libere in prima fila [*in the first row*]. Il resto è tutto occupato.

Mara: C'è veramente _____ gente. Perché non torniamo un'altra sera?

Luigi: Vuoi dire di tornare quando c'è _____ gente, vero?

Mara: Sì! Andiamo!

Luigi: Chiediamo il rimborso [*refund*] del biglietto. Secondo te è possibile perché ci sono _____ spettatori e _____ spettatrici stasera nella sala?

Mara: Non sono sicura, ma possiamo provare.

Luigi: Se non danno il rimborso, torniamo in sala.

Mara: Va bene. Sei _____ tirchio [*stingy*]!

Luigi: Non sono tirchio, ma non voglio buttare via i soldi!

Scriviamo!

Form eight complete sentences in Italian using **molto**, **tanto**, **troppo**, and **poco**: four sentences must include one of each as an adjective and four of them must include one of each as an adverb.

Lavoriamo con altre studentesse o altri studenti

Check over the exercises above with another student.

Parliamo!

Ask another student the questions below, alternating roles. Take note of the answers of your classmate and share them with the class.

1. Cosa ti piace fare molto?
2. Cosa ti piace fare poco?
3. Cosa fai troppo?
4. Cosa fai troppo poco?
5. Studi tanto o studi poco?
6. Quanto cucini? Tanto o poco?
7. Cosa mangi troppo? Cosa mangi troppo poco?
8. Guardi poco la televisione oppure guardi troppa televisione?
9. Vai molto o poco al cinema?
10. Fai molto sport o poco sport?
11. Viaggi tanto o viaggi poco?
12. Hai molti amici e molte amiche? Oppure hai pochi amici e poche amiche?
13. Quanto stai sul social media? Tanto/molto, poco oppure troppo?
14. Quanto ti piace parlare al cellulare? Tanto/molto, poco oppure troppo?

Ask four more questions of your choice to your classmates using a formal register and making sure that they use **molto**, **tanto**, **troppo**, and **poco** when responding to you:

1. _____
2. _____
3. _____
4. _____

6.3 I PARTICIPI PASSATI

In Italian, **il participio passato**, or past participle (such as *been*, *done*, *driven*, *eaten*, or *read*) is used together with the present tense of the auxiliary verbs **essere** and **avere** to form a compound past tenses called **passato prossimo**. Like in English, **il participio passato** is also often used as a noun and/or adjective.

6.3.1 I PARTICIPI PASSATI REGOLARI

Regular past participles are formed by dropping the infinitive endings **-are**, **-ere**, or **-ire** and adding, respectively, the suffixes **-ato**, **-uto**, or **-ito**.

-are → **-ato** (mangi**are** → mangi**ato**)	The verbs in **-are** change from **-are** to **-ato**
-ere → **-uto** (av**ere** → av**uto**)	The verbs in **-ere** change from **-ere** to **-uto**
-ire → **-ito** (dorm**ire** → dorm**ito**)	The verbs in **-ire** change from **-ire** to **-ito**

Based on the rules above, fill the chart below with the regular past participles:

AMARE	
PARLARE	
CREDERE	
SAPERE	
FINIRE	
SENTIRE	

Most of the regular verbs in **-are** have regular past participles, while some irregular verbs have regular past participles, such as **andare** (**andato**), **dare** (**dato**), and **stare** (**stato**). Furthermore, the verbs **essere** and **stare** have the same past participle, **stato**, which is irregular for the former. The verb **avere** has a regular past participle (**avuto**).

When used as nouns and adjectives, past participles change in gender and number. Examples among those that can be used include **amato/a/i/e** and **finito/a/i/e**. Look at the examples below:

1. L'**amata** del poeta Dante è Beatrice. (*noun*)
2. I tempi d'oro della nazionale di calcio italiana maschile sembrano **finiti**. (*adjective*)

Like in English, not every past participle can be converted into an adjective or a noun.

Esercitiamoci!

Form the past participles of the verbs below in the masculine singular form:

studiare	_____	cucinare	_____
piovere	_____	volere	_____
capire	_____	spedire	_____
guardare	_____	potere	_____
giocare	_____	votare	_____
vendere	_____	dovere	_____
guidare	_____	partire	_____
sapere	_____	tenere	_____
pulire	_____	chiarire	_____

Esercitiamoci di più!

Form the past participle of the verbs below in the masculine (m.) or feminine (f.) forms, singular (s.) or plural (pl.) based on the directions:

costruire	_____ f.s.	volere	_____ f.pl.
andare	_____ m.pl.	guarire	_____ m.s.
cadere	_____ f.pl.	sedere	_____ m.pl.
sapere	_____ m.s.	trovare	_____ f.s.
volare	_____ f.pl.	vendere	_____ f.pl.
ricevere	_____ m.pl.	pulire	_____ m.s.
venire	_____ f.s.	ballare	_____ f.s.
suonare	_____ f.pl.	sostituire	_____ m.pl.

Lavoriamo con altre studentesse o altri studenti

Check over the exercises above with another student.

6.3.2 I PARTICIPI PASSATI IRREGOLARI

There also are many verbs that have irregular past participles, such as **essere** (**stato**). Many verbs, particularly those of second conjugation in **-ere,** have irregular past participles. In the chart below, you will find the most common, some of which have been introduced in the previous chapters.

Participi passati dei verbi irregolari in -ARE		
Andare → andato Dare → dato Fare → fatto		

Participi passati irregolari dei verbi in -ERE		
Bere → bevuto Chiedere → chiesto Chiudere → chiuso Conoscere → conosciuto Correggere → corretto Correre → corso Crescere → cresciuto Cuocere → cotto Decidere → deciso Deludere → deluso Difendere → difeso Dipingere → dipinto	Eleggere → eletto Essere → stato Leggere → letto Mettere → messo Nascere → nato Perdere → perso, perduto Piacere → piaciuto Piangere → pianto Prendere → preso Proteggere → protetto Rendere → reso Ridere → riso	Rispondere → risposto Scendere → sceso Scorgere → scorto Scrivere → scritto Sorprendere → sorpreso Sorridere → sorriso Spendere → speso Tacere → taciuto Vedere → visto, veduto Vincere → vinto Vivere → vissuto

Participi passati irregolari dei verbi in -IRE		
Aprire → aperto Coprire → coperto	Dire → detto Offrire → offerto	Scoprire → scoperto Soffrire → sofferto

Esercitiamoci!

Form the irregular past participle of the verbs below in the **masculine, singular form**:

bere	_____	scrivere	_____
aprire	_____	scoprire	_____
stare	_____	leggere	_____
perdere	_____	dire	_____
essere	_____	vedere	_____
fare	_____	correggere	_____

Then, write down the endings for the **feminine singular**, the **masculine plural**, and the **feminine plural**.

Esercitiamoci di più!

Form the irregular past participle of the verbs below in the masculine (m.) or feminine (f.) forms, singular (s.) or plural (pl.), based on what is requested:

soffrire	_____	m.pl.	offrire	_____	f.s.
dare	_____	f.s.	essere	_____	m.s.
prendere	_____	f.pl.	chiudere	_____	f.pl.
scendere	_____	m.pl.	fare	_____	f.s.
perdere	_____	m.s.	coprire	_____	m.s.

Lavoriamo con altre studentesse o altri studenti

Check over the exercises above with another student.

6.4 IL PASSATO PROSSIMO

In Italian, a form of past tense called **passato prossimo** was originally used (and still is) to talk about past events in more recent times, while another past tense called **passato remoto** was reserved for events in the distant past. In current times, **passato remoto** is mostly used in written works (books and written formal Italian) and rarely used in everyday conversation, except in some dialects. Currently, one uses mostly **passato prossimo** to talk about all events in the past that are finished.

In Italian, **il passato prossimo** is formed with the auxiliary verbs **avere** or **essere** in the present tense followed by the **participio passato** of the action verb. This formulation is translated into English with the simple past (*I worked*), the past emphatic (*I did work*), or the present perfect (*I have worked*).

When verbs are built with **avere**, the past participle does not change: it ends in **-o** for all the subjects; when verbs are built with **essere**, the past participle changes based on the gender and number of the subject that performs the action: it can end in **-o**, **-a**, **-i**, or **-e**.

6.4.1 IL PASSATO PROSSIMO DI *ESSERE* E *AVERE*

The passato prossimo of verbs **essere** and **avere** are built, respectively, with the past participles **stato** and **avuto**, as in the examples below:

1. Ieri sera **sono stata** bene, dice Chiara.
2. Ieri **ho avuto** la febbre, dice Francesca.

For the negation, place **non** before the conjugated forms of the present tense of **essere** and **avere**, like in the examples below:

3. Ieri sera **non** sono stata bene, dice Chiara.

4. Ieri **non** ho avuto la febbre, dice Francesca.

To ask if someone has **ever** been in a place, add **mai** between **essere** or **avere** conjugated in the present tense and the past participle, as in the examples below:

1. — Giulio, sei **mai** stato in Italia? – No, **non** sono **mai** stato in Italia.

2. — Marinella, sei **mai** stata in Giappone? – No, **non** sono **mai** stata in Giappone.

Esercitiamoci!

Fill the blanks with the **passato prossimo** of **essere** or **avere**. Pay attention to the context and, in case of **essere**, to the subject pronouns (if masculine/feminine, singular/plural).

Example: Ieri io _____ho avuto_____ freddo tutto il giorno.

　　　　Camilla, _____sei stata_____ al mare la scorsa estate?

1. Amit _____ davvero molta fortuna con la lotteria: ha vinto [won] il primo premio!

2. Nicoletta, Giuseppina e Djenniflore _____ molto bene sabato scorso alla festa di laurea di Giuseppe.

3. Domenica ho festeggiato il mio compleanno. _____ tanti bei regali e un sacco di biglietti di auguri!

4. Con il trasloco, tu e la tua famiglia _____ tanto da fare.

5. Gli studenti e le studentesse _____ troppa fretta di finire l'esame di fisica: hanno fatto tanti errori.

6. Eduardo, Jamal e José _____ tutti insieme a trovare il loro amico Guglielmo.

7. Jasmine è una gran viaggiatrice, ma non _____ in Italia. Mai, nemmeno una volta!

8. Le mie cugine _____ a Firenze alle due del pomeriggio in pieno luglio e __ _____ un caldo terribile.

9. Due settimane fa ho preso il COVID-19 e io (m.) _____ davvero tanto male.

10. Le mie sorelle e io _____ una settimana intensa per i festeggiamenti della nonna: ha compiuto 100 anni!

Scriviamo!

Write six full sentences with the **passato prossimo** of **avere** and six full sentences with the **passato prossimo** of **essere** using all subject pronouns: **io**, **tu**, **lui** or **lei**, **noi**, **voi,** and **loro**. See the examples from the previous exercise.

Lavoriamo con altre studentesse o altri studenti

Check over the exercises above with another student.

Parliamo!

Ask as many questions as possible to a classmate and alternate roles.

1. Dove sei stato/a lo scorso fine settimana?
2. Come sei stata/o? Bene, male, così così?
3. Dove sei stato/a di bello l'estate scorsa?
4. Come sei stata/o in vacanza? Bene, male, così così?
5. Dove sei stato/a di bello lo scorso anno?
6. Come sei stata/o? Bene, male, così così?
7. Sei mai stato/a all'estero?
8. Sei mai stato/a in Italia?
9. Sei mai stata/o all'opera?
10. Sei mai stato/a allo stadio?
11. Cosa hai avuto di regalo per il tuo compleanno?
12. Quanti libri hai avuto in regalo in vita tua, pochi o tanti?
13. Hai mai avuto paura di qualcosa?
14. Hai mai avuto dei brutti voti a scuola?
15. Hai dovuto studiare molto per entrare all'università oppure è stato facile?
16. Hai mai avuto un cane o un gatto?

Ask two more questions of your choice in a formal register, one with the **passato prossimo** of **avere** and one with the **passato prossimo** of **essere**:

1. _____
2. _____

6.4.2 IL PASSATO PROSSIMO CON *AVERE*

The majority of verbs use **avere** as an auxiliary when the **passato prossimo** is formed. In Chapter 4, when we studied the regular verbs in **-are**, we also talked about **transitive and intransitive verbs**: do you recall what they are? We ask this question because, in most cases, the **passato prossimo** of transitive verbs are formed with the auxiliary **avere** in the present tense followed by past participles. Now complete the chart below following the example:

MANGIARE	TO EAT
IO HO MANGIATO	I ATE/I HAVE EATEN
TU	YOU ATE/HAVE EATEN
LEI/LUI	SHE/HE ATE/HAS EATEN
NOI	WE ATE/HAVE EATEN
VOI	YOU ALL ATE/HAVE EATEN
LORO	THEY ATE/HAVE EATEN

Look at the examples below to start learning about the use of this past tense:

1. Ieri a pranzo Mohammed **ha mangiato** un panino.
2. Sabato scorso Preya e Paola **non hanno mangiato** la pizza.

The past participle does not change with the auxiliary **avere** in the **passato prossimo**, as you can see from the examples above. Now conjugate the three verbs below in the **passato prossimo**:

	FARE	LEGGERE	FINIRE
IO			
TU			
LUI/LEI			
NOI			
VOI			
LORO			

Look at the examples below:

1. Marta e Giuseppe **hanno guardato** un film lo scorso fine settimana.
2. Stamattina non **ho visto** il mio amico Gary al bar.
3. Yoji, Carine e io **abbiamo studiato** tutto il giorno per l'esame di italiano.
4. Architetta Modigliani, **ha consegnato** il progetto in tempo?
5. Il regista Federico Fellini **ha ricevuto** numerosi e prestigiosi premi.
6. Marianna **ha detto** molte cose interessanti.
7. Signor Massello, **ha finito** il lavoro per la sua cliente?
8. Carlo, **hai chiuso** la finestra della tua camera?
9. Non **ho viaggiato** tanto in vita mia. Peccato!
10. Ieri **abbiamo passeggiato** nel parco, ma **abbiamo avuto** freddo.

Tu cosa hai fatto nel fine settimana? Scrivi la risposta sotto:

_____

Hai **mai** mangiato la trippa alla fiorentina? Scrivi la risposta sotto:

_____

LE ESPRESSIONI IDIOMATICHE CON *FARE*

With the idiomatic expression with **fare** (see Chapter 4) related to weather, you must use the auxiliary **avere**, as in the examples below:

1. Ieri **ha fatto** brutto tempo.
2. Lo scorso fine settimana **ha fatto** proprio freddo.
3. La scorsa estate ad Aruba **ha fatto** bel tempo ed è stato bellissimo.

Esercitiamoci!

Conjugate the infinitives in parentheses in the **passato prossimo**:

1. Io non _____ (*vedere*) l'ultimo film di Gabriele Muccino.

2. Marco _____ (*perdere*) il suo libro di italiano.

3. Dottoressa Cavaliere, _____ (*leggere*) la relazione sul nuovo progetto del dipartimento?

4. Giada, cosa _____ (*costruire*) con il legno che _____ _____ (*comprare*) due mesi fa [*ago*]?

5. Tu e Samantha non _____ (*presentare*) la vostra ricerca a una conferenza la scorsa primavera.

6. Il mio migliore amico e il suo ragazzo _____ (*aprire*) una cineteca a Bologna.

7. Ingegnere Galimberti, _____ (*guardare*) quei progetti che io _____ (*sottoporre*) alla sua attenzione la scorsa settimana?

8. La professoressa di italiano _____ (*correggere*) gli esami: meno male io ____ _____ (*prendere*) un buon voto!

9. Elisabetta e io _____ (*bere*) un prosecco alla salute di tutti gli amici e di tutte le amiche che abbiamo in Italia.

10. La famiglia di Bebe Vio _____ (*festeggiare*) la campionessa paralimpica.

Esercitiamoci di più!

Complete the paragraph below conjugating the following infinitives in the **passato prossimo**. Pay attention to the context and the subjects when choosing one verb or the other.

fare	parlare	scorgere	mangiare	gridare	bere
finire	vedere	scoprire	passeggiare	decidere	prendere

Il mese scorso, la mia famiglia e io _____ un nuovo bar e stamattina io _____

_____ un caffè proprio in quel bar prima di andare a lezione. Al bar _____

_____ il mio amico Chris e la mia amica Amalia: anche loro _____ un

espresso e _____ una pasta alla crema per uno. Il barista _____

_____ dei caffè davvero molto buoni: non tutti sanno fare l'espresso bene! Noi tre _____

_____ di film: siamo appassionati di cinema! Dopo che _____ la co-

lazione, _____ di fare una passeggiata. A un certo punto io _____

_____ Young e Sigrid da lontano e _____: "Ciao ragazzi! Siamo qua!"

Alla fine _____ per il parco senza andare all'università! Bella mattinata di relax!

Scriviamo!

Write five full sentences answering these questions:

1. Che cosa hai fatto stamattina?

2. Che cosa hai fatto ieri?

3. Che cosa hai fatto lo scorso fine settimana?

4. Che cosa hai fatto la settimana passata?

5. Che cosa hai fatto la scorsa estate?

Lavoriamo con altre studentesse o altri studenti

Check over the exercises above with another student.

Parliamo!

Talk with another classmate asking and responding to the following questions. Ask as many questions as possible, alternating roles.

1. Che cosa hai mangiato stamattina a colazione?

2. Che cosa hai mangiato e bevuto ieri sera a cena?

3. Che cosa hai studiato ieri?

4. Che cosa hai fatto l'altro ieri?

5. Che cosa hai guardato alla televisione lo scorso fine settimana?

6. Che cosa hai visto l'ultima volta che sei andata/o al cinema?

7. Quale libro hai letto di recente?

8. Hai viaggiato la scorsa estate? Se sì, dove sei stato/a?

9. Hai mai prenotato niente online? Se sì, che cosa hai prenotato?

10. Hai mai comprato niente online? Se sì, che cosa hai comprato?

11. Hai mai fatto la pizza fatta in casa? E la pasta?

12. Hai mai visitato l'Italia?

Ask two more questions that are not listed above using a formal register:

1. _____

2. _____

6.4.3 IL PASSATO PROSSIMO CON *ESSERE*

The **passato prossimo con essere** is formed with the present tense of the verb **essere** followed by the past participle: the past participle's endings change based on the gender and number of the subject that performs the action, as with adjectives. Most verbs of movement (except **camminare**, **passeggiare**, **nuotare**, and **viaggiare**) are built with **essere**, as well as the verbs of state (**essere**, **stare**, **restare**, and **rimanere** among others), and those referring to the life cycle and physical development (**nascere**, **invecchiare**, or **morire**). Now complete the chart below following the example:

ANDARE	TO GO
ANDATO/O	I WENT/HAVE GONE
TU	YOU WENT/HAVE GONE
LEI/LUI	SHE/HE WENT/HAVE GONE
NOI	WE WENT/HAVE GONE
VOI	YOU ALL WENT/HAVE GONE
LORO	THEY WENT/HAVE GONE

Look at the examples below:

1. **Gianni** è andat**o** allo stadio domenica scorsa.
2. **Marina** è andat**a** alla festa sabato sera.
3. **Carla e Michela** sono andat**e** all'università per un evento speciale sul cinema.
4. **Marco e Giulio** sono andat**i** insieme alle paralimpiadi.

LE PAROLE CONTANO

Traditional grammar states that when referring to a group of people where both men and women are present, the masculine plural of the past participle must be used, such as in this sentence: **Marco, Giulio, Serena, Marina e Sara** sono andati al cinema a vedere *Perfetti sconosciuti* di Paolo Genovese. However, there are a variety of options to avoid this exclusive use of the language. In everyday written communication, the use of the asterisk can help create a more inclusive sentence and to break the traditional binary system: **Marco, Giulio, Serena, Marina e Sara** sono andat* al cinema a vedere *Corpo celeste* di Alice Rohrwacher. However, while being more inclusive, using the asterisk also introduces the issue of further invisibility of women in the language. In oral communication, the use of the **schwa**, might solve the issue of pronunciation: **Marco, Giulio, Serena, Marina e Sara** sono andatə al cinema a vedere *Viola di Mare* di Donatella Maiorca. Yet, the matter of women's invisibility in language also persists with this solution. Furthermore, as we learned in the previous chapters, this vowel is present in some Italian dialects, such as Neapolitan; however, standard Italian speakers do not use it. The rules can also be bypassed by repeating the *participio passato* twice: **Marco, Giulio, Marina, Serena e Sara** sono andati e andate al cinema a vedere *La pazza gioia* di Paolo Virzì. Becoming proficient in the language will help also to find solutions to traditional grammar rules, and other suggestions might become available by playing a bit with Italian, such as in this sentence: **Marina, Serena e Sara** sono andate al cinema con Marco e Giulio a vedere *Vergine Giurata* di Laura Bispuri.

Dove sei andata/o nel fine settimana? Scrivi la risposta sotto:

_____

Sei **mai** andato/a in Italia? Se sì, quando? Scrivi la risposta sotto:

_____

As mentioned previously, verbs of movement and state are constructed with the verb **essere**:

VERBI DI MOVIMENTO	VERBI DI STATO, DI SVILUPPO FISICO E ALTRI VERBI		
Andare	Apparire	Diventare	Parere
Arrivare	Arrossire	Durare	Piacere
Cadere	Avvenire	Esistere	Restare
Correre*	Bastare	Essere	Rimanere
Entrare	Cambiare*	Finire*	Ringiovanire
Fuggire	Capitare	Guarire	Riuscire
Partire	Costare	Ingrassare	Sembrare
Ritornare	Crescere	Invecchiare	Stare
Salire	Dimagrire	Mancare	Succedere
Scappare	Dipendere	Morire	Vivere
Scendere	Dispiacere	Nascere	
Tornare			
Uscire			
Venire			

Look at the examples below:

1. **Siamo venute** alla festa in macchina.
2. Non **siamo tornati** a casa tardi ieri sera.
3. Ieri non **sono rimasto** a casa come da programma, ma **sono uscito** con gli amici e con le amiche.

4. Ingegnera Zangrilli, quando **è arrivata** in ufficio stamattina?
5. **Sono nata** a Roma, ma ho vissuto a Milano per quindici anni.
6. Il regista Sergio Leone **è morto** nel 1989.
7. Avvocato Quarantotto, quando **è uscito** dal tribunale ieri mattina?
8. L'attrice Giulietta Masina **è morta** nel 1994.

CORRERE	CAMBIARE E FINIRE
* **Correre** [*to run*] can be constructed with **essere** or **avere**, and the choice of the auxiliary is given by the context: if you use it to say that you jog or you run without a fixed destination, you use the verb **avere**; however, if you specify the destination of your run, you must build the **passato prossimo** with **essere**. Look at the examples below: 1. Ieri **ho corso** per il parco dalle 8 del mattino alle 10. 2. Ieri **sono corsa** a casa dopo l'università.	* **Cambiare** [*to change*] and **finire** [*to finish, to end*] can be constructed with either **avere** or **essere**, but they hold different meanings. Look at the examples below: 1. **Ho cambiato** idea sui film di Lina Wertmüller: mi piacciono proprio! 2. La mia migliore amica **è cambiata** ultimamente. 3. **Ho finito** di vedere l'ultimo film di Ferzan Özpetek, il cineasta turco-italiano. 4. La classe di italiano **è finita** puntualmente alle 15.

Quando sei nata/o? Scrivi la risposta sotto:

_____

Dove sei nato/a? Scrivi la risposta sotto:

_____

Certain verbs of movement are constructed with **avere**, such as:

CAMMINARE	PASSEGGIARE	VIAGGIARE	ATTRAVERSARE
RAGGIUNGERE	GIOCARE*	NUOTARE	CORRERE (see the table above)

* **Giocare:** also when movement is involved.

Look at the examples below:

1. Sara **ha camminato** due ore.
2. **Abbiamo passeggiato** per la città sotto il sole cocente.
3. Signora Martini, **ha viaggiato** molto di recente?
4. **Avete attraversato** l'Europa in treno per lungo e per largo.
5. Signor Marsala, **ha raggiunto** Venezia in aereo da Palermo per vedere l'ultimo film di Paolo Sorrentino, *La mano di Dio*?
6. **Ho giocato** a tennis con Michaela ai campi da tennis della Giannella.
7. Alex e Chris **hanno nuotato** tutto il pomeriggio in piscina.
8. **Ho corso** tutto il giorno come una matta.

Esercitiamoci!

Conjugate the infinitive forms of the verbs in the **passato prossimo**, creating complete sentences. Do not forget to put the words and the verb in the correct order and pay attention whether the verbs need the auxiliary **essere** or **avere**!

andare/alla Scala/Giada/ieri/di Milano	
camminare/da/all'università/io/stamani/casa	
scendere/Giulio/dall'autobus/di corsa/stamattina	
attraversare/l'Atlantico/1928/Amelia Earhart/nel	
nascere/noi/2002/nel	
nuotare/in/voi/stamattina/piscina	

Esercitiamoci di più!

Conjugate the following verbs in the **passato prossimo** paying attention to the subjects and the context:

uscire	nascere	entrare	costare	uscire	durare
andare	essere	tornare	nascere	andare	venire

Ciao! Mi chiamo Amal e _____ a Roma. Ho diciassette anni e vado al Liceo Maria Montessori. I miei genitori, Aisha e Bilal, _____ in Marocco, ma _____ _____ in Italia venti anni fa per lavorare. Per la legge italiana, sono marocchina perché i miei genitori sono marocchini e non hanno la cittadinanza italiana, ma io posso prenderla [*get it*] a 18 anni. Con la mia famiglia, _____ spesso in Marocco a trovare i miei nonni che vivono là, ma adesso andiamo di meno. Ho due migliori amiche italiane, Ivana e Mery, e un migliore amico, Metello. Noi quattro siamo sempre insieme! Lo scorso fine settimana Ivana e io _____ presto di casa per andare al cinema. All'entrata abbiamo incontrato Mery e Metello, e tutti e quattro _____ _____ al cinema un minuto prima dell'inizio. Il film _____ due ore ed ___ _____ davvero molto bello. Noi quattro _____ dal cinema alle 20, giusto in tempo per la cena. _____ in pizzeria, ma la cena non ___ _____ poco: trenta euro a testa!! Dopo la pizza e il conto salato, io _____ _____ a casa in autobus alle undici di sera. Che bella serata!

Scriviamo!

Write ten full sentences with the **passato prossimo** utilizing the auxiliary **essere**. Make sure you use all different subject pronouns.

Scriviamo di più!

Tell your classmates? What you did yesterday. Write at least five full sentences in Italian.

Lavoriamo con altre studentesse o altri studenti

Check over the exercises above with another student.

Parliamo!

Talk with another classmate, asking and responding to the following questions. Ask as many questions as possible, alternating roles.

1. Quando e dove sei nata/o?
2. Dove sei cresciuto/a?
3. Dove sei vissuta/o negli ultimi dieci anni?
4. Quando sei uscito/a di casa stamattina per venire all'università?
5. Quando sei arrivata/o all'università oggi?
6. Quanto è costato il libro di italiano?
7. Sei mai mancato/a alle lezioni di italiano?
8. Quando sei tornata/o a casa la sera sabato scorso?

9. Che cosa è successo di importante il mese scorso? Scegli un evento significativo.
10. Dove sei stato/a la scorsa estate?
11. Dove sei andata/o in vacanza l'ultima volta che hai fatto le vacanze o preso le ferie?
12. Sei mai stato/a in Italia? Se sì, dove?
13. Sei mai stata/o in Europa? Se sì, dove?
14. Sei mai stato/a all'estero? Se sì, dove?

Ask two more questions beyond those listed above using a formal register:

1. _____
2. _____

6.5 ALTRI USI USI DEL PASSATO PROSSIMO

The construction of the **passato prossimo** of the verb **piacere** and of the modal verbs **dovere**, **potere**, and **volere** are essential for communicating in everyday life.

6.5.1 IL PASSATO PROSSIMO CON *PIACERE*

Do you remember the Italian construction that corresponds to the English **I like** [*mi piace*]? **Piacere** in the **passato prossimo** is built with the auxiliary verb **essere** followed by the past participle **piaciuto/a/i/e**. The ending of the past particle varies based on the gender (masculine or feminine) and number (singular or plural) of the thing(s) or people you liked. When you need to express that you liked to have done something, you must use the past participle ending in **-o** (**piaciuto**), followed by the infinitive of the action/activity that you liked to do, as in this example: **Mi è piaciuto andare** a Milano a vedere *L'ultima cena* di Leonardo da Vinci.

Now complete the chart below following the example:

	I LIKED IT	I LIKED THEM
IO	MI È PIACIUTO/A	MI SONO PIACIUTI/E
TU	TI	TI
LUI/LEI	GLI/LE	GLI/LE
NOI	CI	CI
VOI	VI	VI
LORO	GLI	GLI

Look at the examples below:

1. Ieri sono andata al cinema a vedere **il film di Emma Dante,** *Le sorelle Macaluso.* **Mi è piaciuto** molto.
2. Una settimana fa abbiamo mangiato al nuovo ristorante indiano in Piazza Dalmazia a Firenze. **Ci sono piaciuti** molto **i piatti** del menù.
3. **Elena è piaciuta a tutti** quando ha parlato di uguaglianza e diversità.
4. **Le barbabietole rosse** non **gli sono piaciute** per niente.
5. **A Barbara e a Marino è piaciuto** molto **trascorrere** qualche giorno di vacanza sulle Alpi.
6. Dottoressa Cristoforetti, **Le è piaciuta la terra** dallo spazio durante la missione della primavera del 2022?
7. **Mi è piaciuto l'ultimo libro** di Michela Murgia: questa scrittrice scrive sempre cose molto interessanti!
8. **A Jamal è piaciuto andare** alle terme di Saturnia, in Toscana. Per lui è stata un'esperienza nuova.

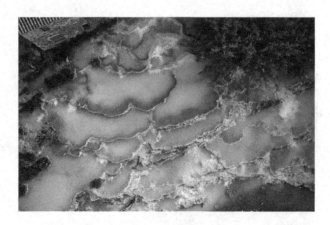

Esercitiamoci!

Fill in the blanks with the verb **piacere** in the **passato prossimo**:

1. A Daniela _____ molto l'ultimo libro di Michela Marzano.

2. Ti _____ gli ultimi film di Roberto Benigni?

3. Vi _____ le crostatine alla frutta fatte dal fratello di Khalid?

4. A Francesca, Margherita e a me _____ l'amica di Emanuele: è veramente molto simpatica! Si chiama Giulia.

5. A Ridoi _____ visitare il museo della Ferrari con Angelo.

6. A Mariella e Irma non _____ il cornetto del bar: troppo secco e con poca cioccolata.

7. Ieri ho visto il mio amico Federico al cinema e abbiamo parlato del doppiaggio. Mi ha detto che a Michela _____ la sua ultima interpretazione.

8. Mi _____ molto i saggi delle studentesse e degli studenti. Sono stati e state bravissimi e bravissime.

Esercitiamoci di più!

Conjugate the infinitive forms of the verbs in the **passato prossimo**, creating complete sentences. Do not forget to put the scrambled words and verbs in the correct order.

piacere/a Paolo e Alessandro/a teatro/ieri/andare	
a Laura/**piacere**/cucinate/da sua sorella/per pranzo/ le portate	
a voi/non/**piacere**/di ieri sera/il film	
mi/poesie/le tue/**piacere**/molto	
a loro/gli antipasti/**piacere**/non/di pesce	
ti/lo spettacolo/**piacere**/del comico?	

Scriviamo!

Che cosa ti è piaciuto fare questo mese? Write five full sentences in Italian saying what you enjoyed doing this month using the construction with **piacere** in the **passato prossimo**.

Lavoriamo con altre studentesse o altri studenti

Check over the exercises above with another student.

⊙⊙⊙ *Parliamo!*

Talk with another classmate, asking and responding to the following questions. Ask as many questions as possible alternating roles.

1. Che cosa hai fatto ieri? Che cosa ti è piaciuto fare di più?

2. Che cosa hai fatto lo scorso fine settimana? Che cosa ti è piaciuto fare di più?

3. Che cosa hai fatto la settimana scorsa? Che cosa ti è piaciuto fare di più?

4. Che cosa hai fatto il mese passato? Che cosa ti è piaciuto fare di più?

5. Che cosa hai fatto di bello l'estate scorsa? Che cosa ti è piaciuto fare di più?

6. Che cosa hai fatto di bello l'anno passato? Che cosa ti è piaciuto fare di più?

Ask two more questions that are not listed above using a formal register:

1. _____

2. _____

6.5.2 IL PASSATO PROSSIMO CON *DOVERE, POTERE* E *VOLERE*

When followed by an infinitive, the modal verbs **dovere**, **potere**, and **volere** in the **passato prossimo** take the auxiliary of the verb in the infinitive form. Look at the examples below:

1. Mario **ha dovuto studiare** per l'esame. (***studiare*** *takes* ***avere***)
2. Mario è **dovuto partire** per Roma. (***partire*** *takes* ***essere***)
3. Gina **ha potuto prendere** il treno delle 20. (***prendere*** *takes* ***avere***)
4. Gina è **potuta venire** da noi a cena ieri sera. (***venire*** *takes* ***essere***)
5. **Ho voluto vedere** il Castello di Santa Severa, sulla costa laziale. (***vedere*** *takes* ***avere***)

6. Siamo volute/i andare a Vieste, sulla costa pugliese, a tutti i costi. (*andare* takes *essere*)

Pay attention to gender and number if you use the verb **essere** as auxiliary, such as in the examples 2, 4, and 6.

Esercitiamoci!

Fill in the blanks conjugating the verbs **dovere**, **potere**, and **volere** in the **passato prossimo**.

1. Ieri Maurizio _____ (*dovere*) andare a trovare sua zia in ospedale.

2. La settimana scorsa Carla non _____ (*potere*) vedere il film a causa di un esame.

3. Per andare in vacanza, la scorsa estate le mie amiche e io _____ (*dovere*) partire da Milano invece che da Roma, il nostro aeroporto di riferimento.

4. Chiara e Tania _____ (*volere*) comprare la torta al pistacchio per il compleanno di Filippo.

5. Dottore, _____ (*dovere*) rientrare dalle ferie prima del previsto?

6. Ieri sera la mia famiglia e io non _____ (*dovere*) cucinare perché abbiamo preso la pizza al taglio prima di venire a casa.

7. Con mio grande rammarico, non _____ (*potere*) ancora vedere l'ultimo film di Cristina Comencini.

8. Tu non _____ (*volere*) festeggiare la promozione con i tuoi colleghi e le tue colleghe di lavoro per via della pandemia, ma quando lo fai allora?

9. Purtroppo, tu e le tue sorelle _____ (*potere*) fare la gita all'Argentario ieri per il brutto tempo.

10. Professoressa, (noi) _____ (*dovere*) studiare anche l'ultimo libro di Vera Gheno per l'esame di sociolinguistica!

Scriviamo!

Write three full sentences with **dovere** in the **passato prossimo**, three full sentences with **potere** in the **passato prossimo**, and three full sentences with **volere** in the **passato prossimo**.

 Lavoriamo con altre studentesse o altri studenti

Check over the exercises above with another student.

 Parliamo!

Talk with another classmate, asking and responding to the following questions. Ask as many questions as possible alternating roles.

DOVERE
1. Che cosa hai dovuto fare stamattina?
2. Che cosa hai dovuto fare ieri?
3. Che cosa hai dovuto fare lo scorso fine settimana?
4. Che cosa hai dovuto fare la settimana passata?
5. Che cosa hai dovuto fare lo scorso anno?
POTERE
6. Che cosa hai potuto fare stamattina?
7. Che cosa hai potuto fare ieri sera?
8. Che cosa hai potuto fare sabato scorso?
9. Che cosa hai potuto fare il mese scorso?
10. Che cosa hai potuto fare l'estate passata?
VOLERE
11. Che cosa hai voluto fare stamattina?
12. Che cosa hai voluto fare due giorni fa?
13. Che cosa hai voluto fare domenica scorsa?
14. Che cosa hai voluto fare tre mesi fa?
15. Che cosa hai voluto fare durante il liceo?

Ask three more questions (one for each verb) that are not listed above using a formal register:

1. _____

2. _____

3. _____

NOTA CULTURALE

Il movimento #Metoo. #Metoo is not only a popular hashtag on social media to denounce sexual abuse and harassment, but it also is one the symbols of the fight against them in the film industry. In October 2017, actress Alyssa Milano posted the following well-known tweet: "If all the women who have been sexually harassed or assaulted wrote 'Me too' as a status, we might give people a sense of the magnitude of the problem," leading other celebrities to repost it, and it quickly reached all corners of the world. The hashtag had been invented by activist Tarana Burke in 2006, yet it went viral after Milano's post. After the Harvey Weinstein case in October 2017, prominent women started to report numerous sexual abuses in the film industry and media. In Italy, in 2018, a letter against sexual harassment and assault was signed by more than 300 women working in Italian television and cinema; it went viral on social media with the hashtag **#dissenso comune**. In Italy, women posted with the hashtag **#quellavoltache** launched by the activist Giulia Blasi.

LA PAGINA CULTURALE

IL CINEMA ITALIANO

Italian cinema has a long history and is regarded as one of the most important in the world. Having collaborated with the Lumière Brothers, **Vittorio Calcina** is known to have been the first Italian film director, and he was followed by a big constellation of well-known names, especially from the onset of Neorealism (mid-1900s) onwards: from **Lina Wertmüller** and **Federico Fellini** to **Liliana Cavani** and **Michelangelo Antonioni**, from **Roberto Benigni** and **Gianfranco Rosi** to **Antonietta De Lillo** and **Marina Spada** as well as **Roberta Torre, Ferzan Özpetek,** and **Paolo Sorrentino**, just to name a few from what would be a very long list. Italian films have won many important awards in film festivals around the world, including many Academy Awards for Best Foreign Language Film (the most of any country) as well as Golden Lions in Venice, Palmes d'Or in Cannes, and Golden Bears in Berlin.

which already showed elements of Neorealism at the beginning of the twentieth century, when silent movies were still the norm and Neorealism was far from even being theorized in the mid-1900s. The canon excluded Bertini as a filmmaker, yet the early stage of Neorealism owes much to this prominent woman of Italian cinema. The **Neorealist movement** flourished in post-World War II Italy, with prominent figures such as directors **Luchino Visconti**, renowned for the first neorealist film *Ossessione* (1943), **Roberto Rossellini**, **Vittorio De Sica**, and **Giuseppe De Santis**. Rossellini's *Roma città aperta* (1945) and De Sica's *Ladri di biciclette* (1948) are still reference points in world cinema, while *Sciuscià* (1947) by De Sica won the first Honorary Award at the 20th Academy Awards the following year, inaugurating the category that would later become the Academy Award for Best Foreign Language Film. *Ladri di biciclette* was awarded the same Honorary Award in 1949.

One of the first films deserving mention is *Assunta Spina*, which was directed in 1915 by **Gustavo Serena**, who was strongly influenced by **Francesca Bertini,** the leading actress and

Cecilia Mangini, the first female documentarian, released *Ignoti alla città* in 1958, written by **Pier Paolo Pasolini**, an intellectual, poet, writer, and film director well-known for films such as *Accattone* (1961) and *Mamma Roma* (1962) starring actress Anna Magnani.

In the 1950s, the visibility of Italian cinema also increased exponentially all over the world; celebrities such as **Sophia Loren, Vittorio Gassman, Silvana Mangano**, and **Marcello Mastroianni** achieved recognition not only in Italy, but also internationally.

Another famous actor is known as **Totò** (Antonio De Curtis), *il principe della risata* [*The Prince of Laughter*]. He portrayed a variety of characters in notable films such as *Guardie e ladri* (1951) by film directors Steno and Mario Monicelli, *Totò a colori* (1952) by Steno, *L'oro di Napoli* (1954) by Vittorio De Sica, and *Uccellacci e uccellini* (1966) by Pier Paolo Pasolini.

In the early 1960s, the *Commedia all'italiana* genre, which includes masterpieces by filmmakers **Dino Risi** and **Mario Monicelli**, took center stage; meanwhile, many other stars, such as **Silvana Pampanini**, **Gina Lollobrigida**, and **Alberto Sordi,** continued to be acclaimed in Italy and around the world.

At the same time, **Pietro Germi**'s *Divorzio all'Italiana* (1961) with **Stefania Sandrelli** was one of the most watched films of its time, and **Federico Fellini**'s *La dolce vita* (1960) won the Palme d'Or at the Cannes Film Festival and the Academy Award for Best Costumes.

The 1960s were also the years of **Sergio Leone** and the *spaghetti western* (particularly the *Dollars Trilogy*). Leone also directed two major films: *Once upon a Time in the West* (1968) and *Once upon a Time in America* (1984), which were

echoed more recently in Quentin Tarantino's film, *Once upon a Time in Hollywood* (2019).

In the 1970s and 1980s, **Ugo Fantozzi**, a stereotypical hard-luck Italian employee character interpreted by **Paolo Villaggio**, had such an impact on Italian society that the adjective *fantozziano* entered the lexicon. Also in the 1970s, **Loredana Rotondo**, **Rony Daopulo**, **Paola De Martis**, **Annabella Miscuglio**, **Maria Grazia Belmonti,** and **Anna Carini** directed *Processo per stupro* (1979), the first documentary to address rape culture on Italian national television; an original copy of the film can also be found at the MoMa in New York City.

The 1980s also saw the rise of the so-called *cinepanettone*, comedies released every year during the Christmas holidays. **Neri Parenti**, who also directed the Fantozzi series with Villaggio, is one of the leading filmmakers in this genre. In the past few decades, **Roberto Benigni** has risen to prominence in Italy and beyond, particularly with *La vita è bella* (1997), a film about the holocaust as seen through the eyes of a child whose father converts their existence in a concentration camp into a type of game to help the son survive the traumatic experience. Among its many awards, *La vita è bella* also won the Academic Award for Best Foreign Language Film in 1999.

More recently, in 2017, **Luca Guadagnino**'s *Chiamami col tuo nome* became one of the biggest international successes of Italian cinema. The movie portrays the romantic relationship between Elio (Timothée Chalamet) and Oliver, and it won 107 awards and garnered 254 nominations worldwide.

Despite the fact that ever more female directors in the film industry are also being highly praised for their works, it is not as easy to be recognized as it is for male directors, both in Italy and globally. As director **Francesca Archibugi** states: "Quando sei una donna tendono sempre ad accorciarti la statura, rispetto ad un regista maschio. Cioè prima di riconoscerti uno status di persona che ha delle cose da dire devi faticare di più [When you are a woman they always tend to cut you down, compared with a male director. That is before they'll recognize your status as a person who has things to say, you have to work harder]" (quoted in Bernadette Luciano and Susanna Scarparo, *Reframing Italy: New Trends in Italian Women's Filmmaking*, West Lafayette-IN, Purdue University Press, 2013, p. 3).

However, Italy has a long list of distingui-shed women filmmakers who have won impor-tant awards nationally and internationally, such as **Lina Wertmüller**, who, in 2019, received the Academy Honorary Award to honor her exten-sive career as a director.

Similarly, **Alice Rohrwacher**, who directed *Lazzaro Felice* (2018) and several episodes of the globally acclaimed series, *L'amica geniale*, based on **Elena Ferrante's** *Neapolitan Novels*, was part of the 2019 Cannes Film Festival Jury, which is considered a prestigious honor.

Furthermore, **Cristina Comencini**'s *La bestia nel cuore* (2006), shot in part at the University of Virginia in Charlottesville, was nominated for Golden Lion and for the Best Foreign Language Film category at Academy Awards.

Many women filmmakers have also brought gender inequality to the forefront in recent years. Out a very long list, these include **Angela Tor-re**'s *Angela* (2002), **Teresa Iaropoli**'s *Passo a due* (2005), one of the first documentaries to depict the life of a lesbian couple in their 80s in Milan, **Alina Marazzi**'s *Vogliamo anche le rose* (2007), **Donatella Maiorca**'s *Viola di mare* (2009), and **Laura Bispuri**'s *Vergine giurata* (2015). A trio of women filmmakers, **Francesca Comencini**, **Su-sanna Nicchiarelli**, and **Paola Randi,** recently directed the third Italian Netflix original series, *Luna Nera* (2019), based on **Tiziana Triana's** fan-tasy novel about seventeenth-century witches in central Italy. Parts of the series were shot in Farnese, a small village at the border between Lazio and Tuscany, where **Luigi Comeninci** also directed several scenes of *Pinocchio* in 1972.

In the past thirty years, Italian filmmakers and documentarians have continued to be recognized internationally. This is the case of **Paolo Sorrentino**, whose film *La grande bellezza* (2013) won the 86th Academy Award for Best Foreign Language Film, the most recent Italian film to win this prestigious award.

Diana Dell'Erba directed *Registe* in 2014, casting a light on the story of **Elvira Notari**, Italy's earliest woman filmmaker, who made an astonishing number of feature films, documentaries, and film shorts. This film also stars **Cinzia H Torrini**, **Giada Colagrande**, and **Maria Sole Tognazzi**,. Other filmmakers of renown are **Nanni Moretti** with *Caro diario* (1993) and *Il caimano* (2006), **Gianni Amelio** with *Lamerica* (1994) and *Così ridevano* (1998), **Emanuele Crialese** with *Nuovomondo* (2006) and *Terraferma* (2011), **Matteo Garrone** with *Gomorrah* (2008), **Paolo Virzì** with *Il capitale umano* (2013) and *La pazza gioia* (2016), **Gabriele Muccino** with *The Pursuit of Happiness* (2006) and *Seven Pounds* (2008), and, last but not least, **Paolo Genovese** with *Tutta colpa di Freud* (2014) and *Perfetti sconosciuti* (2016), which focuses on the impact of social media in everyday life.

Documentarist **Gianfranco Rosi** has been internationally recognized for *Sacro GRA* (2013) and for *Fuocoammare* (2016), depicting the immigrant crisis in Lampedusa, Italy.

Gianni Amelio

Paolo Genovese

Italian-Turkish director **Ferzan Özeptek** has established himself with films such as *Le fate ignoranti* (2001), with **Margherita Buy** and **Stefano Accorsi**, *La finestra di fronte* (2003) with **Giovanna Mezzogiorno** and **Raoul Bova**, and *Mine vaganti* (2010). He often focuses on gay, lesbian, transgender, and bisexual identities.

Matteo Garrone

Paolo Virzì

Margherita Buy

Gabriele Muccino

Stefano Accorsi

Raul Bova

Pif

Italy is also well known for producing movies dealing with the mafia (see the second edition of Dana Renga's *Mafia Movies: A Reader*, 2019, for an overview of the genre), and Pierfrancesco Diliberto-**Pif**' *La mafia uccide solo d'estate* (2013) is considered one of the best films on the Italian mafia ever made, while **Fiorenza Infascelli**'s *Era d'estate* (2016), about **Paolo Borsellino** and **Giovanni Falcone**, was nominated for the Award David di Donatello for Best Adapted Screenplay.

Among the emerging voices of Italian cinema, one should keep an eye out for the works of **Emma Dante,** who recently directed *Le sorelle Macaluso* (2020), **Francesca Lolli**, the director of *Nostra signora del silenzio* (2020), and **Fred**

Kuwornu, whose works raise awareness concerning diversity and inclusion on screen on both sides of the Atlantic.

Emma Dante and Alba Rohrwacher

ESERCITIAMOCI CON LA CULTURA

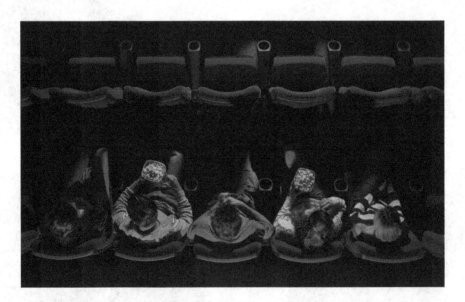

A. Al cinema. You are waiting in line with friends to watch a movie. Write a short dialogue (12 lines) where you re-use words learned in this chapter.

B1. Luisa Ranieri è Donna Carmela in *La Vita Promessa*. Read the extract below about the Italian TV series, *La vita promessa*, and answer the questions.

Parole utili

Interamente: *fully*

Interpretata: *starred*

Talentuosa: *gifted*

Assassinio: *murder*

Scalcinata: *shabby*

Tenace: *persistent*

Nonostante: *despite*

Dolorosa: *painful*

Affrontare: *to face*

La vita promessa è una serie televisiva strutturata [*structured*] su due stagioni, diretta da [*directed by*] Simona Izzo e Ricky Tognazzi, con protagonista l'attrice italiana di grande carisma Luisa Ranieri, e girata [*filmed*] tra Monopoli, Taranto e Sofia in Bulgaria.

La prima stagione de *La vita promessa* apre con scene della Sicilia degli anni '20 ed è interamente centrata [*centered*] sulla figura di Donna Carmela (cognome Carrizzo-Rizzo), interpretata dalla talentuosa Luisa Ranieri. Carmela, dopo aver assistito [*after having assisted*] all'assassinio del marito e all'aggressione del figlio, azioni entrambe [*both*] compiute [*accomplished*] dal boss criminale Vincenzo Spanò, **vuole** partire per gli Stati Uniti per inseguire il sogno di una vita migliore [*better*] e per mettere al sicuro [*to secure*] la sua famiglia. Qui, all'interno di una scalcinata *Little Italy*, Donna Carmela **deve** lottare per integrarsi [*to assimilate*] in un mondo e in una cultura non sua. Carmela è una donna tenace che **sa** rimboccarsi [*to roll up*] ripetutamente le maniche e **riesce** a dimostrare coraggio. Ad assisterla [*To assist her*], ci sono alcuni uomini che **riescono** a creare con lei legami importanti, comunque secondari rispetto [*in comparison to*] al ruolo centrale di Donna Carmela.

Nella seconda stagione ambientata [*taken place*] tra gli anni '30 e '40, la famiglia Rizzo ha una nuova casa e Donna Carmela è un'affermata proprietaria di un ristorante a *Little Italy* che serve specialità italiane. Nonostante le dolorose perdite che **ha dovuto** affrontare, Donna Carmela crede di avere trovato [*to have found*] finalmente *la vita promessa* [*promised*] in America. Carmela è sempre l'anima dell'intera famiglia e ora **può** pensare anche alla propria felicità e alla propria realizzazione come donna, oltra che come madre e moglie. Tuttavia, arriva in città l'uomo che ha ucciso [*killed*] suo marito in Italia.

CHI È LUISA RANIERI? Read her short bio below:

Luisa Ranieri è un'attrice e conduttrice [*anchorwoman*] italiana. Attiva a teatro e in televisione e al cinema, inizia la sua carriera grazie al film *Il principe e il pirata* di Leonardo Pieraccioni. Nel 2004 diventa la protagonista di *Eros*, diretto da Michelangelo Antonioni e l'anno dopo è presente in alcune serie tv come *Callas e Onassis* e *'O professore*. Tra il 2009 e il 2010 è a teatro con *L'oro di Napoli*, e dopo diverse fiction televisive è la madrina del Festival del Cinema di Venezia nel 2014.

Nel 2016 interpreta [*perform*] l'imprenditrice [*businesswoman*] italiana Luisa Spagnoli nell'omonima [*of the same name*] fiction di Rai 1 e a partire dal [*starting from*] 2018 è protagonista insieme a Francesco Arca nella fiction Rai *La vita promessa* con la regia di [*with the direction of*] Simona Izzo e Ricky Tognazzi. Inizialmente Luisa era [*was*] molto scettica e non voleva [*did not want*] interpretare il personaggio di Donna Carmela, ma poi, leggendo [*reading*] il copione [*script*], **ha riconosciuto** la ricchezza del personaggio e **ha deciso** di interpretare un ruolo di donna complesso. A Luisa Ranieri **è piaciuta** Donna Carmela e la sua conquista dell'emancipazione e della felicità come donna.

Lettura e comprensione. Choose the correct answer:

1. **Chi è Carmela Rizzo?**
   A. Un'attrice
   B. Un'immigrata siciliana a New York
   C. La regista di un film
   D. Informazione non presente
2. **Perché la famiglia Rizzo va negli Stati Uniti?**
   A. Per povertà
   B. Per amore
   C. Informazione non presente
   D. Per cercare una vita felice

3. **Qual è la grande difficoltà che Carmela incontra inizialmente a New York?**
   A. Adattamento a tradizioni culturali diverse dalle sue
   B. Informazione non presente
   C. La lingua
   D. Fatica a incontrare nuovi amici e nuove amiche

4. **Carmela dopo qualche anno riesce ad affermarsi professionalmente, perché:**
   A. Diventa un'attrice talentuosa
   B. Riesce ad aprire un punto di ristoro
   C. I suoi figli diventano ricchi
   D. Informazione non presente

5. **Quale evento sconvolge la serenità di Carmela?**
   A. L'apertura del ristorante
   B. L'arrivo in città dell'uomo che aveva ucciso [killed] suo marito
   C. Informazione non presente
   D. La morte di un'amica

6. **Perché Luisa Ranieri ha accettato di interpretare un personaggio come Donna Carmela?**
   A. Informazione non presente
   B. Perché Carmela rappresenta una donna moderna, nonostante il film ambientato negli anni '20-'40
   C. Perché Carmela è l'emblema dell'emancipazione femminile e rappresenta il cuore di un vero e proprio nucleo matriarcale
   D. Perché Carmela è una donna intelligente

B2. More about Donna Carmela. Complete the paragraph below about Donna Carmela with **dovere**, **potere**, or **volere** in the present tense.

Donna Carmela _____ partire per gli Stati Uniti per cercare una nuova vita. Qui fa fatica [struggles] ad adattarsi [to adapt herself] ma _____ dimostrare coraggio per realizzare il suo sogno. Dopo alcuni anni riesce ad aprire un ristorante e _____ aprire un ristorante italiano grazie al suo duro lavoro. Purtroppo la sua felicità è messa alla prova [is tested by] dall'arrivo di Spanò. Adesso Donna Carmela _____ essere forte e lottare per la sua felicità.

C1. Raffaella Carrà, nome d'arte di Raffaella Maria Roberta Pelloni (1943-2021), è stata una cantante, ballerina, attrice, conduttrice televisiva e radiofonica, e autrice televisiva italiana. Research Raffaella Carrà online (reputable sources!) and write about what you have learned.

Tutto su Raffaella Carrà!

C2. Ennio Morricone (1928-2020) è stato un compositore italiano; ha scritto le musiche per più di 500 film e serie TV, oltre che opere di musica contemporanea. Research Ennio Morricone online (reputable sources!) and write about what you have learned.

Tutto su Ennio Morricone!

[8] Activity primarily contributed by Ida Ferrari. Copyright © Kendall Hunt Publishing Company.
[9] Activity primarily contributed by Michela Valmori. Copyright © Kendall Hunt Publishing Company.

GLOSSARIO

Avverbi

Abbastanza [*sufficiently, enough*]

Adesso [*now*]

Affatto [*absolutely, by all means, by any means, absolutely not, not at all*]

Ancora [*again, one more time, once again, still, even now, so far, even*]

Appena [*barely, scarcely, only, just*]

Assai [*very, extremely, rather*]

Bene [*well*]

Così [*so, thus, in this way, like this*]

Così così [*so so*]

Davanti [*in front, across from, opposite from*]

Davvero [*really, truly*]

Dentro [*inside, in*]

Dietro [*back, behind*]

Di mattina [*in the morning*]

Di notte [*at night, during the night*]

Di nuovo [once *again, once more*]

Di pomeriggio [*in the afternoon*]

Di solito [*usually*]

Domani [*tomorrow*]

Domattina [*tomorrow morning*]

Dopo [*later, afterwards, after*]

Fuori [*outside*]

Già [*already, before*]

Giù [*down*]

Ieri [*yesterday*]

Intorno [*around*]

Là [*there*]

Lì [*there*]

Lontano [*far, far away*]

Mai [*never, ever*]

Male [*badly, poorly, wrongly, erroneously*]

Meno [*less, to a lesser extent*]

Molto [*very, highly*]

Oggi [*today*]

Ogni [*each*]

Ogni giorno [*every day*]

Ogni tanto [*sometimes, every now and then*]

Ora [*now*]

Ormai [*by now, at this point*]

Parecchio [*quite a lot, a lot*]

Per niente [*at all*]

Per nulla [*at all*]

Più [*more, most, plus, no more*]

Piuttosto [*rather, instead*]

Poco [*little*]

Poi [*then*]

Presto [*early, soon, in a little while, in a short while, quickly*]

Prima [*before, earlier, previously, once, at one time, sooner, earlier, first of all*]

Purtroppo [*unfortunately*]

Qua [*here*]

Qualche volta [*sometimes*]

Qui [*here*]

Raramente [*rarely, infrequently*]

Recentemente [*recently, lately*]

Sempre [*always, endless, never-ending, continuously, still*]

Solo [*only*]

Soltanto [*only*]

Sopra [*above, upper, previously, earlier*]

Soprattutto [*above all, especially*]

Sotto [*underneath, under, below*]

Spesso [*often, frequently*]

Stamani [*this morning*]

Stamattina [*this morning*]

Stanotte [*tonight*]

Stasera [*this evening*]

Su [*upstairs, up, overhead, upwards*]

Successivamente [*later, at a later time*]

Talvolta [*sometimes*]

Tanto [*a lot, very much, as much as*]

Troppo [*too much, in excess, excessively*]

Tutti i giorni [*every day*]

Un po' [*a bit, a little*]

Vicino [*nearby, close by*]

Volentieri [*gladly, willingly, certainly, surely, of course*]

Verbi modali

Dovere [*must, to have to, to need to*]

Potere [*can, may, to be able to*]

Volere [*want*]

Verbi di movimento con *essere*

Andare [*to go*]

Arrivare [*to arrive, to reach, to come, to achieve, to accomplish*]

Cadere [*to fall*]

Correre [*to run*]

Entrare [*to enter*]

Fuggire [*to escape*, to run away, to flee]

Partire [*to leave*]

Ritornare [*to go back, to return*]

Salire [*to get in, to climb up, to come up*]

Scappare [*to run away*]

Scendere [*to descend, to go down, to get off*]

Tornare [*to go back, to come back, to return*]

Uscire [*to exit, to go out, to leave*]

Venire [*to come, to go*]

Verbi di movimento con *avere*

Attraversare [*to cross, to go through, to pass through*]

Camminare [*to walk*]

Correre [*to run*]

Giocare [*to play*]

Nuotare [*to swim*]

Passeggiare [*to walk*]

Raggiungere [*to reach, to arrive at*]

Viaggiare [*to travel*]

Verbi di stato con *essere*

Apparire [*to appear*]

Avvenire [*to happen*]

Cambiare [*to change*]

Dimagrire [*to lose weight*]

Dispiacere [*to be sorry*]

Diventare [*to become*]

Durare [*to last*]

Essere [*to be*]

Ingrassare [*to gain weight*]

Restare [*to stay, to remain*]

Rimanere [*to stay, to remain*]

Stare [*to stay, to remain*]

Verbi di vita con *essere*

Crescere [*to grow, to raise*]

Esistere [*to exist*]

Guarire [*to heal, to recover*]

Morire [*to die*]

Nascere [*to be born*]

Vivere [*to live*]

Altri verbi con *essere*

Bastare [*to be enough, to suffice, to be sufficient*]

Capitare [*to happen, to occur*]

Costare [*to cost*]

Dipendere [*to depend on*]

Finire [*to finish*]

Mancare [*to miss*]

Parere [*to seem, to appear*]

Piacere [*to like*]

Riuscire [*to be able to, to manage to*]

Sembrare [*to seem, to appear, to look like, to feel like*]

Succedere [*to happen, to occur*]

APPENDICE

IL CONDIZIONALE PER ESPRIMERE *I WOULD LIKE*

There is a more polite way of saying *I would like*, compared to the less polite *I want*, and this is expressed with the conditional mood in the present tense. See below the six forms:

IO VORREI	I WOULD LIKE
TU VORRESTI	YOU WOULD LIKE
LEI/LUI VORREBBE	SHE/HE WOULD LIKE
NOI VORREMMO	WE WOULD LIKE
VOI VORRESTE	YOU ALL WOULD LIKE
LORO VORREBBERO	THEY WOULD LIKE

In the same way as **volere** and **to want**, the conditional **vorrei** in all its forms can be followed by an infinitive or can express a desire for something, like in the examples below:

1. **Vorrei** un caffè.
2. **Vorrei bere** un caffè.
3. Che cosa **vorresti** fare dopo l'università?
4. **Vorremmo vedere** un film interessante, ma questi non ci piacciono.

I VERBI IN -RE AL PRESENTE E AL PASSATO PROSSIMO

There are some verbs in Italian that end in **-re** in the infinitive, such as **porre** [*to put, to place*], **comporre** [*to compose*], **supporre** [*to suppose, to presume*], **sovrapporre** [*to overlap*], **imporre** [*to impose*], and **tradurre** [*to translate*]. Below is the conjugation of **porre** in the present tense:

PORRE	TO PUT
IO PON–G–**O**	I PUT
TU PON–**I**	YOU PUT
LEI/LUI PON–**E**	SHE/HE PUTS
NOI PON–**IAMO**	WE PUT
VOI PON–**ETE**	YOU ALL PUT
LORO PON–G–**ONO**	THEY PUT

As we saw in the previous chapters, some Italian verbs are conjugated from the Latin infinitive, and the verb **porre** (and its derivative) follows the same pattern: it is in fact conjugated from the Latin infinitive, *ponere*. The irregularity is seen in the first-person singular (**io**) and in the third-person plural (**loro**) where a **g** is added to the conjugated forms: **pongo**, **pongono**.

Now, conjugate the verb **comporre**:

Io _____   Noi _____

Tu _____   Voi _____

Lui/Lei _____   Loro _____

E tu componi nel tempo libero? Answer the question below with a complete sentence in Italian:

_____

Puoi tradurre da una lingua straniera in inglese? Answer the question below with a complete sentence in Italian:

_____

The past participles of the verbs in -re are irregular and they include **posto** (porre), **composto** (comporre), **supposto** (supporre), **sovrapposto** (sovrapporre), and **imposto** (imporre).

The **passato prossimo** is formed with the verb **avere**. For negation, one adds **non** before the conjugated auxiliary verb: *Noi non abbiamo supposto niente*. Now complete the chart below following the example:

SUPPORRE
IO HO SUPPOSTO
TU
LEI/LUI
NOI
VOI
LORO

For **tradurre**, the past participle is **tradotto**.

Hai mai tradotto da una lingua straniera in inglese? Se sì, in quale lingua? Answer the question below with a complete sentence in Italian:

_____

TITOLI DI CODA

FM

Page ix (Icons and as recurring icons throughout): *Esercitiamoci!* Icon: Fox Design/Shutterstock.com; *Scriviamo!* Icon: Vladvm/Shutterstock.com; *Lavoriamo con altre studentesse o altri studenti* Icon: howcolour/Shutterstock.com; *Parliamo!* Icon: Linefab Portfolio/Shutterstock.com.

CAPITOLO 01

Page 1: atk work/Shutterstock.com; **Page 2:** Row 1 (Left to right): Kakigori Studio/Shutterstock.com, Shanvood/Shutterstock.com, spyarm/Shutterstock.com; Row 2 (Left to right): Noor-shine/Shutterstock.com, Natykach Nataliia/Shutterstock.com, Anastasia Mazeina/Shutterstock.com; Row 3 (Left to right): yusufdemirci/Shutterstock.com, HappyPictures/Shutterstock.com, Moloko88/Shutterstock.com; **Page 3:** Row 1 (Left to right): Sashatigar/Shutterstock.com, jongcreative/Shutterstock.com, ann131313.s/Shutterstock.com; Row 2 (Left to right): Yindee/Shutterstock.com, Abscent/Shutterstock.com, kate3155/Shutterstock.com; Row 3 (Left to right): brichuas/Shutterstock.com, NTL studio/Shutterstock.com, Milano M/Shutterstock.com; Row 4 (Left to right): Sentavio/Shutterstock.com, ProStockStudio/Shutterstock.com, TotemArt/Shutterstock.com, Row 5 (Left to right): ghrzuzudu/Shutterstock.com, Dreamcreation/Shutterstock.com, BudOlga/Shutterstock.com, Chikovnaya /Shutterstock.com, siridhata/Shutterstock.com, FARBAI/Shutterstock.com; **Page 5:** Top left: Virinaflora/Shutterstock.com; Top Right: suesse/Shutterstock.com; Middle: Lightspring/Shutterstock.com; Bottom left: Barone Firenze/Shutterstock.com; Bottom left: Barone Firenze/Shutterstock.com; Bottom right: Christian Delbert/Shutterstock.com; **Page 6:** Row 1 (Left to right): Vectors bySkop/Shutterstock.com, Intellson/Shutterstock.com; Row 2 (Left to right): AnkaFed/Shutterstock.com, Sanches11/Shutterstock.com; Row 3 (Middle): ESB Professional/Shutterstock.com; **Page 7:** KadirOrhan/Shutterstock.com; Top left: Dmitrii Ivanov/Shutterstock.com; Top right: fizkes/Shutterstock.com; **Page 8:** Top right: Rasto SK/Shutterstock.com, Top right: Buffy1982/Shutterstock.com, Middle: Ursula Ferrara/Shutterstock.com; **Page 9:** Row 1 (Left to right): Kuznetsov Alexey/Shutterstock.com, Africa Studio/Shutterstock.com, Row 2 (Left to right): Boerescu/Shutterstock.com, Fabio Michele Capelli/Shutterstock.com; Row 3 (Middle): Everett Collection/Shutterstock.com; **Page 10:** Row 1 (Left to right): New Africa/Shutterstock.com, zentilia/Shutterstock.com; Row 2 (Middle): K.Decha/Shutterstock.com; Bottom left: Francesco83/Shutterstock.com: Bottom right: JeniFoto/Shutterstock.com; **Page 11:** Row 1 (Left to right): Lustrator/Shutterstock.com, Sun_Shine/Shutterstock.com, Row 2 (Left to right): springtime78/Shutterstock.com, Robert Kneschke/Shutterstock.com, Row 3 (Middle): Ppictures/Shutterstock.com; ; **Page 13:** (Left to right): Christos Georghiou/Shutterstock.com, Channarong Pherngjanda/Shutterstock.com;   **Page 14:** Row 1: Cindy Lee/Shutterstock.com, Studio_G/Shutterstock.com, Row 2: Ovchynnikov Oleksii/Shutterstock.com, RetroClipArt/Shutterstock.com, Row 3: vladwel/Shutterstock.com, Nadia Snopek/Shutterstock.com, Row 4: iD_studio/Shutterstock.com, Vector DSGNR /Shutterstock.com, Row 5: Martial Red/Shutterstock.com, BNP Design Studio/Shutterstock.com; **Page 15:** Row 1: Martial Red/Shutterstock.com, mhatzapa/Shutterstock.com, Row 2: Nadia Snopek/Shutterstock.com, Jan Babak/Shutterstock.com, Row 3: Christos Georghiou/Shutterstock.com, DKDesignz/Shutterstock.com, Row 4: Mukesh Kumar/Shutterstock.com, Scott Maxwell LuMaxArt/Shutterstock.com; **Page 16:** GoodStudio/Shutterstock.com; **Page 17:** Top: Antonio Guillem/Shutterstock.com, Middle: Lucky Business/Shutterstock.com, Bottom: Rainer Fuhrmann/Shutterstock.com; **Page 18:** Top: Klever LeveL/Shutterstock.com, Bottom: Rido/Shutterstock.com; **Page 19:** Rawpixel.com/Shutterstock.com; **Page 20:** Top: Krakenimages.com/Shutterstock.com, Middle: Luis Molinero/Shutterstock.com, Bottom: imtmphoto/Shutterstock.com; **Page 21:** AmpYang Images/Shutterstock.com; **Page 22:** Top: EugeneEdge/Shutterstock.com, Bottom: Drazen Zigic/Shutterstock.com; **Page 23:** Top: Dean Drobot/Shutterstock.com, Bottom: Olena Hromova/Shutterstock.com; **Page 24:** White Space Illustrations/Shutterstock.com; **Page 25:** lev radin/Shutterstock.com, Bottom: YAKOBCHUK VIACHESLAV/Shutterstock.com; **Page 26:** Albachiaraa/Shutterstock.com; **Page 27:** cardopoli/Shutterstock.com; **Page 28:** Top: WineDonuts/Shutterstock.com, Middle:

cardopoli/Shutterstock.com, Bottom: HBRH/Shutterstock.com; **Page 29:** Top: Krakenimages.com/Shutterstock.com, Bottom left: doom.ko/Shutterstock.com, Bottom right: VectorMine/Shutterstock.com; **Page 30:** Igor Levin/Shutterstock.com.

CAPITOLO 02

Page 33: metamorworks/Shutterstock.com; **Page 35:** Top: Iconic Bestiary/Shutterstock.com, (Words have power word cube Icon and as recurring icons throughout) Sinart Creative/Shutterstock.com; **Page 37:** Middle: oneinchpunch/Shutterstock.com; **Page 39:** BlueDesign/Shutterstock.com; **Page 40:** nexus 7/Shutterstock.com; **Page 42:** Top: G-Stock Studio/Shutterstock.com, Bottom: MUNGKHOOD STUDIO/Shutterstock.com; **Page 44:** Olena Yakobchuk/Shutterstock.com; **Page 45:** Top: Matteo Chinellato/Shutterstock.com, Bottom: GaudiLab/Shutterstock.com; **Page 46:** as-artmedia/Shutterstock.com; **Page 52:** Row 1: Tim UR/Shutterstock.com, Row 2: foodstck/Shutterstock.com, Row 3: Valentina Razumova/Shutterstock.com, Row 4: Valentyn Volkov/Shutterstock.com; **Page 053:** Pixsooz/Shutterstock.com, Row 1: marcociannarel/Shutterstock.com, Row 2: MicroOne/Shutterstock.com; **Page 54:** Row 1: Olena Yakobchuk/Shutterstock.com, Row 2: PARALAXIS/Shutterstock.com, Row 3: ZinaidaSopina/Shutterstock.com; **Page 55:** jane55/Shutterstock.com; **Page 57:** Top: MuchMania/Shutterstock.com, Bottom: Vincenzo De Bernardo/Shutterstock.com; **Page 58:** Row 1(Left): Dean Drobot/Shutterstock.com, Row 2(Left): guruXOX/Shutterstock.com, Row 3(Right): melhijad/Shutterstock.com, Row 4(Left): Blue Planet Studio/Shutterstock.com; **Page 59:** Row 1(Left): Minerva Studio/Shutterstock.com, Row 1(Right): Everett Collection/Shutterstock.com, Row 2(Left): Kreangkrai Naktaku/Shutterstock.com, Row 2(Right): Sorbis/Shutterstock.com, Row 3(Right): Monkey Business Images/Shutterstock.com; **Page 61:** Top: Alexandros Michailidis/Shutterstock.com, Bottom: Krakenimages.com/Shutterstock.com; **Page 62:** Top: Rawpixel.com/Shutterstock.com, Middle: Anna Nahabed/Shutterstock.com, Bottom: Stefano Guidi/Shutterstock.com; **Page 63:** Top: Stefano Guidi/Shutterstock.com, Bottom: Massimo Todaro/Shutterstock.com; **Page 64:** Top: Paolo Bona/Shutterstock.com, Bottom: Polonio Video/Shutterstock.com; **Page 65:** Top right: Roman_studio/Shutterstock.com, Bottom middle: leoks/Shutterstock.com; **Page 66:** Kristi Blokhin/Shutterstock.com; **Page 67:** BGStock72/Shutterstock.com; **Page 68:** Igor Levin/Shutterstock.com.

CAPITOLO 03

Page 73: Vasilyev Alexandr/Shutterstock.com; **Page 74:** romeovip_md/Shutterstock.com; **Page 77:** Top right: VAKS-Stock Agency/Shutterstock.com, Bottom left: michelangeloop/Shutterstock.com, Bottom right: graja/Shutterstock.com; **Page 78:** Top right: hanohiki/Shutterstock.com, Row 1: pirke/Shutterstock.com, Row 2: posztos/Shutterstock.com, Row 3: yanikap/Shutterstock.com; **Page 79:** Row 1: Rawpixel.com/Shutterstock.com, Row 2: Monkey Business Images/Shutterstock.com, Row 3: Serhii_Tesliuk_Tesla/Shutterstock.com, Row 4: Alex Segre/Shutterstock.com; **Page 80:** Top: artbesouro/Shutterstock.com, Row 1: Ramon Espelt Photography/Shutterstock.com, Row 2 : Dragon Images/Shutterstock.com, Row 3: Ljupco Smokovski/Shutterstock.com, Row 4: CandyBox Images/Shutterstock.com, Row 5: RESTOCK images/Shutterstock.com; **Page 81:** ProStockStudio/Shutterstock.com; **Page 87:** Row 1 (Left to right): Artem Avetisyan/Shutterstock.com, Nassoy Daniel/Shutterstock.com, Row 2 (Left to right): Dmytro Shapoval/Shutterstock.com, showcake/Shutterstock.com, Row 3: Lipik Stock Media/Shutterstock.com; **Page 88:** Top: Angelo Cordeschi/Shutterstock.com, Bottom Image: New Africa/Shutterstock.com; **Page 91:** Top row 1 (Left to right): Rido/Shutterstock.com, Monkey Business Images/Shutterstock.com, Top row 2 (Left to right): Roman Samborskyi/Shutterstock.com, Rawpixel.com/Shutterstock.com, Bottom: Azindianlany/Shutterstock.com; **Page 94:** Row 1: neftali/Shutterstock.com, Row 2: spatuletail/Shutterstock.com, Row 3: spatuletail/Shutterstock.com; **Page 95:** Row 1: EreborMountain/Shutterstock.com, Row 2: Tinxi/Shutterstock.com, Row 3: D-VISIONS/Shutterstock.com, Bottom: Sentavio/Shutterstock.com; **Page 97:** Bottom left: Yayayoyo/Shutterstock.com, Bottom right: Maxim999/Shutterstock.com; **Page 98:** Row 1 (Left to right): Vectorfair.com/Shutterstock.com, Yayayoyo/Shutterstock.com, Row 2 (Left to right): Cristian Barrios/Shutterstock.com, Yayayoyo/Shutterstock.com, Row 3: (Left to right): Igillustrator/Shutterstock.com, Yayayoyo/Shutterstock.com, Row 4: (Left to right): Yayayoyo/Shutterstock.com, AmazeinDesign/Shutterstock.com, Row 5 (Left to right): Yayayoyo/Shutterstock.com, Arcady/Shutterstock.com; **Page 99:** Bottom left: Tomas Ragina/Shutterstock.com, Bottom right (Up to down): Gunter Nezhoda/Shutterstock.com, GOOD LUCK 2 U/Shutterstock.com; **Page 100:** Top left (Up to down): MIKHAIL GRACHIKOV/Shutterstock.com, Morphart Creation/Shutterstock.com; Top right: M. Unal Ozmen/Shutterstock.com, Bottom row 1 (Left to right): Prostock-studio/Shutterstock.com, Cast Of Thousands/Shutterstock.com, Bottom row 2 (Left to right): PR Image Factory/Shutterstock.com, Olena Yakobchuk/Shutterstock.com; **Page 101:** Top: Nomad_Soul/Shutterstock.com; **Page 102:** Left: Denis Makarenko/Shutterstock.com, Right: Denis Makarenko/Shutterstock.com; **Page 103:** Matteo Chinellato/Shutterstock.com, Matteo Chinellato/Shutterstock.com; **Page 106:**

Top: Pensee Sauvage/Shutterstock.com, Bottom: Drazen Zigic/Shutterstock.com; **Page 107:** karelnoppe/ Shutterstock.com; **Page 108:** Macrovector/Shutterstock.com; **Page 109:** UncleFredDesign/Shutterstock.com; **Page 111:** Bottom left: Tomas Marek/Shutterstock.com, Bottom right: federico neri/Shutterstock.com; **Page 112:** La Gorda/Shutterstock.com; **Page 113:** Alessandro Pintus/Shutterstock.com; **Page 114:** Top: adriaticfoto/Shutterstock .com, Bottom: Nancy Beijersbergen/Shutterstock.com; **Page 115:** Top: Tijana Moraca/Shutterstock.com, Middle: Monkey Business Images/Shutterstock.com, Bottom: bbernard/Shutterstock.com; **Page 116:** MikeDotta/ Shutterstock.com; **Page 117:** Row 1: Photographee.eu/Shutterstock.com, Row 2: Diego Cervo/Shutterstock.com, Row 3: simona pilolla 2/Shutterstock.com, Row 4: Marina Andrejchenko/Shutterstock.com; **Page 118:** Row 1: TravnikovStudio/Shutterstock.com, Row 2: CroMary/Shutterstock.com, Row 3: Grek Irina/Shutterstock.com, Row 4: Tijana Moraca/Shutterstock.com, Row 5: wavebreakmedia/Shutterstock.com; **Page 119:** Igor Levin/Shutterstock .com; **Page 126:** xenia_ok/Shutterstock.com.

CAPITOLO 04

Page 127: Yuganov Konstantin/Shutterstock.com; **Page 128:** nito/Shutterstock.com; **Page 129:** Qvasimodo art/ Shutterstock.com; **Page 130:** Evgeny Atamanenko/Shutterstock.com; **Page 133:** ricochet64/Shutterstock.com; **Page 138:** Sinart Creative/Shutterstock.com; **Page 139:** S.Borisov/Shutterstock.com, Olga Gavrilova/Shutterstock .com; **Page 143:** Top: Jiri Sebesta/Shutterstock.com, Bottom: unpict/Shutterstock.com; **Page 144:** Top left: Alphonse Leong/Shutterstock.com, Top right: CreativeFireStock/Shutterstock.com, Bottom left: Tamas Gabor/ Shutterstock.com, Bottom right: Oksana Mizina/Shutterstock.com; **Page 146:** Linefab Portfolio/Shutterstock.com; **Page 147:** armshare/Shutterstock.com; **Page 148:** Marian Weyo/Shutterstock.com; **Page 149:** Top: vectorfusionart/ Shutterstock.com, Bottom: Maryna Pleshkun/Shutterstock.com; **Page 150:** norikko/Shutterstock.com; **Page 151:** Left Resul Muslu/Shutterstock.com, Right: JeniFoto/Shutterstock.com; **Page 152:** Top left: massimofusaro/ Shutterstock.com, Top right: bbernard/Shutterstock.com, Bottom Middle: Victor Maschek/Shutterstock.com; **Page 153:** Sinart Creative/Shutterstock.com, Right row 1: Alextype/Shutterstock.com, Right row 2: Tinxi/ Shutterstock.com **Page 153:** Marian Weyo/Shutterstock.com; **Page 155:** dcwcreations/Shutterstock.com, Table row 1: Alessandro Tumminello/Shutterstock.com; **Page 156:** Table row 2: Alessandro Tumminello/Shutterstock .com, Table row 3: My name is boy/Shutterstock.com, Table row 4: My name is boy/Shutterstock.com, Table row 5: Alessandro Tumminello/Shutterstock.com; **Page 157:** Table row 6: Alessandro Tumminello/Shutterstock.com, Table row 7: Miyuki Satake/Shutterstock.com, Table row 8: Gemenacom/Shutterstock.com, Table row 9: All For You/Shutterstock.com, Table row 10: All For You/Shutterstock.com; **Page 159:** alice-photo/Shutterstock.com; **Page 160:** olegganko/Shutterstock.com; **Page 161:** Top: adriaticfoto/Shutterstock.com, Bottom: Paladin12/ Shutterstock.com; **Page 162:** Top: Alessio Orru/Shutterstock.com, Middle: DisobeyArt/Shutterstock.com, Bottom: Alessio Orru/Shutterstock.com; **Page 163:** Top: Dmytro Zinkevych/Shutterstock.com, Middle: Andrewshots/ Shutterstock.com, Bottom: Ilia Baksheev/Shutterstock.com; **Page 164:** Top: balabolka/Shutterstock.com, Bottom: Sergio Delle Vedove/Shutterstock.com; **Page 165:** Top: Raywoo/Shutterstock.com, Bottom: Leka Leck/Shutterstock .com; **Page 166:** GoodStudio/Shutterstock.com; **Page 167:** Igor Levin/Shutterstock.com; **Page 169:** alanadesign/ Shutterstock.com; **Page 170:** Top: Olga Nayashkova/Shutterstock.com, Bottom: bonchan/Shutterstock.com; **Page 171:** Top: Stefano_Valeri/Shutterstock.com, Bottom: All For You/Shutterstock.com.

CAPITOLO 05

Page 173: Marzolino/Shutterstock.com; **Page 175:** ImYanis/Shutterstock.com; **Page 176:** Top: Laura Bartoli/ Shutterstock.com, Bottom: Pixel-Shot/Shutterstock.com; **Page 178:** giuseppelombardo/Shutterstock.com; **Page 179:** Row 1 (Left to right): Alexandros Michailidis/Shutterstock.com, M. Cantile/Shutterstock.com, Juli Hansen/ Shutterstock.com, Row 2(Left): Evgeny Atamanenko/Shutterstock.com, Row 2(Right): Evgeny Atamanenko/ Shutterstock.com; Row 3(Left): Jacob Lund/Shutterstock.com, Row 3(Right): Jacob Lund/Shutterstock.com, Row 4(Left): Vitalii Vodolazskyi/Shutterstock.com; **Page 181:** Syda Productions/Shutterstock.com; **Page 183:** Top: RPBaiao/Shutterstock.com, Bottom: Everett Collection/Shutterstock.com; **Page 184:** Top: Takashi Images/ Shutterstock.com, Bottom: PSHAW-PHOTO/Shutterstock.com; **Page 185:** Row 1: Intellistudies/Shutterstock.com, Row 2: hedgehog94/Shutterstock.com, Row 3: DELBO ANDREA/Shutterstock.com; **Page 188:** Miljan Zivkovic/ Shutterstock.com; **Page 190:** pathdoc/Shutterstock.com; **Page 191:** Tinxi/Shutterstock.com; **Page 194:** Top: Catarina Belova/Shutterstock.com, Bottom: posztos/Shutterstock.com; **Page 197:** Linefab Portfolio/Shutterstock .com; **Page 200:** AS Food studio/Shutterstock.com; **Page 201:** Olga Gavrilova/Shutterstock.com; **Page 202:** Row 1: Cristian Puscasu/Shutterstock.com, Row 2: Balate Dorin/Shutterstock.com, Row 3: Adriano Castelli/Shutterstock .com, Row 4: iacomino FRiMAGES/Shutterstock.com; **Page 203:** Row 1: Vereshchagin Dmitry/Shutterstock.com,

Row 2: Stefano_Valeri/Shutterstock.com; **Page 204:** Row 1: Massimo Todaro/Shutterstock.com, Row 2: Creative Lab/Shutterstock.com; **Page 205:** Row 1: REPORT/Shutterstock.com, Row 2: Iara martone/Shutterstock.com, Bottom: cristiano barni/Shutterstock.com; **Page 207:** Row 1 (Left to right): Pixel-Shot/Shutterstock.com, Photosite/Shutterstock.com, Row 2 (Left to right): Christian Nastase/Shutterstock.com, Breadmaker/Shutterstock.com, Row 3 (Left to right): LifeCollectionPhotography/Shutterstock.com, SUPACHART/Shutterstock.com, Row 4 (Left to right): pongsakorn chaina/Shutterstock.com, SUPACHART/Shutterstock.com, Row 5 (Left to right): FooTToo/Shutterstock.com; **Page 208:** Top: Matyas Rehak/Shutterstock.com; Bottom: Obs70/Shutterstock.com; **Page 209:** Top: FooTToo/Shutterstock.com, Middle: Simona Sirio/Shutterstock.com, Bottom: TY Lim/Shutterstock.com; **Page 210:** JJFarq/Shutterstock.com; **Page 211:** Top: Diego Fiore/Shutterstock.com, Middle: Furiarossa/Shutterstock.com; Bottom: Davide Trolli/Shutterstock.com; **Page 212:** Row 1: Fred Mays/Shutterstock.com, Row 2: kumachenkova/Shutterstock.com, Row 3: Luca Grandinetti/Shutterstock.com, Row 4: bibiphoto/Shutterstock.com; **Page 213:** Row 1(Left to right): Marti Bug Catcher/Shutterstock.com, ChiccoDodiFC/Shutterstock.com, Row 2(Left to right): Catarina Belova/Shutterstock.com, cge2010/Shutterstock.com; **Page 214:** Top: Kuznetsov Alexey/Shutterstock.com; Bottom: Uffizi Museum, Florence, Italy (No reproduction or duplication is permitted); **Page 215:** Row 1(Left): Geert Smet/Shutterstock.com, Row 2(Right): spatuletail/Shutterstock.com, Row 3(Left): Catarina Belova/Shutterstock.com, Row 4(Left): Paolo Gallo/Shutterstock.com; **Page 216:** Row 1(Left to right): Everett Collection/Shutterstock.com, Olga Popova/Shutterstock.com, Row 2(Left to right): Olga Popova/Shutterstock.com, RiumaLab/Shutterstock.com; **Page 217:** Top: Elisa Locci/Shutterstock.com, Middle: Elisa Locci/Shutterstock.com, Bottom: jorisvo/Shutterstock.com; **Page 218:** YueStock/Shutterstock.com; **Page 220:** Igor Levin/Shutterstock.com.

CAPITOLO 06

Page 225: nito/Shutterstock.com; **Page 226:** Alexander Reuter/Shutterstock.com; **Page 227:** Fabio Nodari/Shutterstock.com; **Page 228:** Row 1: Olga Popova/Shutterstock.com, Row 2: rarrarorro/Shutterstock.com, Row 3: Dean Drobot/Shutterstock.com, Row 4: Robert Kneschke/Shutterstock.com; **Page 229:** Row 1: Simona Bottone/Shutterstock.com, Row 2: Monkey Business Images/Shutterstock.com, Row 3: Elnur/Shutterstock.com, Row 4: itsflowingtothesoul/Shutterstock.com; **Page 229:** Top: Milan Ilic Photographer/Shutterstock.com, Bottom: fizkes/Shutterstock.com; **Page 231:** Row 1: silky/Shutterstock.com, Row 2: Rawpixel.com/Shutterstock.com; Row 3: Fabio Pagani/Shutterstock.com, Row 4: Antonio Guillem/Shutterstock.com; **Page 242:** Kanuman/Shutterstock.com, **Page 245:** Chiragsinh Yadav/Shutterstock.com; **Page 247:** FocusDzign/Shutterstock.com; **Page 249:** Roberto Lusso/Shutterstock.com; **Page 252:** aaltair/Shutterstock.com; **Page 254:** leoks/Shutterstock.com; **Page 255:** canbedone/Shutterstock.com; **Page 257:** Left: Piotr Piatrouski/Shutterstock.com, Right: neftali/Shutterstock.com; **Page 258:** Top left: neftali/Shutterstock.com; Bottom left: Elliott Cowand Jr/Shutterstock.com, Top right: Kathy Hutchins/Shutterstock.com, Bottom right: Roberto Lusso/Shutterstock.com; **Page 259:** Top left: Kraft74/Shutterstock.com, Bottom left: spatuletail/Shutterstock.com, Top right: spatuletail/Shutterstock.com, Bottom right: Ovidiu Hrubaru/Shutterstock.com; **Page 260:** Top left: Ovidiu Hrubaru/Shutterstock.com, Bottom left: Featureflash Photo Agency/Shutterstock.com, Right: Kathy Hutchins/Shutterstock.com; **Page 261:** Top Left: Andrea Raffin/Shutterstock.com, Middle left: Kathy Hutchins/Shutterstock.com; Bottom left: Andrea Raffin/Shutterstock.com, Top right: Claudio Bottoni /Shutterstock.com; **Page 262:** Top left: Matteo Chinellato/Shutterstock.com, Bottom left: Featureflash Photo Agency/Shutterstock.com; Top right: Adriano Castelli/Shutterstock.com, Bottom right: Matteo Chinellato/Shutterstock.com; **Page 263:** Top Left: Matteo Chinellato/Shutterstock.com, Middle Left: Matteo Chinellato/Shutterstock.com, Bottom left: GIO_LE/Shutterstock.com, Top right: Matteo Chinellato/Shutterstock.com, Middle right: Andrea Raffin/Shutterstock.com, Bottom right: GIO_LE/Shutterstock.com; **Page 264:** Top left: Vincenzo De Bernardo/Shutterstock.com, Top right: GIO_LE/Shutterstock.com, Middle right: Matteo Chinellato/Shutterstock.com, Bottom: Stock-Asso/Shutterstock.com; **Page 265:** Ringo Chiu/Shutterstock.com; **Page 266:** Matteo Chinellato/Shutterstock.com; **Page 268:** DELBO ANDREA/Shutterstock.com; **Page 269:** Dziurek/Shutterstock.com; **Page 270:** Igor Levin/Shutterstock.com; **Page 273:** Top: Rawpixel.com/Shutterstock.com, Middle: panitanphoto/Shutterstock.com, Bottom: cybrain/Shutterstock.com.